T0270519

JAMES BOND
AND THE
SIXTIES SPY CRAZE

JAMES BOND AND THE SIXTIES SPY CRAZE

Thom Shubilla

APPLAUSE
THEATRE & CINEMA BOOKS
Essex, Connecticut

APPLAUSE
THEATRE & CINEMA BOOKS

An imprint of Globe Pequot, the trade division of
The Rowman & Littlefield Publishing Group, Inc.
4501 Forbes Blvd., Ste. 200
Lanham, MD 20706
www.rowman.com

Distributed by NATIONAL BOOK NETWORK

Library of Congress Cataloging-in-Publication Data

Names: Shubilla, Thom, 1984- author.
Title: James Bond and the sixties spy craze / Thom Shubilla.
Description: Essex, Connecticut : Applause, [2024] | Includes bibliographical references
    and index. | Summary: "Of all the novel cultural confections to appear during the 1960s,
    one of the more peculiar was the nearly insatiable hunger of audiences for spy stories.
    Bubbling with sex and violence, and marrying pop-culture cool with a funhouse-mirror
    vision of Cold War geopolitics, the obsession with spy stories found its most popular
    and lucrative outlet in the James Bond franchise. But beyond 007, there were a host
    of competing movies and television programs that ranged from inspired to hopelessly
    derivative-among them the Flint and Harry Palmer movies, The Man from U.N.C.L.E.,
    Mission: Impossible, The Avengers, and countless others. James Bond and the Sixties
    Spy Craze delves into the cultural trends that produced such a flowering of interest in
    spy stories, from the Cold War and JFK's enthusiasm for Ian Fleming's novels to the
    unexpected success of the five original Bond movies by Eon Productions, all of them
    starring Sean Connery. Covered here are the cinematic spin-offs and television take-offs
    on the genre, as well as the explosion of merchandising in the form of toys, comic books,
    and model kits. The book also features interviews with some of the key players of the
    sixties spy trend who are still with us, such as Lana Wood, Caroline Munro, Martine
    Beswick, Madeline Smith, George Lazenby, and others. Packed with behind-the-scenes
    anecdotes and illuminating insights, this is a loving tribute to a venerable pop-culture
    genre"-- Provided by publisher.
Identifiers: LCCN 2023033542 (print) | LCCN 2023033543 (ebook) | ISBN
    9781493079766 (cloth) | ISBN 9781493079773 (epub)
Subjects: LCSH: Spy films—History and criticism. | Spy television programs—History and
    criticism.
Classification: LCC PN2287.T18 S58 2024 (print) | LCC PN2287.T18 (ebook) | DDC
    791.43/6581--dc23/eng/20231124
LC record available at https://lccn.loc.gov/2023033542
LC ebook record available at https://lccn.loc.gov/2023033543

∞™ The paper used in this publication meets the minimum requirements of
American National Standard for Information Sciences—Permanence of Paper
for Printed Library Materials, ANSI/NISO Z39.48-1992.

CONTENTS

INTRODUCTION

History is moving pretty quickly these days and the heroes and villains keep on changing parts.

—Ian Fleming, *Casino Royale*

At the end of World War II, two world superpowers emerged, the Soviet Union and the United States. Both nations, allies during the war, fought in proxy wars; competed in a space race; sought to overthrow, influence, and control a number of world governments; attempted to achieve nuclear superiority; and engaged in international espionage.

Seemingly every day, newspaper headlines were splashed with tales of the uncovering of Communist spy rings and the possible activities of the Soviet counterintelligence agency that went by the acronym SMERSH (Dederer "The LO Heist"; "Yes, Virginia").

Fear of Communist spies was brought to American classrooms. Jack Webb, star of the police procedural *Dragnet* (1951–1959 and 1967–1970), narrated an educational short subject film, *Freedom and You* (a.k.a. *Red Nightmare*) in 1962 that told the story of a "typical" American, English-speaking town set up behind the Iron Curtain in the middle of the Soviet Union. The town's goal was for its residents to learn to become like Americans to infiltrate, sabotage, and spy when they were sent to American towns and cities.

To make matters worse, both world superpowers feared the possibility of the rise of the Fourth Reich somewhere on the globe, headed by Nazi spies—high commanders or possibly their offspring—who escaped Germany following World War II.

Secret agents and spies, typically working for Western governments, were also being romanticized. Not much was known about them, but spies were fictionalized and stylized in pop culture. Inspired by Las Vegas lounge lizard cool and traditional British style, spies were portrayed as swinging international jet-setters; suave, sophisticated, and well-dressed playboys. Tough and incredibly smart and cunning, they were an antithesis to the beatnik and emerging hippie counterculture lifestyle, with perhaps the exception of the break with sexual morals.

> *He was a secret agent, and still alive thanks to his exact attention to the detail of his profession.*
>
> —Ian Fleming, *Casino Royale*

The trend was kicked off by James Bond, a British Secret Intelligence Service MI6 "double-O" agent with a license to kill. Created by Ian Fleming, 007 James Bond was featured in fourteen novels by the author, starting with 1953's *Casino Royale*.

Portrait of James Bond creator Ian Fleming. *Author's collection*

The novels *really* took off in popularity when President John F. Kennedy listed *From Russia with Love* as one of his favorite books in 1961 (Mootz "James Bond"; Wallenstein "James Bond").

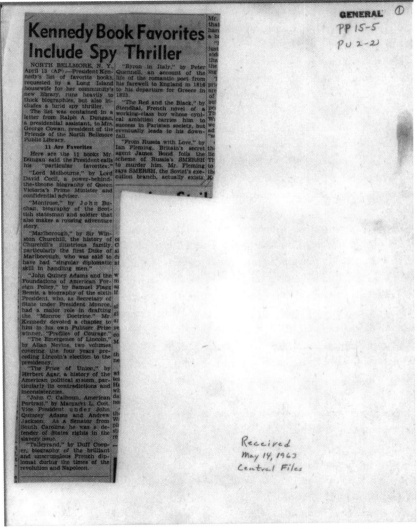

This newspaper clipping found in John F. Kennedy's archive lists Ian Fleming's *From Russia with Love* as one of the President's favorite books. *John F. Kennedy Library: Arthur M. Schlesinger Folder*

President Kennedy even introduced the books to CIA director Allen W. Dulles. President Kennedy and Dulles often talked privately about Ian Fleming's Bond novels, and in 1964 Dulles spoke about them in the same breath as when discussing American operations in Cuba—alluding to the fact that both he and Kennedy looked to Bond's adventures for inspiration when dealing with Cuba and the Soviet Union during the Bay of Pigs and Cuban Missile Crisis (Dulles, interview).

Before making it to the big screen, James Bond started taking over many different forms of media and pop culture. In 1954 CBS aired an Americanized teleplay of *Casino Royale*, starring Barry Nelson (as "Jimmy" Bond) and Peter Lorre, on the anthology series *Climax!* (1954–1958), presented by Chrysler. The novel *Moonraker* was turned into a radio drama in South Africa in 1958, and in the same year, the British newspaper *Daily Express* began running a James Bond comic strip.

When the first James Bond big screen adventure, *Dr. No* (1962), was released to theaters, it was reported that over twenty-two million copies of James Bond adventures were sold worldwide (Johnson "Sean Connery"). By 1964, 007 was a cultural phenomenon in the United States. Longtime *Washington Post* columnist Peter Potomac (a.k.a. Roy H. Hoops) even compared Bond to the Beatles, calling him "the grownup's Beatle." In his column he opined that Bond is "the intellectual's very own Beatle, without the crazy hairdo . . . the teen-agers have their Beatles fan clubs, but Bond lovers are not to be outdone: There is a 'Bond cult' at Harvard, and at Oxford there is a 50-member James Bond Club dedicated 'to carrying on the finer traditions of Bondmanship as they apply to good eating, stylish drinking, high stakes gambling and women.'" Concluding with "So take that, Bond lovers. And let's hear less of these comments about the Beatles not even playing good rock 'n' roll!" (Potomac "James Bond Mania," 18).

Not everyone felt that watching James Bond was for everyone. Dr. Fredric Wethman, a well-known New York psychiatrist, said in 1966 that the James Bond movies were "strictly sadistic and snobbish," adding, "I object to the killing and snobbishness toward sex. The world gets more violent every day, and with movies like these, young people get more and more used to violence. It becomes a natural part of life." Wethman made headlines that same year when he declared that he could "confirm" that the stories of the *Batman* television show "are psychologically homosexual" (Reiter "How Do Shore"). In the same vein, erotic/sexploitation film magazine *Adam Film Quarterly* discussed Bond's sexual prowess, the psychology behind why he chooses the women he becomes involved with, and the question of whether Bond is homosexual and secretly hates women (R. Black "The Case").

> *The world is not enough.*
>
> —Sean Connery as James Bond, *On Her Majesty's Secret Service* (1963), written by Richard Maibaum

Weeks after the North American premiere of *Dr. No* in May 1963, New York *Daily News* reporter Kate Cameron predicted "a thriller film trend," and she could not have been more correct; in addition, the trend flooded many other forms of media (Cameron "Thriller" 28). Spy shows quickly filled the television airwaves throughout the decade. All three major American television networks (NBC, ABC, and CBS) had their share of espionage to fill their prime-time lineups, and spy shows from Great Britain could not be imported fast enough to keep up with the demand.

Even Jethro Bodine (Max Baer Jr.) in *The Beverly Hillbillies* (1962–1971) longed to be a "double naught" spy, in the third season episode "Double Naught Jethro." Herman Munster (Fred Gwynne) was captured by the Russians while scuba diving on vacation and was thought to be a "new type of American spy," in "Herman the Master Spy" on *The Munsters* (1964–1966). *The Monkees* (1966–1968) were caught up in international intrigue, in the episode "The Spy Who Came In from the Cool" when they were asked to be undercover spies, after singer Davy Jones accidentally purchased red maracas with microfilm inside. On *My Favorite Martian* (1963–1966) Tim O'Hara (Bill Bixby) wrote an article in the newspaper criticizing the government's spending on the space program, using knowledge from his Martian "Uncle" Martin (Raymond Walston), and was, of course, accused of being of course, a Russian spy in the episode "Russians 'R' in Season."

Scores of cheap spy pulp novels and magazines were published. The novels, with titles akin to *Spy from the Grave* and *The Spy Who Came Home to Die*, and magazines with titles like *Real Men* and *Men in Combat* included articles such as "I Fought the Reds with Girl Guerrillas" and "I Escaped the Russians" and featured lurid covers with violent scenes, scantily clad women, and tough-as-nails spies.

Some took a more serious approach. John le Carré's *The Spy Who Came In from the Cold* (1965) and *The Looking Glass War* (1965) achieved critical praise and financial success. Published in 1964, children's novel *Harriet the Spy*, written and illustrated by Louise Fitzhugh, gave junior spy aficionados someone their own age to look up to and read about. The book's success upon its release was not a coincidence; it coincided with the peak of the spy craze.

Books parodying Bond were abound. In 1965, former newspaper man Sol Weinstein wrote the book *Loxfinger*, filled with Yiddish phrases and references to Jewish food and kosher delicatessens, about a Hebrew secret agent "Oy-Oy 7 Israel Bond." Weinstein was asked by columnist Earl Wilson, "Isn't that getting to be old hat now? I don't know anybody who isn't spoofing *Goldfinger*." Weinstein responded that "he did it first" in a comedy routine he wrote for Joe E. Lewis a year prior. "I anticipated that the Bond Craze would become impactful as it did. Joe E. talked about being a Hebrew secret agent" (Wilson "Another James Bond," 8). The *Harvard Lampoon* published the James Bond parody *Alligator*. The book was sent to President Kennedy in 1963 by Special Assistant to the President Arthur M. Schlesinger Jr. and can be found in President John F. Kennedy's personal archives (Schlesinger "Papers of John F. Kennedy").

James Bond spy toys were among the hottest-selling children's toys for Christmas 1965 and 1966. Most popular were the James Bond attaché case, James Bond 007 "Action Pack" (which included a secret agent pen, watch with a hidden compartment, vapor paper, and decoder ring), *Thunderball* action figures, and model kits of Bond's signature Aston Martin.

James Bond Aston Martin DB5. Corgi Diecast model no. 261. Issued in 1965. *My Childhood Memories/Alamy Stock Photo*

Television's *Get Smart, The Avengers, Danger Man, The Man from U.N.C.L.E.*, and *The Girl from U.N.C.L.E.* toys and merchandise were not far down the aisle from James Bond in department stores. Commercials filled the television airwaves for toys like the Secret Sam Spy Kit, by Topper Toy. The commercial featured kids, not adults, in trench coats and sunglasses playing with the spy kit. The kit included an attaché case that contained a working periscope, toy pistol with optional silencer and attachable rifle stock that shot short- and long-range bullets or a secret message–carrying missile, and a camera that took actual pictures. Bullets could also be fired from the attaché case. Also included in the kit, according to the box, was

> Secret Sam's fantastic arsenal of secret weapons. The unbelievable Camera Book takes real pictures—black and white or color—from inside or outside—also fires bullets. Secret Sam's Bomb Binoculars really work and fire a bomb besides. The amazing Pipe Shooter—fires [by] squeezing with your teeth. Sixfinger—looks like a finger but fires bullets, missiles, bombs, sends messages and writes with a ball point pen. . . . Bazooka Bat—fires exploding grenades. The Cane Shooter—looks like a harmless cane but fires a bomb and bullets. Secret Sam Spy Kit—complete with bullet and missile firing pistol, detachable stock, silencer, periscope and camera that takes pictures inside or outside of case. They're all official Secret Sam Weapons from Secret Sam.

Topper Toys 1966 Secret Sam Exploding Bomb Binoculars and Pipe Shooter. *My Childhood Memories/Alamy Stock Photo*

A young Kurt Russell, future star of films ranging from *Escape from New York* (1981), *The Thing* (1982), and *Big Trouble in Little China* (1986) to *Overboard* (1987), *Sky High* (2005), and *Guardians of the Galaxy* (2014) starred in three commercials for Mattel's Agent Zero line of spy toys, which included a radio rifle, a movie camera gun, and a sonic blaster. Breakfast cereal Chex even got in on the act. Commercials featuring a trench coat and sunglasses–wearing Butch Patrick, who formerly played Eddie Munster on *The Munsters* (1964–1966), advertised spy-themed prizes. Each box of Wheat Chex included a decoder ring, a secret agent invisible ink pen came with Rice Chex, and a secret message watch (with a secret compartment) was found in boxes of Corn Chex.

The toys that were found under many Christmas trees, despite some back-lash from parental and religious groups. One such critic was Canadian minister Thomas Knott, who also panned "sexy" NHL beer commercials. Knott scolded parents, stating that "children are being encouraged to imitate a brutal, sadistic, hard-drinking killer by parents who buy their children James Bond toys" ("007 Hit," 4).

For adults, a line of official James Bond clothes, with the tagline "Be a Bond Man," was released. The clothing line included James Bond "his and hers" pajamas, shoes, raincoats, money clips, belts, and even gold lamé *Goldfinger* panties and "secret agent baby doll nighties" for ladies. James Bond brand golf clubs and beer were also later unveiled (Moss "Bond," 26; Cullen "James Bond Undies?," 20; Lazarus "More Punch"). Retail stores reported having "fantastic success" with James Bond–themed sales. James Bond–branded products, such as pajamas and cologne were "selling briskly," and James Bond toys were called "the hottest thing on the market" by merchants (Reiter "How Do Shore," 41).

Bond even became part of the common vernacular. The latest technology routinely became described as "James Bond gadgets." Tiny radios, portable TV sets, pocket-sized tape recorders, wearable jewelry that would double as a phone, and a "tiny computer for personal use" were described as such in an article by the Associated Press (Dawson "James Bond Gadgets," 2).

That's as bad as listening to the Beatles without earmuffs.

—Sean Connery as James Bond in *Goldfinger* (1965),
written by Richard Maibaum and Paul Dehn

Scores and theme songs, both official and cover recordings, were released for Bond and practically every spy movie and television show. The first six James Bond films released in the 1960s—*Dr. No* (1962), *From Russia with Love*

(1963), *Goldfinger* (1964), *Thunderball* (1965), *You Only Live Twice* (1967), and *On Her Majesty's Secret Service* (1969)—were not only box office hits. Their theme songs were on seemingly every turntable. *Dr. No* featured the now iconic "James Bond Theme," composed by Monte Norman and arranged and performed by John Barry. *From Russia with Love*'s theme was sung by famous British baritone Matt Monro and composed by Lionel Bart. Brassy-voiced Shirley Bassey recorded the theme for *Goldfinger*; the movie's soundtrack would also reach number one on *Billboard*'s pop album charts. Bassey would later do the theme for later Bond films *Diamonds Are Forever* (1971) and *Moonraker* (1979). Sex symbol Tom Jones belted out the theme to *Thunderball* (1965). Two American singers finished off the 1960s. Nancy Sinatra sang the theme to *You Only Live Twice* (1967). Louis Armstrong sang and played trumpet for the theme to *On Her Majesty's Secret Service* (1969): "We Have All the Time in the World." All the James Bond movie theme songs were covered by artists ranging from Pérez Prado to Glen Campbell.

A number of unauthorized albums featuring the music from the first several James Bond films were released in the mid-1960s. *Author's collection*

Smokey Robinson and the Miracles released the title track to spy spoof *Come Spy with Me* as a B side to "More Love" in 1967. Nancy Sinatra recorded "Last of the Secret Agents?" the theme to the 1966 film of the same name. She also appeared in the film, which starred the comedy team Marty Allen and Steve Rossi. *Get Smart* star Barbara Feldon recorded the spy novelty track "99," along with the B side "Max."

Originally recorded by the Challengers, Johnny Rivers's "Secret Agent Man" was the theme song for the American version of *Danger Man* (1960–1968), which was retitled *Secret Agent* in the states, and it reached number three in 1966 on the *Billboard* Hot 100 charts. The song was most notably covered by surf rockers the Ventures, crooner Mel Tormé in 1966 and the Sam and Dave Orchestra in 1967. The iconic instrumental "Theme from *Mission: Impossible*" by composer Lalo Schifrin reached number forty-one on the *Billboard* Hot 100 and jumped to number nineteen on the Easy Listening Charts.

Between 1966 and 1968 the dance club at the Shelborne Hotel in Miami transformed into a Bond-themed nightclub called the "007½ Go-Go." Herb Kelly of the *Miami News* called the nightclub a "wild place for watusi, frug, swim and others." Unescorted girls received their first drink free on Sunday and Monday nights, and the club featured acts such as Bobby Sands, Lisa the Bat-woman, the Soul Twisters, and Dr. Go (Kelly "Parents Request," 12; "Actress Visiting").

> *If you fail at the large things it means you have not large ambitions.*
>
> —Ian Fleming, *Dr. No*

Subsequent spy films took over the movie screens in the 1960s, following the success of the James Bond films. Espionage, occasionally called "the world's second-oldest profession," was not new to the Cold War, and spy films were not new to the 1960s. They had been made in the silent era and continued to be popular especially from the 1930s to the 1950s. A combination of Cold War fears, technological advancements in filmmaking, increased film production spending, 1960s style, and, of course, 007 James Bond, helped the genre explode in popularity throughout the decade.

A number of spy films from around the world did not make it to movie theaters stateside. Although there was not a language barrier to overcome, British films such as *Die Slowly You'll Enjoy It More* (1967), which was also released as *Spy Today, Die Tomorrow*, never made it to theaters across the pond. On the continent of Asia, a number of unauthorized Tagalog-language Filipino "James Bond" films were made, such as *Dolphfinger*, *Genghis Bond*, and *Dr. Yes*. Unfortunately, prints of these films cannot be found and have been lost to history. However, *James Batman* (1966), which exploited both the James Bond/spy craze and Batmania of 1966, is available but was not discovered in the United States until decades later on VHS. In Japan, Bond-style parody *International Secret Police: Key of Keys* (1965) was not seen in theaters in the United States in its original form; instead it was famously redubbed with new dialog for the Woody Allen film *What's Up, Tiger Lily?* (1966).

German superspy Kommissar X was featured in seven films from 1965 to 1971, beginning with *Kiss, Kiss . . . Kill Kill* (1965). Although the films were dubbed into English and made their way to America in the late 1960s, they all were introduced to American viewers via television screens. Eurospy flicks made around the European continent, like *Requiem of a Secret Agent* (1966), *Death on the Run* (1967), and *Operation Skybolt* (1968), were never shown in American theaters but often did make excellent late-night television in the 1970s and 1980s.

Arguably Mexico's second most popular masked luchador (professional wrestler), Blue Demon, starred in the groovy and stylized *Blue Demon: Destructor de espías* (1968; a.k.a. *Blue Demon: Destructor of Spies*) and the film's sequel *Pasaporte a la muerte* (1968; a.k.a. *Passport to Death*). Mexico's top luchador, El Santo, had starred in *Operation 67* (1966; a.k.a. *Operación 67*) two years earlier, and it played a *very* limited run north of the border. El Santo, Blue Demon, and a number of other luchadores more famously starred together and separately in "creature feature"–style monster movies.

Spanish director Jess Franco directed two French-language superspy films that paid homage to James Bond, starring Europe's number-one tough guy Eddie Constantine: *Residence for Spies* (1966) and *Attack of the Robots* (1966). Constantine was not a stranger to the French spy genre, having previously starred in *There's Going to Be a Party* (1960) and *Jeff Gordon, Secret Agent* (1964).

Aside from England, Italy was the European country most enthralled with the spy genre. It was also easy to import Italian films because Italian filmmakers used a "Tower of Babel"–style of filmmaking, where all the actors spoke in their native language and later the film was dubbed into any applicable language. Many Italian spy flicks never made it to the American silver screen in the 1960s, most famously *Secret Agent 777* (1965), *008: Operation Exterminate* (1965), *Operation White Shark* (1966), and *Danger!! Death Ray* (1967). Even Italy's wrestling superhero and answer to Mexico's El Santo, Superargo, in *Superargo versus Diabolicus* (1966) and *Superargo Meets the Faceless Giants* (1968), took numerous elements from the era's spy flicks.

> *I shall not waste my days in trying to prolong them. I shall use my time.*
>
> —Ian Fleming, *You Only Live Twice*

But secret agent films flooded theaters, drive-ins, and television sets in the United States throughout the 1960s, starting with the first James Bond adventure to hit the big screen, *Dr. No* (1962). This is the story, from a historical perspective, of those films and television shows and how they became a part of American pop culture.

1

007 JAMES BOND

Mine's Bond—James Bond.

—Ian Fleming, *Casino Royale*

The 1960s spy craze all started with MI6 Agent 007, James Bond of Her Majesty's Secret Service. There were seven films that officially feature James Bond released between 1962 through 1969: six by Eon Productions and one noncanon, James Bond spoof by MGM.

Dr. No (1962)

Selling twenty-two million books worldwide and being a favorite of President John F. Kennedy get the attention of the press and the general public. So in August 1961 when it was announced that Ian Fleming's James Bond adventure novel *Dr. No* would be sold to producers Albert "Cubby" Broccoli and Harry Saltzman, who collectively formed Eon Productions, and would be financed and released by United Artists, there were a buzz of excitement and lots of speculation (Johnson "Sean Connery"; Graham "Private Citizen").

The biggest question was, Who would take on the role of James Bond? In the 1955 novel *Moonraker*, Ian Fleming described Bond as "certainly good-looking" and that Bond had "black hair falling down over the right eyebrow," "there was something a bit cruel in the mouth," and his "eyes were cold." Fleming personally gave the casting directors guidance as to who should be cast as James Bond, advising, "Bond is quiet, hard, ruthless, sardonic and fatalistic. . . . All his movements are relaxed and economical" ("Top Hero," 8).

Stack of ten of Ian Fleming's James Bond novels. *Chris Howes/Wild Places Photography/Alamy Stock Photo*

Actors David Niven, Richard Todd, Rex Harrison, Stanley Baker, and Trevor Howard were all rumored to have been in talks or at least considered for the part; however, in November 1961 it was announced that the role of James Bond would be played by a relatively unknown Scottish actor, Sean Connery (Ibid.). Saltzman called the role the "acting plum of the decade" (Ibid.).

Connery talked about preparing for the role: "I see Bond as a complete sensualist. His senses are highly tuned and he's awake to everything. He likes his women. He's quite amoral." He added, "I particularly like him because he thrives on conflict—a quality lacking in present day society" (Ibid.).

In his first film adventure, 007 James Bond is sent to Jamaica to investigate the murder of MI6 agent Strangways. Bond determines that his death was because of his assignment, which was in cooperation with the American CIA, to find the cause of sabotage missiles launched from Cape Canaveral, Florida. With the help of a CIA agent and local fisherman Quarrel (John Kitzmiller),

Bond discovers the island, feared by the locals, which is responsible for the sabotage and discovers the lair of Dr. No (Joseph Wiseman), who has a far more sinister plot in mind.

Bond's first film establishes him as an MI6 "Double O" agent with a license to kill and introduces a number of characters that would be used in many future James Bond films: head of the UK's Secret Intelligence Service MI6, "M" (Bernard Lee), secretary to "M," Miss Moneypenny (Lois Maxwell)—with whom Bond has a flirtatious yet never physical relationship—and American CIA agent Felix Leiter (Jack Lord). Lee would play the role of M in the first eleven Eon-produced James Bond films, the last one being *Moonraker* (1979), before his death in 1981. Maxwell continued with her role as Miss Moneypenny for the first fourteen Eon-produced Bond films until *A View to a Kill* (1985). She was replaced by Caroline Bliss in *The Living Daylights* (1987), when Timothy Dalton took over the role of James Bond. Felix Leiter would be played by an ever-revolving door of actors including Cec Linder, Rik Van Nutter, and Norman Burton.

Dr. No also included the "James Bond Theme," which was composed by Monte Norman and was arranged and performed by John Barry; Bond's signature introduction (My name is Bond, James Bond), the famous "Gun Barrel Sequence" that opened the film; and James Bond acquiring his infamous handgun (Walther PPK). It establishes Bond's preferred drink as a vodka martini "shaken, not stirred" and the introduction of evil criminal organization SPECTRE (Special Executive for Counterintelligence, Terrorism, Revenge and Extortion), which Bond fights until *For Your Eyes Only* (1981). In addition, it introduced the "Bond Girl," a girl who is typically caught up in international intrigue, who sleeps with and is usually saved by James Bond, and who is typically never seen or referenced after the conclusion of the film. Ursula Andress was the first "Bond Girl," playing skin diver/shell collector Honey Ryder, whom Bond meets on Dr. No's island.

The director's chair was occupied by Terence Young, who had previously directed a number of British films—most notably, *Corridor of Mirrors* (1948), which was both Young's directorial and Christopher Lee's film debut; *Safari* (1956), with Victor Mature and Janet Leigh; *Zarak* (1957), with Victor Mature; and *Too Hot To Handle* (1960), with Jayne Mansfield.

With a production cost of just under a million dollars, much of *Dr. No* was filmed on location in London, England, and the British colony of Jamaica, where Bond creator Ian Fleming worked on many of his James Bond novels at his Jamaican estate, "GoldenEye." Jamaica became the setting and inspiration of many of his James Bond novels ("*Thunderball* Bond Film").

Still of Ursula Andress in *Dr. No* (1962), wearing her iconic bikini and collecting shells on Dr. No's island. *Author's collection*

On October 5, 1962, at *Dr. No*'s premiere at the London Pavilion, for the first time, audiences saw the famous and often parodied gun barrel sequence—where stuntman Bob Simmons (not Sean Connery) walks across the screen while being followed by a gun barrel, jump-pivots, and fires his gun at the barrel as blood flows down the screen—and heard the now iconic "James Bond Theme" blaring from the theater's speakers. The film did not premiere in the United States until May 8, 1963, and did not make it to America's two largest markets, Los Angeles and New York City, until May 29, 1963.

Birmingham, England, *Sunday Mercury* writer F. Leslie Withers wrote that *Dr. No* was the antithesis of the realistic "kitchen sink" dramas that were popular in England at the time, such as *A Taste of Honey* (1961). "Aren't you, too, getting a bit tired of the kitchen stove, back-to-back houses, smoking industrial chimneys, slouching delinquents, pick-up girls and the blowsy mums and inarticulate dads?" Withers added the film is a "rattling 'boys' adventure yarn . . . and it crams in everything—seascapes, tropical beaches, gorgeous women, a Chinese master crook with millions, Cape Canaveral, lush club settings, fast cars, crashes, explosives, gun-play but thank heaven, not a kitchen stove in sight." Perhaps the most predictive statement was made by Withers as well when he said, "I hope this film is the only forerunner of a series if only it could be guaranteed that they wouldn't let the pace flag or realities intrude" (Withers "What, No Kitchen Sink?," 18).

Newcastle, England's Lynn Fenton, of *The Journal*, remarked that Bond was a "tough, sadistic, sensual operator, who can kill a man without qualm and who can make love to a dame he has just met," adding, "You have got to take it in gulps or not at all. You either like your violence and sex straight out of Bond or you don't. There are no half measures about James Bond. He gives everything and everybody the works, and it works" (Fenton "James Bond Is No Gentleman," 10). Ernest Betts of London newspaper *The People* tore the film apart, writing, "[With] a million dollars spent in the process, I expected something better than this. We get a clumsy script which [*sic*] boobs in your face and some hammy situations that send thrills skidding into laughs" (Betts "Oh, No!," 16).

In America, *New York Times*'s critic Bosley Crowther wrote, "If you are clever, you will see it as a spoof of science-fiction and sex. For the crime-detecting adventure that Mr. Bond is engaged in here is so wildly exaggerated, so patently contrived, that it is obviously silly and not to be believed" (Crowther "Dr. No," 20). Advertisements flooded newspapers, saying, "Now meet the most extraordinary gentleman spy in all fiction! James Bond Agent 007 Adding the Double 'O' means he has a license to kill when he chooses . . . whom he chooses!" (*Dr. No* advertisement). And radio spots filled the airwaves as well, inviting listeners to "meet James Bond. The indestructible agent who thrives on trouble, both violent and voluptuous" while the "James Bond Theme" played in the background. There was even international attention for *Dr. No.* Soviet youth newspaper *Komsomolskaya Pravda* called James Bond part of "the sinister world-wide, anti-Soviet conspiracy centered in Washington" and that James Bond enjoys "great popularity with American propagandists" ("Ian Fleming," 33).

Dr. No, was a worldwide success, earning $2,400,000 in North America alone. Sales of James Bond novels skyrocketed again, selling 1.5 million more books in a six-month period ("Big Rental Pictures of 1963"; J. Black *Politics of James Bond*, 96).

From Russia with Love (1963)

United Artists announced in March 1962 the production of the second James Bond film, *From Russia with Love* (1963). The film was based on the Ian Fleming novel of the same name. Clearly producers foresaw the success of the James Bond franchise, even before releasing *Dr. No* (1962).

Even President John F. Kennedy was a fan of Ian Fleming's novels. Almost every press release and article about the upcoming movie seemed to mention it. Ian Fleming, who met then senator Kennedy in Washington, DC, six months before Kennedy was elected president in 1960, recalled that Jackie Kennedy asked him "Are you *the* Ian Fleming?" which Fleming stated was "music to any writer's ears." From his encounter on, Fleming personally sent a copy to Kennedy whenever he published a new James Bond novel. Fleming was quoted as saying, "It's the least I can do" (Lyons "Pieces of Molding," 9; Cullen "Tarantulas," 8; "JFK's Favorite," 12).

Production of *From Russia with Love* began even before *Dr. No* was released in the United States, on March 25, 1963, and shooting took place in England, Istanbul, and Venice. Sean Connery returned as agent 007 James Bond. Before production began, Connery announced he had a nonexecutive contract to make six more Bond films every fourteen months. However, it did come with a handsome salary bump: Connery reportedly made $15,000 for his work on *Dr. No* a year earlier, but his salary was increased to $100,000 for *From Russia with Love* (Monahan "Second"; Quinn "Of Broadway").

Terence Young also returned to take on directing duties. Additional casting included 1960's Miss Universe runner-up Daniela Bianchi, whose appearance was often likened to both Greta Garbo and Princess Grace Kelly ("Kildare Romance," 61), as Tatiana Romanova, a Soviet consulate clerk and James Bond paramour. The role was originally rumored to be taken on by Jennie Ann Lindstrom, the twenty-four-year-old daughter of Ingrid Bergman. Lotte Lenya played Rosa Klebb, a former Soviet counterintelligence (SMERSH) colonel turned SPECTRE's number three. And Pedro Armendáriz was cast as Ali Kerim Bey, who was head of MI6 in Istanbul. Bernard Lee would return as M, chief of British Intelligence, as would Lois Maxwell as Miss Moneypenny, M's secretary. *From Russia with Love* would mark the first appearance of Desmond Llewelyn as MI6 quartermaster/weapons and gadget expert Major Boothroyd, later known as simply Q who provides Bond with the first of many gadgets, namely, a tear gas bomb–spewing attaché case and a folding sniper rifle. Llewelyn would appear as Q in seventeen Eon-produced James Bond films, his last appearance being in *The World Is Not Enough* (1999) (Thomas "Sean Connery"; Johnson "Heart Thumper"; Parsons "Rita Wins"; "Wanted"; Graham "Gleason").

From Russia with Love also marked the first appearance of SPECTRE's number-one and soon-to-be archrival of James Bond: Ernst Blofeld. Blofeld, who's torso and hand petting his cat was only seen on screen, was credited as "?" but was played by Anthony Dawson, who also played Professor R. J. Dent in *Dr. No*, and was voiced by Eric Pohlmann.

In the film, while SPECTRE was still attempting to get revenge on Bond for killing Dr. No, Bond was on a mission to retrieve a Soviet encryption-decoding device known as the Lektor. The hunt for the device took Bond for an action-packed ride on the Orient Express to Istanbul, where he believed the Lektor was located. Of course, Bond makes time to be intimate with several women along the way.

As production progressed, entertainment pages kept readers abreast of the latest updates from the set. *From Russia with Love* boasted a seventy-two-member production unit and was the first movie to shoot on two continents on the same day, due to Istanbul being located between Asia and Europe. Reports from the set stated that "director Terence Young finished scenes sooner than he had expected at the St. Sophia Mosque, on the European side, and was able to make an afternoon set-up across the Bosporus in Uskudar." Young was quoted as saying, "I suppose it's nothing for record books, but it was certainly an unusual experience for this crew" ("Movie Shot" 9).

While shooting *From Russia with Love*, it was clear the fervor for Bond and the spy craze were not going away, as Sean Connery began receiving upward of five hundred fan letters a week (Steele "From 'Idiot'"). The set even had a VIP guest visit while shooting in London. James Bond author and creator Ian Fleming was on hand to watch the production (McClure "Fleming Autographs").

When shooting on location in Istanbul, Turkey, director Young had trouble getting silence on the set due to the calls to Muslim prayer five times a day. Eventually he decided to work around the calls to prayer since, he said, it was "part of the authentic color of Istanbul" (Scheuer "Visitors," 69). Meanwhile, Mexican actor Pedro Armendáriz, who was cast as a Turkish British Secret Service MI6 agent Ali Kerim Bey, was interviewed about refusing to play stereotypical Mexican roles and noted that he also refused to play a stereotypical Turk. When asked about his costume fitting, he said he would be wearing "ordinary suits, but they said they wanted them to look a little Turkish. Whatever that may mean." He added, "But no fez. It may be a myth—but it's a modern one" (Garret and Cleave "Man from South," 10). Armendáriz would not be able to fight against Hollywood stereotype casting following his role in *From Russia with Love*. Armendáriz committed suicide before the film's release in June 1963 at age fifty-one, following late-stage cancer treatment ("Mexican Star").

One of the actors in the film sparked ire in Egypt. Focusing on movies and television, Egypt's minister of culture decreed that belly dancers (or harem dancers, as he called them) must "keep their art in the consistence with public morality" and asked dancers to keep their dancing "respectable." He added, "Hip swinging, shaking, quivering and shivering are out. The back and abdomen must be covered. Skirts must be full with no side or front openings." Lella Guirael, a professional Lebanese belly dancer, whose role in the film was to seduce James Bond through her belly dancing while in Istanbul openly defied any decrees from the minister of culture in Egypt (where belly dancing is said to originate). She stated why she felt any attempt to change her occupation would fail: "The dancing is older than the pyramids" (Johnson "Harem Dancers," 2).

After production wrapped, entertainment pages in the United States and the United Kingdom throughout 1963 were filled with still shots promoting the film's highly anticipated release. The film's poster exclaimed, "James Bond is Back! . . . Meet James Bond, secret agent 007. His new incredible women! His new incredible enemies! His new incredible adventures!"

From Russia with Love premiered on October 10, 1963, at the Odeon Leicester Square in London and reviews came pouring in from critics in London papers. Penelope Gilliatt of *The Observer* wrote that the opening sequence for the film "is so good that anyone but the James Bond film makers might be frightened they couldn't top it." But she felt this film did not have the same "coarse-grained" humor as in *Dr. No* and that James Bond needed to use more logic and intellect instead of violence. "Heroes in this sort of film can't afford not to be bright. You have to be able to admire heroes for something, and you can't exactly admire Bond for his character." She added, "I wish he thought his way out of more situations, instead of always kicking his way out" (Gilliatt "Laughing," 27).

Jack Bentley of the *Sunday Mirror* was surprised that *From Russia with Love* escaped the British Board of Film Censors with an A rating, that is, suitable for all audiences. "Sex and sadism on a scale to make most Continental* X films like Disney trailers abound throughout," wrote Bentley. He added, "And surely it must be the first film in history to touch on the subject of lesbianism[†] and escape the brand X." However, aside from the ratings issue, Bentley felt that *From Russia with Love* was the kind of film that could "stop the rot in the movie industry. For, as a piece of escapism it is superb. . . . It's one of the few films I wouldn't mind seeing twice" (Bentley "From the Censor," 31).

Patrick Gibbs of the *Daily Telegraph* felt "Bond was slipping" because "morally it seems safer than its predecessor; the sex and sadism formula has been toned down. Artistically, if one can use the word in this context, I miss Mr. Young's earlier tendency to laugh up his sleeve, as it were" (Gibbs "In the Bed-Sitter," 13). *The Guardian*'s Richard Roud criticized *From Russia with Love* because the movie "didn't seem quite so lively, quite so fresh, or quite so

---

* Mainland Europe.
  † Rosa Klebb (SPECTRE Number Three) had several lines of dialogue and acting that alluded to lesbianism.

rhythmically fast moving." Roud also felt that "there aren't so many juicy girls" (Roud "New Films," 9).

Those in the United States had to wait six more months until *From Russia with Love* made its debut. However, President Kennedy, who in 1961 had listed Ian Fleming's Bond novel *From Russia with Love* as one of his favorite books, was given a special screening of the film at the White House on November 20, 1963. The screening took place two days before he was assassinated in Dallas, Texas, on November 22, 1963, and is believed to be the last movie the late president watched (Zenou "JFK's Secret Weapon").

On April 8, 1964, the movie premiered in the United States at New York's Astor Theater. It ran in other Showcase theaters throughout the city and opened nationwide on April 10, 1964. *New York Times* critic Bosley Crowther urged readers not to miss the movie and called the characters "deliciously fantastic and delightfully well played" and the film "a mad melodramatization of a desperate adventure of Bond with sinister characters in Istanbul . . . and in a dashing style thoroughly illogical, but younger blithely wedged in cheek" (Crowther "James Bond Travels," 25).

Associated Press correspondent Bob Thomas believed Bond adventures too formulaic. "A logical continuity cannot be written because there is none. These films are a throwback to the Saturday matinee serials that were a Hollywood staple for many a year," wrote Thomas. "The formula is simple. Every five or ten minutes, Bond is bottled in a tight or deadly situation. Will he get out? Of course. The only difference between these films and the old-time serials is that you don't have to wait until next Saturday to find out what happens" (Thomas, "James Bond," 10).

Joel Anastasi of the *Asbury Park Press*, in Asbury Park, New Jersey, compared James Bond to Superman when it comes to being seemingly invincible. "There's a new model super male out handsomer, and more suave, who has become the ultimate weapon in the battle of intrigue between nations," Anatasi wrote. He noted that Bond got into "some wild situations loaded with color and suspense. Example: some eerie trips though the rat-infested subterranean canals of Istanbul; some spectacular fights between bullies, a helicopter and an outrageously contrived but beautifully executed scene where Bond blows up a small fleet of motor boats that have him cornered." Anastasi also made a remark about the women in the picture, saying that "when (Bond) isn't making love to them, we're ogling them" (Anastasi *"From Russia,"* 29).

Just as when *Dr. No* was released a year earlier, James Bond book sales went through the roof. Between 1956 and April 1964, Ian Fleming's book *From Russia with Love* had sold more than six million copies around the world ("Sells").

And the movie was the highest-grossing film in England in 1963, earning £800,000 in the UK (approximately $2.5 million) by year's end and over $3,849,000 in the United States, $700,000 of which was earned in New York during the film's opening week ("Most Popular Films"; Portis "Is Cloak-and-Dagger"; "Big Rental Pictures 1964"). Along with box office numbers, Connery's popularity also skyrocketed. The London bureau of New York's *Motion Picture Herald* reported that Sean Connery's popularity in England rose from the tenth most popular star in 1962 to fourth in 1963, due to the popularity of *From Russia with Love*. Pop singer Cliff Richard took the list's top spot that year ("Cliff Richard").

Even though Bond was popular with filmgoers and was a favorite of President Kennedy, Bond's creator did not see the appeal. "I've never made Bond out to be a hero, but only a competent professional," said Fleming following the release of the film version of *From Russia with Love*. "That's why I'm amazed to see the teen-agers take him up and idolize him." However, Fleming was quick to defend his character when British weekly magazine *Today* called Bond the "nastiest and most sadistic writing of our day . . . disgusting drivel." The magazine also called James Bond a "cheap and very nasty upper class thug" who engaged in sadistic sexual acts. "The world has read enough about torture used during the Algerian war to know that these things happen," responded Fleming. "Bulldog Drummond would have been hit over the head with a cricket bat, but nowadays he would be subjected to much more refined torture. I try to get as near the truth as I can without scaring the daylights out of people" (Cullen "Tarantulas," 8).

Goldfinger (1964)

The ending credits in *From Russia with Love* (1963) announced, "Not Quite the End. James Bond Will Return in Ian Fleming's *Goldfinger*." The next year Bond did just that, pitted against the gold-obsessed, German, red-haired villain Auric Goldfinger. Goldfinger conspired to set off a nuclear bomb (provided by the Red Chinese) in Fort Knox to both disrupt the American monetary system for the Chinese and to make his personal gold reserve worth ten times as much. His plot was known as "Operation Grand Slam."

As early as January 1963, when *Dr. No* was still in theaters and before *From Russia with Love* began production, Eon Productions/James Bond franchise producers Albert "Cubby" Broccoli and Harry Saltzman began discussing plans to produce the Ian Fleming James Bond novel *Goldfinger*. They even tapped Jack Lord to reprise his role as CIA agent/American counterpart to James Bond, Felix Leiter, a character that did not appear in *From Russia with*

Love. However, an eventual contract dispute with Lord over where his name would appear on the movie's billing caused Lord to drop out of the film and to eventually be replaced by Cec Linder (Hopper "Curtis' Marriage," 8).

In early 1964, although he reportedly signed a six-picture deal, Sean Connery announced that he would not reprise the role of James Bond in *Goldfinger* because he was afraid of being typecast. But Connery quickly changed his mind, thanks to a healthy pay increase, by the time production began in April. Connery also was reported to have held up production when he injured his back during a fight sequence and demanded a cut of the film's profits. Connery later announced that he would require a salary of one million dollars, per film, to continue to play the character of James Bond following *Goldfinger* (Graham "Johnson Cheered"; Cohen "In One Ear").

The main Bond villain, the gold-obsessed member of SPECTRE Auric Goldfinger, was played by German actor Gert Frobe, in his first English-language role, which yielded his interesting and very distinctive delivery (Scheuer "Gilbert to Direct"). Frobe's casting did cause some controversy upon the film's release. In 1965 Frobe was quoted by the British newspaper *Daily Mail* as saying that during World War II, "naturally I was a Nazi." Frobe later denied the quote saying, "What I told an English reporter during an interview was that during the Third Reich I had the luck to be able to help two Jewish people, although I was a member of the Nazi party." The original quote even reportedly delayed *Goldfinger*'s release in Israel until a Jew, Mario Blumenau, informed the Israeli Embassy in Vienna that his life and his mother's had been saved when Mr. Frobe hid them from the Nazis ("Gert Frobe," 14).

Professional wrestler and 1948 US Olympic weightlifting silver medalist Harold Sakata (known around the world in the wrestling ring as Tosh Togo) was cast as Goldfinger's mute Korean henchman Oddjob. Saltzman and Broccoli got the idea to cast Sakata after seeing him in the main event of a televised professional wrestling program. Sakata won the duo over in his audition when he kicked the mantle of Saltzman's fireplace off with his bare foot. Although Sakata would be associated with the role of Oddjob the rest of his life, at first he thought it would benefit his already impressive wrestling career. "I'm so mean in this picture that promoters may have trouble finding opponents for me after it is shown," laughed Sakata. Sakata's portrayal of Oddjob became the prototype for all future James Bond villain henchmen ("Former Konan," 20).

English actress Honor Blackman was cast as the personal pilot for Goldfinger and, of course, eventual lover of James Bond. The United Press International (UPI) press service described Blackman as "a slender, long-haired blonde with a gleaming smile who could pass for 30 if she did not insist on telling her right age" (Blackman was thirty-eight at the time of filming) and added that script-writers wanted a somewhat more mature woman who would be both intelligent and tough. They found this a problem to put down on paper until Miss Black-man said, "Just write as though she were a man. I'll do the rest" ("Mayhem on Males," 11).

After being cast, Blackman was quoted as saying, "I can hardly wait, I met [Connery] once when he was just Sean Connery and he's gorgeous. *Very* sexy" (Richards "Three Men," 14). It was reported that Blackman earned £10,000 in 1964 (approximately $33,305) for two months of work filming *Goldfinger* (Ibid.). Prior to *Goldfinger*, she costarred on the popular British spy show *The Avengers* (1961–1969) from 1962 through 1965 as the leather-clad secret agent and anthropologist Dr. Cathy Gale, alongside her partner Patrick Macnee as John Steed. It was reported that Broccoli did not mind that at the time Black-man was primarily known in Europe (*The Avengers* did not premiere in the United States until March 1966), stating, "The Brits would love her because they knew her as Mrs. Gale, the Yanks would like her because she was so good—it was a perfect combination" (Moore *Bond on Bond*, 51).

While Blackman was still on *The Avengers* in 1964, the *New York Times* wrote about the show and Blackman's popularity overseas. In the article, Black-man, a noted judo expert, stated that "about 20 million people spend the time between 10 P.M. and 11 P.M. each Saturday hoping to see [Cathy Gale] climb into her 'fighting suit' and hurl the heavies through plate glass windows." Her "fighting suit" consisted of a leather outfit worn with hip-length boots, which also caused a fad among women in England. Despite her outfit being popular with women, Blackman added her fan mail was "98 percent male" and that "only about 1 percent is concerned with my acting ability." Blackman quipped that if she turned the letters over to the police, "a sizable proportion of the male population of Britain would be liable to arrest." When asked about the reason for her popularity, Blackman bluntly stated, "The explanation doesn't have to be complicated. It's quite simple. One three-letter word: sex." But Blackman did enjoy her tough persona and particularly enjoyed throwing men around on film. "It was really kind of sick," said Blackman. "but I must confess I got a band out of it myself" (Carthew "All Honor"; Thomas "Female 'James Bond,'" 36; Cullen "Judo Societies," 9; Boyle "British Actress," 40).

Blackman enjoyed the attention. Famously and clearly leaning into her own sex appeal, a bikini-wearing Blackman appeared in a promo shot by famed Brit-ish photographer Terry O'Neill for *Goldfinger* with the word "PUSSY" written in the sand. Many articles written about the film in America referred to Black-man's character as simply "Miss Galore" ("Goldfinger Contest," 22).

Infamous promotional photo by Terry O'Neill of Honor Blackman for *Goldfinger* **(1964), where she played villainess Pussy Galore.** *Author's collection*

To complement Blackman, producers went on a nationwide hunt for "six 6-ft-tall sexy beauties" to star in *Goldfinger*. The women cast made up a team of pilots known as "Pussy Galore's Flying Circus" (Wilson "That's Earl," 2). In addition, Shirley Eaton appears as Jill Masterson in one of the film's most iconic scenes. Masterson, a scantily dressed employee and "companion" of Goldfinger who also helps him cheat at cards by using a telescope and radio, double-crosses Goldfinger and (of course) spends the night with 007. The next morning, Bond has breakfast with Felix Leiter and leaves Masterson in the hotel room. Upon his return, Bond finds Masterson covered in gold paint and dead from "skin suffocation." The scene led to urban legends about gold paint actually accidentally killing Shirley Eaton or makeup artists needing to be extra careful not to kill her because skin suffocation is an actual ailment. In the film, Bond even states that dancers in Rio who paint their bodies need to leave a small patch of unpainted skin to avoid the condition. All such ideas are untrue.

Although the previous James Bond adventure, *From Russia with Love*, introduced Desmond Llewelyn as Q, head of MI6's Q branch who supplies agents with weapons, tools, gadgets, and vehicles, *Goldfinger* established the Q branch as a division that creates outlandish devices for Bond and other double O agents at MI6. One such device featured in *Goldfinger* is a parking meter that disperses tear gas when change is inserted. In later movies the gadgets got more unorthodox (and at times zany). *Goldfinger* also established Bond's playfully yet antagonistic relationship with Q that would be seen in all future Bond films.

The Q branch equipped James Bond with gadgets in his Aston Martin DB5: tire-ripping, flick-knife wheels, machine guns, smoke screen exhaust, four-pronged nail sprayer, oil slick sprayer, a bulletproof screen, reversible license plate numbers, passenger ejector seat, and radar scanner. Although the Aston Martin DB5 with all the car's gadgets sold for around £4,400 (approximately $13,222) in 1964, the car cost the film's producers an extra £10,000 (approximately $33,300), making it about ten times more costly than the average car produced that year (Wale "Steering Clear"; "James Bond Comes Back").

While planning *Goldfinger's* production, Broccoli was reported to have contacted White House press secretary Pierre Salinger for permission to film over the vault at Fort Knox in Kentucky. Salinger referred him to the "proper authorities," but he did have one request: "If you have a print of *From Russia, with Love* send it over. Somebody wants to see it." "Somebody" was President John F. Kennedy, who listed Ian Fleming as one of his favorite writers (Hopper "Hollywood," 13).

Goldfinger reportedly cost approximately £900,000 (approximately $3 million) to produce. At the time, it was the most expensive James Bond adventure due to an ever-increasing need to one up the previous film with effect, scenery, and actors, and, of course, the need to keep Sean Connery as 007. In comparison, *Dr. No* cost £504,000 (approximately $1.68 million) and *From Russia with Love* came in at £272,000 (approximately $2.24 million) to produce ("James Bond Said"; "Film with Midas Touch," 10).

Unfortunately, James Bond's creator never got to see the final product. Nearly a month before *Goldfinger* made it to theaters, Ian Fleming died of a heart attack at the age of fifty-four on August 12, 1964. Fleming only got to see two James Bond adventures on the big screen ("Creator of Secret Agent"). *Goldfinger* premiered on September 17, 1964 at the Odeon Leicester Square in London. The showing was a benefit for the Newsvendors Benevolent Association, an organization that provided pensions and financial assistance to newsmen ("Briefing").

The *New York Times* reported that at the film's premiere at Odeon Leicester Square, "the thousands outside the theater made it extremely difficult for the invited audience to get near and the situation was resolved only when police reinforcements arrived and carved a passage through the mob." Subsequent screenings brought success to English movie theaters. "The Odeon Theater's first-week record—set up by the last Bond, *From Russia with Love*—was exceeded by some $9,000, for an all-time London cinema record take of $52,000," reported the *New York Times*, "in spite of the fact that the film was simultaneously having a 'showcase' presentation in nine other London theaters. At one of these, in Hammersmith, where a good average week yields $6,000, *Goldfinger* drew $30,000" (Bart "On Britain's," 13). Cecil Wilson of the *Daily Mail* wrote, "This latest James Bond film remains a lusty memorial to the exotic imagination of Ian Fleming. . . . This is the most violent, complex and self-mocking of the 007 films." Said Donald Zec of the *Daily Mirror*, "If deadly females, death-ray torture, electrocution, strangulation, lung bursting depressurization and dry Martinis beguile your lighter moments, then you are in for the whole gold-plated works" ("New Bond Movie," 9).

Before *Goldfinger* opened to paying audiences in the United States, the film was previewed at an annual sales meeting for Piper Aircraft, which supplied the aircrafts for Pussy Galore and her six pilots ("Goldfinger Has Been"). In the United States, *Goldfinger* premiered on December 21, 1964, at the DeMille Theater in New York City. The film was so popular that the DeMille began running the movie around the clock, showing *Goldfinger* at least twelve times every twenty-four hours, from December 23, 1964, through the end of the year (Crowther "Agent 007," 36; "Theater Open 24").

Herb Michelson, stage and screen writer for the Oakland, California, *Oakland Tribune* noted, "House records are being broken everywhere you look; one theater, the Oaks in Berkeley, had to hire special police to handle traffic; other movie houses in which you could once fire a Howitzer and not injure anyone are packing 'em in." Warren McMillain, owner of the Rancho Drive-In in San Pablo, California, called the movie "one of our top grossers of all time.

It's fantastic. And *Goldfinger* will do even better in the second run." And Sal Enea, who ran the Fremont outdoor theaters in Fremont, California, exclaimed, "Amazing. I've never seen anything like it" when asked about *Goldfinger*'s attendance numbers (Michelson "That Glittering").

Reviews that came in throughout the United States were mostly positive, with some exceptions. Bosley Crowther of the *New York Times* seemingly disliked the film, preferring the two previous James Bond films, and was strangely obsessed with the type of women James Bond was intimate with in *Goldfinger*:

> Old Double-Oh Seven is slipping—or, rather, his script writers are. They are involving him more, and more with gadgets and less and less with girls. . . . Agent 007 of the British Secret Service virtually spurns the lush temptations of voluptuous females in favor of high-powered cars and tricky machines. That is to say, he virtually spurns them in comparison to the way he went for them in his previous cinematic conniptions, *Dr. No* and *From Russia with Love*. In those fantastic fabrications, you may remember, he was constantly assailed by an unending flow of luxurious, exotic and insatiable girls. (Crowther "Agent 007," 36)

Crowther did not even seem to like the type of girls in *Goldfinger* either:

> One is a pliant little number who expires early, sealed in a skin of gold paint, and the other is a brawny pilot who remarkably resembles Gorgeous George. Neither is up to the standard of femininity usually maintained for Mr. Bond. . . . One might question whether Bond really likes girls. So maybe his careful script writers have played down that overly amorous side, delicately displacing dolls with automation and beautiful bodies with electronic brains. (Ibid.)

As for the film itself, Crowther stated that *Goldfinger* "is an excess-of-science-fiction fun, a mess of mechanical melodrama and a minimum of bedroom farce" (Ibid.).

The Associated Press's Bob Thomas wrote that Goldfinger is "a glossy, sexy and slick piece of film entertainment" (Thomas "Latest James Bond," 3). John L. Scott of the *Los Angeles Times* called the film a "rousing melodrama" and noted that for "devotees of Fleming's James Bond" the film is a "must" (Scott "*Goldfinger*," 1964, 17). Even Forest J. Ackerman, the editor of science fiction/horror magazines *Famous Monsters of Filmland* and *Monster World*, was amazed by *Goldfinger*. He wrote in a 1965 edition of *Monster World*, "I thrilled to every [*sic*] minute of it. I would like to see a new James Bond picture every month (Ackerman "Fang Mail," 48). *Goldfinger* became a worldwide box-office hit, grossing $3,849,000 in the United States by the end of 1965 alone ("Big Rental Pictures of 1965").

In addition to great box office numbers, *Goldfinger* was an award-winning film. Norman Wanstall took home an Academy Award for Best Sound Effects Editing, and John Barry was nominated for the Grammy Award for Best Score for a Motion Picture in 1965. The album of *Goldfinger*'s score by John Barry also rose to number one on the *Billboard* Pop Albums charts.

After the release of *Goldfinger,* Connery starred in the Alfred Hitchcock thriller *Marnie* (1964) and reportedly signed a deal to play the role of James Bond in three more pictures for Eon/United Artists (Fiset "Escape from the Office").

Thunderball (1965)

Although *On Her Majesty's Secret Service* was originally planned to be the next Ian Fleming novel turned into a movie for Eon Productions, the ending credits of *Goldfinger* (1965) announced "the End of *Goldfinger*, but James Bond will be back in *Thunderball*." *On Her Majesty's Secret Service* made it to the big screen two years later in 1967 ("4th James Bond").

In *Thunderball*, SPECTRE hijacks two nuclear hydrogen bombs and holds NATO ransom for £100 million in diamonds. Of course, 007 is called in to thwart SPECTRE's plans, follows clues to the Bahamas, and does battle with SPECTRE's number-two man Emilio Largo (Adolfo Celi) and his henchmen in a number of spectacular underwater sequences.

The rights to *Thunderball* were in dispute even before the first James Bond film, *Dr. No* (1962), was made. In 1961 scriptwriter Jack Whittingham and producer Kevin McClory took Ian Fleming to court over his novel *Thunderball*, which was released in 1961. The three men worked on a similar film script together, and later Fleming independently released the book. Whittingham and McClory attempted to stop the release of the book and get the court to acknowledge the fact that *Thunderball* was not a solo effort by Fleming and thus all three men were entitled to compensation and rights ("Dispute over Copyright"). Whittingham settled out of court and would sign away his rights to *Thunderball*. However, McClory received the film rights to the novel and announced that production of his own version of *Thunderball* would begin the next year in the Bahamas at an estimated cost of around $2 million. McClory hoped to make it to theaters in time to rival the release of *Goldfinger* in 1964 (Lewis "Even 'M'").

Rumors abounded about who would play the role of James Bond for Kevin McClory's *Thunderball*; Laurence Harvey, Richard Burton, Rod Taylor, and even Sean Connery were rumored to have been offered the role ("Laurence Harvey"; "Burton"; "Rod Taylor"; "New Bond, Perhaps," 11).

Production of McClory's *Thunderball* never commenced. Instead, in September 1964 McClory was named producer on the Eon Productions/United Artists version of *Thunderball*, and he abandoned his own project (Hopper "Bond's Thunderball"). Throughout the years McClory would attempt to produce yet another version of *Thunderball*. Twenty years after his legal battle with Ian Fleming was settled, McClory produced *Never Say Never Again* (1983). Directed by Irvin Kershner, *Never Say Never Again* was based on the Ian Fleming novel *Thunderball* and gave Fleming, McClory, and Whittingham story credit. The film starred none other than Sean Connery, who was fifty-two when the film was released and had not played the James Bond character since *Diamonds Are Forever* in 1971. Prior to being cast, Connery was quoted many times as saying he would "never" play James Bond again (the title an obvious reference to Connery's statement).

Trustees of the estate of Ian Fleming, who died in 1964, attempted to stop the releases of *Never Say Never Again*. The trustees claimed that although Fleming agreed to give McClory the film rights of the novel *Thunderball* and use of the character James Bond in a *Thunderball* film in 1963, *Never Say Never Again* did not follow the story of the novel and the film's release should have been halted. The London High Court struck down the claim. *Never Say Never Again* was released to theaters in 1983; the same year as the Albert Broccoli–produced James Bond film *Octopussy* (1983), starring Roger Moore, was released ("007 Lives").

Metro-Goldwyn-Mayer (MGM), parent company of Allied Artists, purchased the rights to *Never Say Never Again* in 1997 in order to own all James Bond–related properties. In a press release, the president of United Artists, Lindsay Doran, stated, "We have taken this definitive action to underscore the point that the Bond franchise has one home and only one home," adding, "We want to make it undeniably clear to any and all encroachers that MGM will do everything to protect what has been established over 35 years to be the most valuable film franchise in history" ("Metro-Goldwyn-Mayer" press release). As for Eon Productions' *Thunderball* (1965), it was announced that Terence Young, director of *Dr. No* and *From Russia with Love*, would again take the helm as director and Connery would once again take on the role of James Bond. *Thunderball* would be the first film of his new three-film deal. The over four-million-dollar production began in February 1965 and shot on location in France, Miami, and Nassau Island in the Bahamas (Bourke "Work Begins"; "*Thunderball* Bond Film"). When shooting in Miami, Miami area newspapers kept residents abreast of shooting schedules and what to expect to see, such as an early morning "invasion" of "aqua-paratroopers" and military-style planes flying overhead (Bourke "*Thunderball* Unit," 63).

Rik Van Nutter replaced Jack Lord and took on the role as CIA agent Felix Leiter. Originally singer Burl Ives was rumored to take on the role of the villainous Emilio Largo and was even reportedly getting in shape for filming, cutting out alcohol and pills, but casting fell through and the role went to Italian actor Adolfo Celi (Hopper "Bill Wellman Jr.").

A number of actresses' names were attached to the project to play the new Bond girl, Domino. Originally character actress Linda Bennett, known mostly for her television work on *Bonanza* (1959–1973), *Hawk* (1966), *The Adventures of Ozzie Harriet* (1952–1966), and *Flipper* (1964–1967) was rumored to be under consideration (Wilson "It Happened," 1965, 9). Soon afterward, rumors swirled about Austrian arthouse favorite Marisa Mell, who would later star in the 1966 Italian superspy flick *Super Agent, Super Dragon* ("James Bond's Bombshells"). Neither woman got the part.

United Press International (UPI) wrote about the casting search, reporting, "Eon Productions has been deluged by thousands of photographs of starlets and models. [The producers and director] narrowed the list first down to 100 and finally 22." The report added that the list included "blond girls, buxom girls, sexy girls with gorgeous figures, girls who pack a good punch" ("Starlets Hope," 42). After a month of rumors and speculation, in February 1965 it was announced that French actress/model Claudine Auger was selected to take on the role of Domino in *Thunderball* ("Bond's New Girl").

The Associated Press (AP) described Auger as "shapely, sleek, seductive looking" and that her "vital statistics are 37-25-37. She has shiny auburn hair, stunning eyes, exquisitely shaded by long, silked eyelashes." The AP quoted Auger as saying, "I am very proud to have been chosen for this role," adding, "Sean Connery is a modern hero of this world—a fine actor, strong cruel hand, but capable of great tenderness. He is a real man, we have nothing like him in France" ("Bond's 'Friend' Picked," 19).

Many of the scenes in *Thunderball* are in and on the water along the Florida coast, so the Associated Press asked if her diving gear would conceal her figure. Auger responded, "No, no. The equipment will be back, behind my shoulders" (Ibid.).

Thunderball marked the first appearance of Bond's archrival Ernst Blofeld's face. Although the character made his premiere in *From Russia with Love* and made an appearance in *Goldfinger*, audiences only saw his torso. Although he was played by many different actors throughout the series (the change of appearance is explained by plastic surgery), in *Thunderball* the role was taken on by Donald Pleasence.

Bond would fight Blofeld and SPECTRE until *For Your Eyes Only* (1981), when Bond unceremoniously drops Blofeld into a smokestack, due once again to a legal dispute with Kevin McClory and the rights to characters in *Thunderball* (Beck "Moore Ready").

The often-parodied James Bond "gun barrel sequence," which had kicked off every James Bond film, did not feature Sean Connery. Instead stuntman Bob Simmons was featured. However, *Thunderball* marked Connery's first appearance in the sequence; every subsequent Bond film would feature the actor portraying Bond in the gun barrel's sights, and every Bond would have their own take on the sequence.

By April 1965 producers announced the three women who would be joining the existing cast: Martine Beswick, Molly Peters, and Luciana Paluzzi ("Joins *Thunderball* Cast"). Roman actress Paluzzi, who was cast as SPECTRE agent Fiona Volpe, stated that she considered the casting to be the biggest break in her career but that "appearing in a Bond film is like doing four or five years' work in one." When asked about her character, Paluzzi said, "She isn't a very nice woman, but I think she certainly will be a memorable screen character." She added, "Men prefer women who are dangerous" ("Luscious Luciana," 30).

The first three James Bond films (*Dr. No*, *From Russia with Love*, and *Goldfinger*) presented Bond as an incredible secret agent but not necessarily as a *super*agent. Although most, if not all, secret agent movies made after *Dr. No* in 1962 were inspired by, copied, imitated, or straight up ripped off James Bond, those "inspired" films pushed the envelope of the spy genre and had outrageous plots, more suspenseful chases, violent fights, and, of course, over-the-top gadgets—especially films made between 1965 and 1967 and produced in Italy and Mexico. Bond had to catch up with competitors. *Thunderball*'s opening scene includes Bond narrowly escaping with the aid of a Bell Rocket Jetpack, and the film also includes an underwater jetpack, infrared camera, motorcycle equipped with rocket launchers (driven by Luciana Paluzzi's character), a two-man underwater diving bell, underwater sleds with headlights and spear guns, a skyhook rescue device attached to a weather balloon that was picked up by a B-17 military airplane, and a mini underwater breathing apparatus.

Thunderball was at the time the most expensive Bond film. Shooting took seven weeks on location and required a 102-member production crew and twenty-five thousand pounds of camera equipment ("Bond Is Up"). The underwater sequences were choreographed and directed by Ricou Browning, who played Universal Studios' *Creature from the Black Lagoon* (1954) and cocreated *Flipper* (1964–1967). There are a number of breathtaking underwater sequences, including Bond swimming with real tiger sharks that needed to be transported by the underwater crew, one holding the tail and two others on the fins. "As long as you don't give it a chance to get moving under its own power, you're all right," said Browning. "But once it gets a little momentum, look out" (Gray "Training Tiger Sharks," 43).

SPECTRE used divers to hijack atomic bombs from a downed Air Force bomber. Ricou Browning recalled the difficulties he had to find qualified divers. "While filming this sequence we sank a replica of a plane off Nassau and while it was going down shot footage of divers swimming into the fuselage. In the climactic fight between James Bond [and the SPECTRE divers] the first problem was to find skilled divers with motion picture experience." Browning had twenty at his own studio but had to recruit more in the Miami/Fort Lauderdale area who were working as spear fishermen or treasure divers and doing other odd jobs on the set (Ibid.). A special Panavision camera needed to be developed for underwater sequences by cameraman Lamar Boren, and the camera was pressurized and encased in stainless steel, yet buoyant for easy movement in the ocean (Ibid.).

As far back as 1962, Ian Fleming described himself as a "kiss-kiss bang-bang" writer, in reference to the amount of sex and violence found in his novels, and reportedly "Mr. Kiss Kiss Bang Bang" is the title given to 007 James Bond by the Italian public. The term goes back even further and was reportedly the name given to "morally objectionable" films made in the United States by those in other countries. James Bond producers planned on referencing the nickname in the original theme to *Thunderball* (1965), "Mr. Kiss Kiss Bang Bang," which was written by "James Bond Theme" composer John Barry along with Leslie Bricusse (Veysey "Man behind"; Morehouse "Sean Connery Called"; Lenzi "False Picture").

"Mr. Kiss Kiss Bang Bang" was originally recorded by Shirley Bassey and later Dionne Warwick, when Bassey was not available to rerecord the track. However, producers wanted a song with *Thunderball* referenced in the lyrics, so Tom Jones recorded the title track. "Thunderball," was cowritten by John Barry and John Black. An instrumental version of "Mr. Kiss Kiss Bang Bang" appears on the soundtrack and was released as the B side to the "Thunderball" single by Tom Jones.

It was announced that *Thunderball* would be released around Christmas 1965, but theaters started preparing as early as the summer, some running ads for the film and Bond double and triple features of *Dr. No*, *From Russia with Love*, and/or *Goldfinger*. In June 1965 the *New York Times* reported long lines at twenty-six city theaters showing the *Dr. No/From Russia with Love* double feature. Movie patrons waited in line for up to an hour before showtime at the

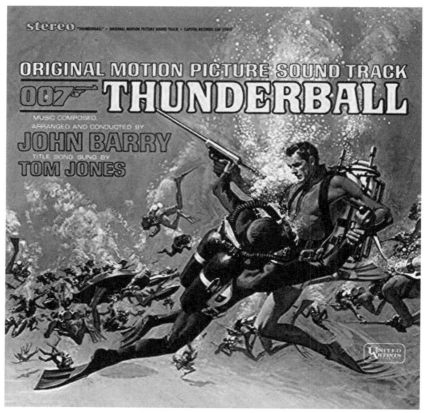

The cover of the soundtrack to *Thunderball* was illustrated by Bob McGinnis, who also provided artwork for *Breakfast at Tiffany's* (1961) and would go on to illustrate the posters for Bond films *You Only Live Twice* (1967), *Diamonds Are Forever* (1971), *Live and Let Die* (1973), and *The Man with the Golden Gun* (1974). *Author's collection*

Victoria Theater on Broadway, which grossed $40,000 in box office sales for the double feature, besting numbers the theater did during the film's respective original runs (Archer "007").

Thunderball opened on December 9, 1965, at the Hibiya Theater in Tokyo, Japan, breaking Japanese box office records. The film premiered in the United States on December 21, 1965, at Grauman's Chinese Theater in Los Angeles and on December 29 in the United Kingdom at the London Pavilion and Rialto Cinemas ("*Thunderball* on Way"; "*Thunderball* to Open"; Walker "Wham!"). As with *Goldfinger,* a number of theaters, such as the Paramount in New York City, ran the film twenty-four hours a day to excited audiences (Paramount Theater advertisement 1965).

A 1965 double feature of rereleased Bond films. © 1965 United Artists Corporation

British entertainment writer Alexander Walker believed that *Thunderball* went too far and almost made Bond a superhero akin to Batman or Superman, writing, "James Bond finally parts company with mere flesh and blood and becomes a fully fledged Superman—a Pop Art hero who makes you expect to see 'Wham!' 'Pow!' or 'Zowie' flashed on the screen every time he flattens the enemy." Walker must have caught a sneak peek at television's *Batman* (1966–1968), which did not premiere in the United States until January 1966 or in the UK until March 1966 (Walker "Wham!" 9).

Bosley Crowther of the *New York Times* had a similar line of thinking. Crowther wrote, "Mr. Fleming's superhero . . . has not only power over women, miraculous physical reserves, skill in perilous maneuvers and knowledge of all things great and small[,] . . . but he also has a much better sense of humor than he has shown in his previous films. And this is the secret ingredient that makes *Thunderball* the best of the lot." Crowther added, "Mr. Connery is at his peak of coolness and nonchalance with the girls. Adolfo Celi is piratical as the villain with a black patch over his eye. Claudine Auger, a French beauty winner, is a tasty skin diving dish and Luciana Paluzzi is streamlined as the inevitable and almost insuperable villainous girl. The color is handsome. The scenery in the Bahamas is an irresistible lure. Even the violence is funny. That's the best I can say for a Bond film" (Crowther "007's Underwater," 23).

The *Los Angeles Times* motion picture editor Philip K. Scheuer felt the film had "action galore" but said, "Cinematically it's a dud . . . it's the same as its predecessors only more too much of everything, from sudden desire to sudden death" (Scheuer "Action Galore," 79). *Variety* wrote that the "action, dominating element of three predecessors, gets rougher before even the credits flash on . . . studded with inventive play and mechanical gimmicks," and it credited Terence Young and the production team for taking "advantage of every situation at fever pitch." *Variety* also stated that *Thunderball* had a larger budget than initially reported: "There's visible evidence that the reported $5.5 million budget was no mere publicity figure; it's posh all the way" ("Thunderball," *Variety Film Reviews*).

Charlotte Observer staff writer Dick Banks noted that although the action was "magically super," he felt that the "cutting room has sacrificed coherence for speed. You hardly get to know what are the good girls and which the bad before another set of bosomy creatures takes their place" (Banks "Icy-Nerved," 15).

In a strange, seven hundred–word official commentary, East German officials, via the Communist East German news agency ADN, wrote that James Bond "personifies fascism" and that 007 movies were "playing a macabre game with the existent fear countless people have about a possible sudden outbreak of atomic war." They added, "Bond is the incarnation of all the wrong and dangerous ideals to the youth of the Western world. He personifies in a frightening way the ideals of fascism, everything which youth should be protected against . . . but the Bond wave continues unabated," after *Thunderball*'s release in West Germany ("Agent 007," 4). Soviet Communist Party newspaper *Pravda* wrote that James Bond was "an unthinking, murderer and rapist" who defended the interests of the "bourgeois ruling class" and was the "successor of Nazi war criminals." The writer added that there was "no difference between the philosophy of Bond and that of the commandant of the Auschwitz concentration camp" and went as far as to say that "Bond is the symbol of the civilization that used napalm in Vietnam" and that "those being sent to kill" in Vietnam, the Congo, and the Dominican Republic used James Bond adventures as textbooks ("*From Russia, with Love*," 2). Bond was even condemned by the Vatican, which considered Bond films "a dangerous mixture of violence, vulgarity, sadism and sex" and added, "Evil, presented in an alluring manner, has a very strong power on poor human nature weakened by original sin" ("Shame, James," 16).

After the film's release, director Terence Young told the *New York Times*, "There will be no more Bond films for me," stating that he was working on other projects "far removed" from the genre. In the next two years, Young would go on to produce *The Poppy Is Also a Flower* (1966), *Triple Cross* (1966), *The Rover* (1967), and *Wait until Dark* (1967). Young would never direct another James Bond film (Weiler "Best Film").

Thunderball was the highest-grossing film of 1966, making $26,000,000 that year in North America ("Big Rental Pictures of 1966"). And it sold even more than tickets. New York's Paramount Theater even reported that *Thunderball* broke records in concession sales, averaging $50,000 a week when the film was being shown. The previous record holder for concession sales was *Goldfinger* (Talbert "007th").

Although wildly popular with audiences, *Thunderball* only won one Academy Award. In 1966 John Stears won for Best Visual Effects for his work on the film.

You Only Live Twice (1967)

Even though Sean Connery was quoted as saying he was "fed up" with the image of James Bond as early as 1964, Connery signed on to continue to play the character, earning one million dollars a picture plus a percentage of each film's profits and merchandising. Following the release of *Thunderball*, Sean Connery was touted as the biggest star based on box office success in both

America and England ("Bond Packs"; Graham "Graham's Grapevine"; Talbert "007th"). Although it was originally believed the next Bond film would be based on Ian Fleming's *On Her Majesty's Secret Service*, in March 1966 Connery headed to Japan to begin production on *You Only Live Twice*.

Early reports of the film indicated Bond would have to "look Japanese," and rumors began that Bond would get married in the film. Both stories turned out to be correct (Graham "Amusement"; Graham "Graham's Grapevine"). Scriptwriter Richard Maibaum, who wrote or cowrote all the previous Bond films, stated that Bond should not get married, because if he did, the film could never fulfill men's escapist fantasies. However, *You Only Live Twice* was not written by Maibaum. The script was written by famed children's author, novelist, and screenwriter Roald Dahl ("Bond to Marry"; Talbert "007th").

After NASA spacecraft Jupiter 16 is captured by an unidentified object in space, the United States immediately assumes the Soviets are to blame. However, the United Kingdom's intel tells a different story. According to the UK, the unidentified craft came down along the shores of Japan. In order to conduct an investigation without his enemies actively looking to kill him, James Bond, while in bed with an undercover female agent (Tsai Chin) in Hong Kong, fakes his own death after being shot at by assassins. Wearing SCUBA gear in his sea casket, Bond is given a burial at sea and is picked up by a British submarine and brought to the Japanese coast. While in Japan, Bond is aided by Japanese Secret Intelligence Service chief Tiger Tanaka (Tetsurō Tamba), agent Aki (Akiko Wakabayashi), Q (Desmond Llewelyn), and MI6's Q branch, which brings Bond a tiny helicopter, "Little Nellie," equipped with dual machine guns, rocket launchers, flamethrowers, a smoke screen, heat-seeking missiles, and aerial mines.

During Bond's investigation, a Soviet spacecraft is also intercepted. The Soviets assume the interception is the work of the Americans, and now Bond must find the location of a secret base to prevent all-out war between the world superpowers. As it turns out, SPECTRE is behind the spacecraft hijackings and has a base at the bottom of a Japanese volcano.

Before an assault on the SPECTRE volcano base, Tiger Tanaka tells Bond that he must "become Japanese" to go undetected and also sent Bond to train with the Japanese Secret Intelligence Service's ninja commando force. Bond is given new clothes, prosthetics to give him a new eye shape, and a wig with a stereotypical Japanese haircut. Also, to better blend in, Bond takes a Japanese bride, Agent Kissy Suzuki (Mie Hama). *You Only Live Twice* also marks the first time that Bond comes face to face with his archrival, SPECTRE number one Ernst Stavro Blofeld (Donald Pleasence).

James Bond (Sean Connery) enjoying Japanese bathing during the filming of *You Only Live Twice* (1967). *Keystone Press/Alamy Stock Photo*

As for Dahl's writing, *New York Times* columnist Bosley Crowther believed that in the script, "there's enough of the bright and bland bravado of the popular British super-sleuth mixed into this melee of rocket-launching to make it a bag of good Bond fun." Stating that Roald Dahl's screenplay was not true to Ian Fleming's book of the same name, the columnist said, "It is notable that only Bond, the title and the location of an Ian Fleming book have been used by Mr. Dahl in writing his screenplay." He added that Dahl put his "touch" on the screenplay "here and there," but it was typical Bond "science-fiction." Crowther also remarked that in the film, "the sex is minimal. But, then, Bond is getting old. And so, I would guess, is anybody who can't get a few giggles from this film" (Crowther "Sayonara," 40).

The credits of *You Only Live Twice* thank Japanese Toho studios "for the services of their producer Kikumaru Okuda as technical advisor." Toho was most famous for producing giant monster films featuring Godzilla, Rodan, King Ghidorah, and Mothra. Toho supplied Eon Productions with actors, including Tetsurō Tamba, Akiko Wakabayashi, and Mie Hama and provided technical support while filming in Japan. Newspapers throughout the United States gave lots of attention to Mie Hama, who at the time of filming *You Only Live Twice* was only twenty-two years old but had appeared in a staggering sixty-seven films—among them, *King Kong vs. Godzilla* (1962) and *The Lost World of Sinbad* (1963)—and would appear in *King Kong Escapes* (1967) the same year *You Only Live Twice* was released in Japan, under the title *007 Dies Twice* (Graham "Bette Davis").

Excitement for *You Only Live Twice* was apparent while filming. While production took place in Tokyo, the notoriously persistent and innovative Japanese press were banned from the studio. Not to be deterred, a pair of Japanese photographers disguised themselves as plumbers to gain access to the set and waited for Connery to enter the men's room. When Connery entered, the duo began taking pictures of the star. Connery, obviously upset at the situation, reportedly started shouting, "They've got me surrounded, surrounded. They're coming out of the plumbing!" ("Silver Lining," 2).

As early as March 1967, theaters began to announce they would be showing *You Only Live Twice* when it was released. A block-long billboard to promote the film was unveiled on Broadway in New York, replacing a billboard for the Dino De Laurentiis epic *The Bible: In the Beginning* ("Coral Ridge Books"; Lazarus "More Punch"; McHarry "Room for All"). Soon media outlets began reporting on all things *You Only Live Twice* and Bond, with such stories as:

Ian Fleming's James Bond novels became a hot commodity in London libraries.

James Bond brand beer hitting shelves.

A "flock" of three-hundred-pound sumo wrestlers were set to appear in the film.

The volcano built for *You Only Live Twice* used two hundred miles of tubular steel and five hundred thousand couplings.

The Toyota GT 2000 that Agent Aki used in the film featured a miniature closed-circuit TV, two-way FM radio, hi-fi receiver and voice-actuated tape recorder and was shown at the "World of Wheels" exhibit in New York.

The increase of Aston Martin sales occurred as a result of the Bond films.

("Coral Ridge"; Lazarus "More Punch"; "Oldsters"; "Bond's Volcano"; "Weighty Menace"; Cochnar and Burgin "Toyota")

There was even excitement when Nancy Sinatra arrived in London to record the theme to *You Only Live Twice*. Nancy Sinatra arrived with her sister, Tina Sinatra, in tow. The arrival marked Tina Sinatra's first public appearance since breaking off her engagement to real estate mogul and future *Mod Squad* (1968–1973) creator Sammy Hess ("Arrives"; "Another Sinatra"). Nancy Sinatra's theme to *You Only Live Twice* reached number eleven on the UK Singles Charts, number forty-four on the US *Billboard* Hot 100 charts, and number three on the US *Billboard* Easy Listening charts.

Two months prior to the release of *You Only Live Twice*, Columbia Pictures released *Casino Royale* (1967), very loosely based on the first Ian Fleming James Bond novel. The rights to *Casino Royale* were originally sold to the producers of anthology series *Climax!*, which ran an episode based on the book. The rights were acquired by producer Gregory Ratoff and later by *Casino Royale* producer Charles K. Feldman several years before Eon Productions began producing James Bond films. In London, billboards for *You Only Live Twice* lined the streets with the caption, "This Man Is James Bond"; however, as soon as a billboard for *You Only Live Twice* went up, a billboard for *Casino Royale* appeared with the tagline "There's Too Much in *Casino Royale* for One James Bond." To make things even more confusing, the trailer for *You Only Live Twice* often appeared after showings of *Casino Royale* (Watts "007 Movie"; Graham "London Billboards"; Terry "Star-Laden").

On March 25, 1967, BBC documentary series *Whicker's World* (1958–1994), which aired on BBC-2 in the United Kingdom and was hosted by Alan Whicker, aired a behind-the-scenes look at the filming of *You Only Live Twice* in Japan. Alan Whicker interviewed Sean Connery, Connery's wife Diane Cilento, producers Albert Broccoli and Harry Saltzman, and screenwriter Roald Dahl. *Whicker's World* also dove into Bondmania and what it took to be a Bond girl, and he unveiled the fact that Connery only read one and a half Ian Fleming novels (Amos "Revenue").

On April 2, 1967, in the United States, NBC ran the special *Welcome to Japan, Mr. Bond* (the title referring to Tiger Tanaka's first words to Bond). Produced by Albert Broccoli and Harry Saltzman, the special was a best-of clip show of *You Only Live Twice* and all the previous Bond films. *Welcome to Japan, Mr. Bond* featured newly shot wraparound sequences with Miss Moneypenny (Lois Maxwell) and Q (Desmond Llewelyn), and it introduced a new character that would not be seen in any future Bond films: Moneypenny's assistant. She was played by Kate O'Mara, who had previously played on television's *Danger Man* (1960–1962 and 1964–1968) and *The Saint* (1962–1969) and would later star in British horror film production studio Hammer Films' *The Vampire Lovers* (1970) and *Horror of Frankenstein* (1970). The wraparound sequences were used to recall past Bond girls, villains, incredible action sequences and gadgets; introduce the new characters featured in *You Only Live Twice*; and speculate on if and whom Bond was going to marry in the film. *Welcome to Japan, Mr. Bond* also contains a subplot of an unseen evil woman plotting to be cast as the "first wife of James Bond." The special preempted an episode of spy program *The Man from U.N.C.L.E.*

Before the premiere, Connery was clearly trying to distance himself from the James Bond role, now sporting grown-out hair with his natural hairline (Connery was wearing a toupee though most of his time playing James Bond), a mustache, and long sideburns. Once again, Connery was quoted as saying he had no interest in returning as James Bond. "I am not James Bond," said Connery. "There are a lot of other roles around, and now I want the opportunity to play some of them" ("Connery Insists," 25).

In addition, Connery would not be doing the seventeen-city tour of the United States to promote the film, nor would he be appearing at the four-theater New York City premiere (Astor, Victoria, Baronet, and Loews Orpheum) of *You Only Live Twice* on June 13, 1967. He would be replaced on the tour by Lois Maxwell, who played Miss Moneypenny (Graham "Movie Attractions").

On Maxwell's seventeen-city tour to promote the film, she confessed that she was far from a method actor. "I can't take dictation," said Lois Maxwell. "And I can type on an Italian typewriter, because I don't seem quite able to find the keys on an English machine. I'm afraid the only thing I could do well in a business office would be to answer the door and take someone's coat." However, many people only wanted to know one thing about Moneypenny and Bond: "Most girls who get involved with Bond either die or meet what used to be called a fate worse than death, but not Miss Moneypenny," adding, "I get many amusing letters from secretaries saying 'You won't ever nip off with that naughty James Bond will you?'" Then she joked, "Well, on or off the screen?—There is little likelihood of that" (Boyle "Bond Film Star," 8).

Connery agreed to attend the film's London premiere on June 12, 1967, at Odeon Theater on Leicester Square, and the premiere would have a very special guest of honor: Queen Elizabeth II. The premiere was sponsored by the Variety Club of Great Britain in an effort to aid the YMCA and Imperial Cancer Research Fund. Dick Van Dyke, who was set to star in the Albert Broccoli–produced and Ian Fleming–written *Chitty Chitty Bang Bang* (1968), was also in attendance at the premiere. Van Dyke was photographed alongside Connery and Queen Elizabeth II (Steel "Let's Chat"; Bradford "Natalie Wood's").

Similar to what many theaters in New York City did for earlier Bond films, the Fox Theatre, a movie palace in downtown Philadelphia, showed the newest James Bond film around the clock on June 14, 1964 ("Fox to Run"). Once again, Bond broke the opening day record at the Odeon Theaters in London. The film was also number one in the United States for seven weeks. Reports indicate *You Only Live Twice* earned $16,300,000 in North America, making it

Britain's Queen Elizabeth II, attending the premiere of *You Only Live Twice* (1967), is greeted by Dick Van Dyke, British actress Diane Cilento, and Sean Connery. *Keystone Press/Alamy Stock Photo*

the second highest grossing film of the year ("Bond Rolls," 11; "National Box-office"; "Big Rental Films of 1967").

You Only Live Twice continued to be shown in theaters and at drive-ins regularly throughout 1967 and 1968. But despite its box office success, critics were not so kind to the newest James Bond adventure. *Time* magazine ripped apart *You Only Live Twice*, writing,

> The previous Bond films have so far grossed $125 million with a surefire combi-
> nation of ingredients: *You Only Live Twice* is the mixture as before. As always,
> Bond is surrounded by a scare 'em harem, this time peach-skinned, almond-eyed
> Japanese dishes. There is the mandatory hardware and gadgetry show, featuring
> a mini-helicopter equipped with such optional extras as flamethrowers and air-to-
> air missiles. There is the ultimate confrontation with the Evil Genius, represented
> by Ernst Stavro Blofeld (Donald Pleasence), an asexual monster with shaved
> head, hideous scar and foreign accent. . . . At the finale, the volcano blows its
> stack. Alas, the effects are ineffective. The outer-space sequences would be more

appropriate in a grade school educational short entitled *Our Amazing Universe*, and the volcanic climax is a series of clumsy process shots that no one took the trouble to fix. Even Connery seems uncomfortable and fatigued, as if he meant it when he said that this would be his last Bond film. ("006-¾," 73)

Clifford Terry of the *Chicago Tribune* wrote, "Budget-wise, the James Bond movies are certainly on the rise," noting that the production cost 1,200,000 more than *Dr. No.* He added, "Unfortunately, however, as the price has gone up, the quality has gone down" (Terry "Budget," 22). In London, Richard Roud of *The Guardian* believed that "the James Bond films have been on the downward spiral" but that *You Only Live Twice* was "more entertaining than the water-soaked *Thunderball*." Roud also felt that "Bond's day would seem to be almost over: "The gadgets just aren't terribly entertaining any more. Added to which, the dialogue has got dopier, the sentiment sloppier" (Roud "New Films," 9).

Felix Barker of the *Liverpool Echo* believed the "extravagance" of *You Only Live Twice*'s budget was not justified: "However much you spend on spectacle you can only achieve the same amount of entertainment." But, he added, "Bond addicts will find their hero in good shape and in the climax with its mass battle in the volcano is very busy" (Barker "Versatile," 5).

One of the most complimentary reviews came from Nadine M. Edwards of the Hollywood newspaper *Valley Times.* "To Roald Dahl goes credit to the suspense-laden screenplay, modern and sophisticated in tone, oftentimes frenetic in pace; but one which catches and sustains interest from beginning to end," wrote Edwards. "There is less farce and more down-to-earth grimness; less fantasy and more factual quality" (Edwards "Excitement Colors," 14).

Shortly after *You Only Live Twice* was released to theaters, Connery officially announced he would never take on the role of James Bond again. Reportedly, he even went so far as telling this to Queen Elizabeth II at the premiere of *You Only Live Twice* ("Connery-Bond"). Although the end credits of *You Only Live Twice* stated that "Bond would be back *On Her Majesty's Secret Service*," news outlets questioned whether Connery leaving the film franchise would signal its death knell or if another actor could fill Connery's shoes.

On Her Majesty's Secret Service (1969)

Following the release of *You Only Live Twice* (1967), Sean Connery, who had become synonymous with the character of James Bond, made it official he would be leaving the franchise. Tom Carlile, of the *Los Angeles Times* and *Washington Post*, said,

Only once or twice in every decade have movie audiences accepted with such warmth and conviction the screen portrayal of a totally fictional character. James Bond is the entertainment phenomenon of this century. The fantastic international box-office grosses of the Bond films make any other concussion inarguable. . . . Three-quarters of the world's movie-going public may think he is, but Connery doesn't agree and he makes no bones about saying so when he is confronted by the press or his fans.

He added,

In a recent interview with *Film Daily* Connery stated that he would only consider appearing in another Bond film for a sum roughly approximating the contents of Fort Knox. Perhaps because he is two pictures too late for such a Goldfingerian raid, the producers in a rebuttal announced a worldwide search for an unknown actor to play James Bond in the sixth of the series, *On Her Majesty's Secret Service*. . . . The principal location sites, a number of new "Q Branch" gadgets and several girls have already been selected.

But Carlile believed that Connery's exit from the franchise would not stop the "Bondwagon" (Carlile "Sean's Exit," 3).

Although Eon Productions' Albert Broccoli and Harry Saltzman held out hope that they could possibly lure Sean Connery back once again to the role of James Bond, despite Connery's continued insistence that he would never play Bond again—and his statement to that effect to Queen Elizabeth II—they realized they needed to look for a replacement. In July 1967, Broccoli said, "We are going ahead with the series without Sean, we don't want an actor to appear in films he is not enthusiastic about. Even if Sean changes his mind, that will not affect our decision. We are looking for a new James Bond." He added, "We don't start filming until August of 1968, so that will give us plenty of time to find a new James Bond." Ten months before the film went into production, in January 1968, Saltzman, who was working on a non–James Bond production, *The Battle of Britain* (1968), was clearly not in a hurry to name a new 007 and was quoted as saying that once he was finished with that project, "Then we'll test some actors for the part of James Bond" (Thomas "Producers Seeking," 20; "Connery-Bond," 8; Benjamin "Listening Post," 88; Graham "Who Plays Bond," 39).

By March 1968, a new James Bond was still not cast. Connery was continuously asked if he would come back to the role he made famous but was quoted as saying he would not return to the James Bond role because he wanted to focus on "more peaceful endeavors." Harry Saltzman begrudgingly admitted, "I think it's time for a change . . . frankly I don't have any idea yet who will be cast for the part" ("Whither James Bond?," 19). Despite his protest, rumors persisted that Connery would be returning to the role. By July 1968, Albert Broccoli conceded that although they persuaded him to return after a hefty pay increase for *You Only Live Twice*, "this time they're not going to bother," and Connery was let out of his six-picture deal (Graham "Anita Louise"; Powers "Nephew of Broccoli Grower," 11; Watts "$8 Million").

Sean Connery said that though playing Bond started out just fine, it became a "Frankenstein's Monster," but Albert Broccoli believed that the role is what made Connery a household name and that he should be more grateful for the role. "Sean wore a sweater and jeans when he first came to us," said Broccoli. "We made him into a snappy dresser and an international star—but if he wants to stop playing Bond, that's his affair" (Watts "$8 Million," 50). Although not made official, in late September 1968, relatively unknown six-foot-tall, twenty-nine-year-old Australian commercial actor George Lazenby was described as "a front runner" on the short list of actors who could possibly be cast as James Bond ("Aussie as 007?"). Then, on October 3, 1968, it was made official that George Lazenby would take on the role of 007 in the sixth James Bond film, *On Her Majesty's Secret Service* ("New Actor").

To replace Connery as Bond, a number of leading men were originally considered for taking on the role of 007; including Pat McGoohan, John Richardson, Anthony Rogers, Robert Campbell, Hans de Vries, Michael Caine, Timothy Dalton, and Peter Purves. Broccoli revealed that over four hundred actors and male models were also considered for the role, but the producers did not want to cast a Connery double. "We were looking for someone with the same sort of qualities," said Broccoli. "Lazenby is everything we hoped for and more. I'm staggered by the way he's picked it up so quickly." Broccoli stated that although they "tested five or six actors" and gave them tough screen tests, they did not make an immediate decision (Watts "$8 Million," 50; Graham "Lawyers Battle," 5).

Lazenby impressed producers on his screen test in a fight scene with 240-pound professional wrestler Yuri Borienko, who played Blofeld's henchman Grunther in *On Her Majesty's Secret Service*. Producers were impressed with Lazenby's aggressiveness during the screen test, from which Borienko walked away with a fat lip. Producers were also impressed by what they called his "virile masculine assurance." Clearly excited for the role, Lazenby stated, "Playing Bond is like having one's childhood dreams come true. You know, all that shooting and stuff. I enjoy it" (Watts "$8 Million," 50).

Immediate criticism was drawn for the pick due to Lazenby's lack of experience. Lazenby became acquainted with Bond producer Albert Broccoli when

The new James Bond is unveiled for *On Her Majesty's Secret Service* (1969).
Keystone Press/Alamy Stock Photo

the pair met in a London barbershop in the Dorchester Hotel. A former car salesman, he had been named Australia's Top Model of the Year in 1966, but his only acting experience came from a series of commercials for Fry's Chocolate Bars in England. Even sharper criticism was given when Lazenby admitted that he took the job for one thing, stating, "I'm in it for the money." He added, "I've never acted before. . . . I'm not exactly Lawrence Olivier but Sean Connery's acting experience was limited when he became 007. I'm doing what he did—placing myself in the hands of the highly successful team that molded Bond into a cinematic figure." Lazenby also assured Bond fans the role was in good hands: "I saw all the Bond films twice. . . . The character of Bond will remain the same in this film, although I'm playing it as myself in a way" (Thomas "SMERSH"; Thomas "Newest James Bond," 43; Watts "$8 Million," 50).

In a press conference to promote the film at the Dorchester Hotel in London, Lazenby was bombarded with questions. Lazenby stated afterward, "It wasn't as bad as I expected. Only three or four of the reporters asked me catty questions, the answers to which I wouldn't even tell my closest friends" (Thomas "SMERSH," 3). Even actor Michael Caine, who had been in the running and had starred as Harry Palmer in Bond coproducer Harry Saltzman's spy drama *The Ipcress File* (1965) and its sequels *Funeral in Berlin* (1966) and *Billion Dollar Brain* (1967), piled on Lazenby by stating, "The difference between Sean [Connery] and George [Lazenby], Sean can act" ("New James Bond"; Graham "Saturday Sit-In," 9).

Lazenby was paid approximately $72,000 for *On Her Majesty's Secret Service* and signed a seven-year deal, where Lazenby would continue to play Bond in future films and take on other roles for United Artists. The deal was said to be worth up to $2.4 million ("New James Bond"; Watts "$8 Million"). Soon after announcing the casting of George Lazenby, Eon Productions revealed that Diana Rigg, who played the popular British superspy Emma Peel on TV's *The Avengers* from 1965 to 1967 and at the time was playing the Royal Shakespeare Company, was set to play Bond girl/love interest Contessa Teresa "Tracy" di Vicenzo.

Lazenby stated that at the time of filming *On Her Majesty's Secret Service*, he was a bachelor with a number of girlfriends. "I'm just not ready for marriage, I like to keep moving," said Lazenby. He also mentioned his preference for "just chicks who wear skirts. . . . I'm basic—an uncomplicated man" (Watts "$8 Million," 50).

Though he spent a lot of time talking about his own sexual prowess, Lazenby's character was a different story. It was publicized in January 1969 that the script called for infamous playboy James Bond to get married in the film's conclusion, to Countess Teresa "Tracy" di Vicenzo and daughter to Count Marc-Ange Draco (Gabriele Ferzetti) who was a noted gangster but loving father. This was to happen despite the fact that four years earlier, Richard Maibaum—who also worked on all the other previous Bond films (with the exception of *You Only Live Twice*) and was the principal writer on *On Her Majesty's Secret Service*—stated that Bond should not get married, because if he did, the films could never fulfill men's escapist fantasies ("Bond to Marry," 72; Talbert "007th," 63).

In the film, Bond falls for Tracy and asks her to marry him. In the final scene of *On Her Majesty's Secret Service*, after their wedding, attended by M, Q, Miss Moneypenny, and Tracy's father, James and Tracy drive away for their honeymoon. Bond's wife is gunned down by Irma Bunt in a car driven by Blofeld. As Bond holds his now dead wife, he says, "We have all the time in the world." James Bond's marriage is only referenced a few times throughout the franchise:

> The first scene of James Bond's next adventure, *Diamonds Are Forever* (1971), features Bond attempting to avenge the death of Tracy by killing Blofeld; however, the film does not explicitly acknowledge the events of *On Her Majesty's Secret Service*.
>
> In *The Spy Who Loved Me* (1977), it is mentioned that Bond had "many lady friends, but married only once. Wife killed."
>
> In the opening sequence of *For Your Eyes Only* (1981), Bond brings flowers to a grave whose headstone reads: "Teresa Bond, 1943–1969, Beloved Wife of James Bond: We have all the time in the World." He is then attacked; soon afterward, he finally gets revenge and unceremoniously kills Blofeld. (Blofeld and SPECTRE were never mentioned again in Bond films due to ongoing legal disputes with Kevin McClory, who worked on the story of *Thunderball* and claimed ownership to several characters and concepts.)
>
> In *License to Kill* (1989), Della Leiter, wife of CIA agent Felix Leiter, asked if she said something wrong to Bond after she made reference to Bond being the one to get married next when Bond caught her garter belt at her and Felix's wedding. Felix replied, "He was married once, but it was a long time ago."

Astute viewers of *No Time to Die* (2021)* will notice "We've Got All the Time in the World" playing throughout the film. However, *No Time to Die* concluded with the death of James Bond (Daniel Craig) instead of his love interest, Madeleine Swann (Léa Seydoux).

Telly Savalas, who may be best known for playing bald-headed, lollipop-eating NYPD detective *Kojak* (1973–1978), took over for Donald Pleasence in the role of SPECTRE number-one Blofeld. Although Blofeld is the ruthless head of a terrorist organization, Savalas wanted to avoid being typecast as a villain, saying that he thought of himself as "soft, sentimental, and nice." He added, "I can understand why people think of me as a villain. I've played a lot

---

* James Bond films from *Casino Royale* (2006) on started a new James Bond timeline, rebooting the franchise.

of different roles, done comedy. Yet people remember you for something like *The Dirty Dozen*. They remember that sexual psychopath" (Ross "Became an Actor," 8).

In *On Her Majesty's Secret Service*, Blofeld brainwashed twelve "Angels of Death" from all corners of the globe to spread his plague, Virus Omega, across the world. Cast as Angels of Death were Helena Ronee, Angela Scoular, Anouska Hempel, Catherina von Schell, Dani Sheridan, Ingrid Back, Jenny Hanley, Joanna Lumley, Julie Ege, Mona Chong, Sylvana Henriques, and an actress simply known as Zara. Out of all the actors cast as Blofeld's Angels of Death, former Israeli beauty queen Helena Ronee seemingly got the most press. Papers throughout the country reported on the twenty-year-old actress, who at the time was attending Queens College in New York, getting the role ("Israeli Queen"). German actress Ilse Steppat was cast as Blofeld's assistant, assassin Irma Bunt. Bernard Lee, Desmond Llewelyn, and Lois Maxwell returned to the franchise as M, Q, and Miss Moneypenny ("New James Bond"; "Agent 007 Filming").

Even the scenery and the vehicles got attention. The script included an avalanche in the Swiss mountains; instead of using stock footage, the *On Her Majesty's Secret Service* crew decided to cause their own avalanche, using dynamite. The film also included a heliport for Blofeld that cost producers $150,000 and was also used for the film's climactic shootout ending. The helicopter used in the film was also used for real-life heroics. During production, the helicopter had to be used to rescue eighty delegates heading to a Universal Postal Union meeting in nearby Bern, Switzerland, who were suspended 150 feet in the air on a cable car ("Ford Cars"; "Unusual Sets"; "007's Helicopter"). The script also called for a spectacular car crash on an ice-racing circuit. The crew used a Ford Escort, driven by Austrian rally driver Erich Glavitza. When the Ford Escort originally refused to roll over, the crew had to dig a trench and add weight to the car to eventually get it to flip ("Ford Cars").

On Her Majesty's Secret Service, which had a budget of $8.4 million, also marked the directorial debut of Peter R. Hunt. Hunt served as an editor on the first five James Bond films.

As filming began in late October 1968 on location in England, Switzerland, and Portugal, United Artists did its best to promote the name and skills of its new Bond, including in a number of press releases the fact that Lazenby was athletic, a skin diver, skier, rifle expert, swimmer, and a veteran of the Australian Army (Watts "$8 Million"; Sparks "Latest Bond"). Lazenby put his skiing ability to good use when filming in Switzerland, when Bond outruns and outguns SPECTRE agents on the eleven-thousand-foot peak of the Schilthorn in the

Swiss Alps. It was reported that it took a cast and crew of 120 to prepare the skiing scene alone ("Agent 007 Filming").

Shooting skills were also put to the test. Lazenby was challenged to a 100 Swiss franc shooting contest by a local hunter, three skiers, and six British stuntmen. The target was a one-inch-diameter flagpole forty yards away, Lazenby walked away 100 Swiss francs richer and was voted "top marksman" by the crew (Kaliff "Magic Carpet").

As production progressed, Lazenby seemingly became more comfortable with his role. "I have made a happy discovery: I *am* James Bond." Lazenby elaborated: "Well, let's say our personalities are similar. I don't feel like I'm really acting. I take chances as they come and, like Bond, I've got an eye for the chicks" (Watts "$8 Million," 50).

By March 1969, cracks in Lazenby's James Bond veneer began to open. On the set, an anonymous crew member called Lazenby an "arrogant egotist." An unnamed actress who played one of Blofeld's Angels of Death recalled, "[George is] a brilliant conversationalist—as long as you want to talk about Australia," adding that "he's only interested in sex." Lazenby did not do himself favors when he attempted to defend himself. "When I came to Murren (Switzerland) for location shooting all the girls were chasing me," said Lazenby. "I can't really blame them, all they wanted was publicity but sooner or later women become ugly and testy." Another actress recalled dropping a load of packages only to have Lazenby "practically walk over her without helping to pick them up" ("George Lazenby: Arrogant," 42).

Lazenby also had issues with producers Broccoli and Saltzman. Although Lazenby signed a seven-year contract, he stated, "No one can make me do what I don't want to do" when asked about his future roles. Lazenby was ordered not to ski while the film was in production, because if he hurt himself, a delay it would be too costly for the picture—the next day Harry Saltzman saw Lazenby skiing down one of the many slopes in Switzerland. Of course, Lazenby stated, "He caught me at a bad time, I was about to ask him for a raise!" (Ibid.).

After the production wrapped, Lazenby created even more drama for *On Her Majesty's Secret Service*'s producers. Lazenby announced in October 1969 that he would not be returning to the role of James Bond because he did not want to be typecast as Bond all his life. He also stated that the makers of the film made him feel like he was "mindless." Lazenby was released from his five-year $2.4 million contractual obligation (Browning "New Monroe?," "Lazenby Quits," 27; "Press Fund").

Even before his announcement, there were doubts that Lazenby would be asked back by Bond producers because of his attitude on set. Syndicated

Hollywood columnist Sheilah Graham asked, "How much can a producer take?" (Graham "Women in Love," 17). *On Her Majesty's Secret Service* was set to premiere in both the United States and England for the Christmas season of 1969. But by early December, Lazenby was already attempting to break free from the role by growing a beard and his hair long. "It's just me doing my own thing," said Lazenby. "I think this'll be the greatest Bond picture ever made . . . the production was perfect but I don't want to do it any more" ("Light Side"; Wilson "Bond Star," 15).

The ads for the film exclaimed the film was "Far Up! Far Out! Far More! James Bond Is Back!" Bond once again took on Ernst Blofeld and SPECTRE, who planned to hold the world ransom by threatening to unleash new bacteria on the world, killing livestock and crops. The bacteria would be spread using his twelve beautiful, brainwashed "Angels of Death," who hailed from all corners of the world. The film contains a not-so-subtle nod to the fact that Bond was being played by a new actor. In the film's opening sequence, after preventing the future Mrs. Bond, Contessa Teresa "Tracy" di Vicenzo from committing suicide on the beach, Bond is ambushed by SPECTRE agents. After the fight, Bond coyly states, "That wouldn't have happened to the other fellow." However the movie establishes that George Lazenby *is* James Bond. *On Her Majesty's Secret Service* is not a James Bond reboot, however. Lazenby is the same character in the same timeline in the same movie universe, much like actors who played vine-swinging Tarzan, English adventurer Bulldog Drummond, or in the Batman serials, before him.

The film's intro contains clips from all previous James Bond films, and the movie references previous Bond gadgets as the individual themes from the movies play in the background. *On Her Majesty's Secret Service* held box office records at the site of the film's English premiere, which George Lazenby famously did not attend, at Odeon Leicester Square. Lazenby stated, "Bond is a brute. I've already put him behind me. I will never play him again. Peace—that's the message now" ("Newsmakers," 2).

Premiering in the United States on December 18, 1969, and in England the following day, the film held the record for highest number of first week ticket sales at Odeon Leicester Square in England. It went on to earn £130,000 (approximately $433,290) in the first three months in the theater ("Press Fund"; "People in the News"). The film was a financial success, earning $1,223,000 in its first week and $9,000,000 throughout 1970, making it the ninth highest grossing film in North America that year. But it did not make as much as previous Bond films, so *On Her Majesty's Secret Service* was considered a flop. To make matters worse, the film was called a disaster by many critics ("Big Rental Films of 1970"; "50 Top Grossing"; Browning "New Monroe?").

A. H. Weiler of the *New York Times* believed that although "serious criticism" of James Bond films "would be tantamount to throwing rocks at Buckingham Palace," *On Her Majesty's Secret Service* does "call for a handful of pebbles" to be thrown. Weiler maintained that although Lazenby was "merely a casual, pleasant, satisfactory replacement" for Sean Connery but also conceded that Lazenby "plays a decidedly second fiddle to an overabundance of continuous action, a soundtrack as explosive as the London Blitz, and flip dialogue and characterizations set against some authentic, truly spectacular Portuguese and Swiss scenic backgrounds, caught in eye catching colors" (Weiler "New James Bond," 68).

The *New York Times'* Vincent Canby placed *On Her Majesty's Secret Service* on his "Ten Worst Films of 1969" list. Canby wrote that George Lazenby "looks as if he'd been chosen by computer to replace Sean Connery as Ian Fleming's James Bond. If you squint your eyes a bit, he does resemble Connery, but he seems ill-at-ease in his beautifully tailored suits." Canby also wrote that "Diana Rigg . . . is such a beautiful, intelligent, responsive, mysterious actress that her presence makes everything around her look even more dull and foolish than is absolutely necessary" (Canby "Ten," 81).

The Daily Telegraph in London stated the film was "an almost isolated example of self-mockery, which used to be such an endearing feature of these films the new director Peter Hunt, appearing to have no taste for it; and with the scriptwriter, Richard Maibaum, having no use for gadgetry, another element of the original style is missing" ("Good Morning," 10).

After the film's release, producers scrambled to find a new Bond to play in their upcoming production; *Diamonds Are Forever*, which was announced at the end credits of *On Her Majesty's Secret Service*. Although a number of actors were considered and rumored (namely, Clint Eastwood, Adam West, Burt Reynolds, Robert Wagner, Brett Halsey, Malcolm Roberts, and Ralph Fiennes), the leading candidate was believed to be *The Saint* star and future James Bond, Roger Moore. Although Moore was spotted having dinner with Bond producer Harry Saltzman to discuss the role, and although Moore was given serious consideration, he had to decline due to contractual obligations to shoot the British action-comedy show *The Persuaders!* (1970–1971), so the role was given to American actor John Gavin ("Press Fund"; Kupcinet "Super Brawl")—that is, until Sean Connery decided to return to his most iconic role one more time (until 1981's *Never Say Never Again*).

Gavin was given a $50,000 check to walk away from the role, and after eighteen months of negotiations, Connery agreed to a contract for one more Bond film, which, according to the *Daily Sun*, gave Connery, who was believed to add an extra $10 million to $15 million to a film's box office based on his name alone, around a million dollars in base salary (numbers were rumored to be as high as $1,200,000 to $2,000,000) and a "healthy share of the new film." Reportedly, Connery donated his entire salary to the Scottish International Educational Trust, which gives financial help to Scots who show "exceptional ability and promise" to further their studies or professional training, an organization Connery helped found a year prior ("Sean's Doing Bond," 27; Harber "Jill Will Join"; "Sean Could," 1; "Trust").

Sean Connery's *Diamonds Are Forever* (1971) costar Jill St. John, who was originally cast to play opposite John Gavin, did not mind the change in leading men. "I'd be happy playing against anyone, but Sean's a fine actor," St. John stated (Harber "Jill Will Join," 72). With the help of Connery's star power, *Diamonds Are Forever* outperformed *On Her Majesty's Secret Service* at the box office and was generally more accepted by Bond fans. Despite the fate of Tracy Bond, *On Her Majesty's Secret Service*'s theme, Louis Armstrong's "We Have All the Time in the World," became a popular wedding song.

Roger Moore replaced Connery as Bond in *Live and Let Die* (1973), went on to play Bond in seven films, and was a much more successful replacement than George Lazenby.

Casino Royale (1967)

Nine years before James Bond became a cultural phenomenon, CBS aired an Americanized teleplay based on Ian Fleming's *Casino Royale*. It starred Barry Nelson and Peter Lorre in 1954 on the anthology series *Climax!*, presented by Chrysler.

Producer Charles K. Feldman scooped up the film rights to *Casino Royale* from the estate of producer Gregory Ratoff, who himself acquired the rights from the producers of *Climax!* prior to the first James Bond film, *Dr. No* (1962). Feldman's ownership of *Casino Royale* prevented James Bond producers Harry Saltzman and Albert "Cubby" Broccoli from producing the first Ian Fleming's James Bond adventure in the first crop of James Bond films. So at the height of Bondmania, Columbia Pictures released their *own* Bond film produced by Feldman, *Casino Royale* (Watts "007 Movie").

Rumors of *Casino Royale*'s production began as early as January 1965. Peter Sellers, star of *The Pink Panther* (1963) and known for his roles in Stanley

Kubrick's *Lolita* (1962) and *Dr. Strangelove: Or How I Learned to Stop Worrying and Love the Bomb* (1964), and Woody Allen's *What's New Pussycat?* (1965) was believed to be in talks to play James Bond ("Bond without Connery"). However, *Casino Royale* producers originally wanted to cast none other than James Bond himself, Sean Connery, for their version of the film ("On Location").

Connery, however, rejected the casting. So David Niven, an actor who was originally considered to play James Bond in *Dr. No* (1962) and was known for his roles in *Separate Tables* (1958) and *Around the World in 80 Days* (1956) was cast as James Bond. But he would not be the only James Bond in the film. In fact, Peter Sellers, *Dr. No* Bond girl Ursula Andress, Joanna Pettet, Daliah Lavi, Barbara Bouchet, and Terence Cooper were *all* also cast to play James Bond.

Casino Royale was originally conceived as a serious Bond adventure, as in the Ian Fleming book, but by 1966–1967, spy spoofs were all the rage not only in Hollywood but around the world. So the producers would attempt to ride that wave and make the ultimate Bond spoof, with the only connection to the *Casino Royale* book being the fact that James Bond plays his signature card game, baccarat. In the film, David Niven plays the original Sir James Bond, who is brought back to MI6 and uses the James Bond name to throw off and confuse Soviet counterintelligence SMERSH agents (which at times confuses the viewer).

Other notable casting includes:

Six-time Academy Award nominee for Best Actress Deborah Kerr, best known for her roles in *From Here to Eternity* (1954), *The King and I* (1956), and *The Sundowners* (1961), as SMERSH Agent Mimi.

Geoffrey Bayldon as MI6 quartermaster, Q. Bayldon. This Shakespearean actor also had noteworthy roles in *Horror of Dracula* (1958) and *King Rat* (1965) and would go on to play in *To Sir, with Love* (1967) and *Frankenstein Must Be Destroyed* (1969), following *Casino Royale*.

William Holden as the CIA's Ransome, who talks Bond out of retirement. Holden at the time found fame with his role as Sgt. J. J. Sefton in *Stalag 17* (1953), a role for which he earned a Best Actor Oscar. Later Holden would play in *The Wild Bunch* (1969) and *Network* (1976).

The casting even included Geraldine Chaplin, daughter of Charlie Chaplin, in an insert that re-created a scene from her father's *Keystone Cops* silent films, and David Prowse, dressed as Frankenstein's monster. Prowse would go on to play Frankenstein's monster in Hammer Films' *Frankenstein and the Monster from Hell* (1974) and, most famously, Darth Vader in the original *Star Wars* trilogy.

Shot and produced in the style of a counterculture psychedelic movie, akin to *Blow-Up* (1966), *Skidoo* (1966), and *The Love-Ins* (1967), which, like spy spoofs, were all the rage at the time. But unlike other psychedelic movies of the time, *Casino Royale* had a budget. In total, five directors were brought in to film different segments. The *New York Times* broke down how many minutes each director contributed to the 129-minute film: John Huston (38 minutes), Kenneth Hughes (25 minutes), Joseph McGrath (20 minutes), Robert Parrish (20 minutes), and Val Guest (26 minutes).

John Huston, the most critically acclaimed of the group, previously directed timeless films such as *The Maltese Falcon* (1941), *The Treasure of the Sierra Madre* (1948), *The Asphalt Jungle* (1950), *The African Queen* (1951), and *The Misfits* (1961). *The Trials of Oscar Wilde* (1960) director Kenneth Hughes would go on to make another movie based on an Ian Fleming novel, *Chitty Chitty Bang Bang* (1967), the next year. Joseph McGrath was known for his work on the BBC radio program *The Goon Squad*, with Peter Sellers. Academy Award winner Robert Parrish won the Oscar for Best Film Editing for *Body and Soul* (1947). Celebrated Hammer Film's horror director Val Guest was tasked to shoot wraparound scenes to fill plot holes and give the film's supposed story a common thread (Canby "007 to Multiply").

Two other directors—among America's most prolific—were on set as well, but they were cast as SMERSH agents: Sir James Bond's nebbish nephew Jimmy Bond was played by Woody Allen, and SMERSH financial officer Le Chiffre was played by Orson Welles. In 1967, auteurs Woody Allen and Orson Welles were on two different career trajectories. Welles, director of what is widely considered by many to be one of greatest films of all time, *Citizen Kane* (1941), along with films such as *The Stranger* (1946), *The Lady from Shanghai* (1947), and *Touch of Evil* (1958), was mostly acting in other people's movies and doing narration work. Welles's directing career would be marred with unfinished projects and rambling, incoherent work such as the docudrama *F for Fake* (1973).

Woody Allen, on the other hand, was set to be one of the leading directors of "New Hollywood," a new generation of filmmakers who were not constrained by the Hays Code and still had an exclusively theatergoing audience. Allen, acclaimed for his stand-up comedy and late-night television appearances, a year prior had written the sex comedy *What's New Pussycat?* (1965), which was directed by *Casino Royale* producer Charles K. Feldman. Allen made his directorial debut with spy spoof *What's Up, Tiger Lily?* (1966). He would go on to write, direct, and star in award-winning and time-honored films like *Bananas* (1971), *Manhattan* (1979), and *Annie Hall* (1977).

Joseph McGrath was tasked with directing the scenes in *Casino Royale* that featured Orson Welles and Peter Sellers, who famously did not get along. The two often refused to be on the same set at the same time together, which required stand-ins and scenes to be filmed separately.

In May 1966 *Casino Royale's* production was announced and filming began in January 1966 (Canby "007 to Multiply"). Production originally was set to cost around $6 million; the budget rose to $8 million and quickly ballooned to $12 million because of an ever-expanding cast and list of directors and writers. The eight-month-long production cost more than any of the previous official Bond films by Eon Productions, even more than *You Only Live Twice*, which was released two months prior to *Casino Royale* (Ibid.).

The *New York Times'* Bosley Crowther chronicled the confusing saga of *Casino Royale's* production. "[Charles K. Feldman] has made it on the premise that the more writers and directors he could put to work and the more actors he could cram into his picture, the more impressive, if not the better, it would be, and the more energy and noise would be projected by the sheer human multiplicity. As a consequence, he had twice as many writers working on the script as the three that are named in the credits." Crowther added,

> "He had six directors shooting segments of it—and so conglomerate are their efforts that you have to consult the program to tell where one left off and another began. And he has a cast of so many, at least 14 of whom are ranking stars that the screen appears to be a demonstration of the population explosion at its peak. Furthermore, since he wasn't paying (Columbia Pictures was), he spared no expense in buying the most elaborate and fantastic sets and the finest outdoor locations in London, Scotland, and points east and west to enclose his completely Brobdingnagian[*] burlesque on the crazy cult of Bond" (Crowther "Population Explosion Victims," 25).

The February 1967 issue of men's magazine *Playboy* featured the "Girls of *Casino Royale*." The film's producers allowed set access to the magazine's photographers to take photos of the women featured in the film, including Ursula Andress, Barbara Bouchet, Deborah Kerr, Joanna Pettet, Geraldine Chaplin (in her *Keystone Cops* costume), and Daliah Lavi, after filming ended. The thirteen-page pictorial spread included text by Woody Allen.

In April 1967, billboards featuring Sean Connery in London for *You Only Live Twice* were soon followed by competing billboards for *Casino Royale*. *Casino Royale's* poster also featured Twiggy, English model and "the face of

---

* Giant.

Casino Royale soundtrack features iconic 1960s model Twiggy on the cover.
Records/Alamy Stock Photo

Swinging London." Twiggy did not appear in the film (Graham "London Bill-boards"; Terry "Star-Laden").

The movie trailer, which presented the film as a madcap comedy, echoed the billboard's sentiment and asked audiences to "Join the *Casino Royale* fun movement." The film's soundtrack, released by Columbia Pictures' recording arm Colgems, was composed by Burt Bacharach with lyrics by Hal David. "The *Casino Royale* Theme" was performed by Herb Alpert and the Tijuana Brass, but perhaps the biggest hit to come out of the soundtrack was Dusty Springfield's "The Look of Love," which was nominated for Best Song by the Academy Awards in 1968.

The UK premiere of *Casino Royale* took place on April 13, 1967, at London's Odeon Leicester Square, the site of the premiere of *From Russia with Love* (1963). The film premiered in the United States two weeks later, on April

28, 1967. Reviews of the film poured in by critics from around the country, and they were less than kind.

Bosley Crowther of the *New York Times* wrote, "Since it's based more on slapstick than wit, with Bond cliché piled upon cliché, it tends to crumble and sprawl. It's the sort of reckless, disconnected nonsense that could be telescoped or stopped at any point. If it were stopped at the end of an hour and 40 minutes instead of at the end of 2 hours and 10 minutes, it might be a terminally satisfying entertainment instead of the wearying one it is" (Crowther "Population Explosion Victims," 25).

Chicago Sun-Times resident critic Roger Ebert opined, "At one time or another, *Casino Royale* undoubtedly had a shooting schedule, a script and a plot. If any one of the three ever turns up, it might be the making of a good movie. In the meantime, the present version is a definitive example of what can happen when everybody working on a film goes simultaneously berserk." And he called the movie "possibly the most indulgent film ever made. Anything goes. Consistency and planning must have seemed the merest whimsy. One imagines the directors . . . waking in the morning and wondering what they'd shoot today" (Ebert "*Casino Royale*," n.p.).

Echoing Ebert's sentiment, Jeanne Miller of the *San Francisco Examiner* called the film "lavish" and said that the movie "brings to mind a huge, gaudy bubble-gum blob which limply deflated into its flaccid components before one's very eyes." She concluded that "for all its effort (and the strain clearly shows), the movie falls far short of the enormous talent of its creators and participants (Miller "Bond's Latest," 8). William Mootz, at the *Courier-Journal* of Louisville, Kentucky, went so far as to say that *Casino Royale* may have "killed off James Bond." He also called the film "heavy-handed," "idiotic," and a "bore" and said that if the "movie doesn't kill off the current spy-spoof craze, nothing will" (Mootz "Bond Spoof," 17).

Some fans did not seem to mind the poor reviews. Less than a month after *Casino Royale*'s debut, the excitement for the film spilled onto the streets of Boston. On May 6, 1967, Boston radio station WRKO sponsored a special 4:00 a.m. showing of *Casino Royale* at the Sack Savoy Theater. The station offered free admission, doughnuts, coffee, and soft drinks to any "spy" who showed up wearing a trench coat. Reportedly anywhere from eight thousand to fifteen thousand people were denied admission, which caused the filmgoers to riot. United Press International (UPI) reported that Deputy Police Superintendent Joseph Sala "mobilized 'every available' patrolman, including a riot squad led by dogs, to quell the mob." The riot was three hours long and saw thirty injuries; items, such as flowers, were thrown at police, stores were looted, and cars were smashed. Inside the theater, the crowd lost control as well. The theater's assistant manager, Frank Dubrawski, reported fighting in the seats, two fires and a broken fire hose "that soaked portions of the audience." "I was scared stiff to shut the projector down," said Dubrawski. Allen Friedberg, general manager of the theater was quoted as saying, "Under no condition will there be another preview of this type. . . . I never dreamed that this reaction would have resulted ("Disappointed Fans," 58).

The excitement was also seen at the box office; the film made $10.2 million in the United States and Canada and a worldwide total of $41.7 million ("Big Rental Films of 1967").

In 1999, James Bond's copyright holder, Danjaq (the company that owns the copyrights to James Bond that was started by Harry Saltzman and Albert "Cubby" Broccoli), finally acquired the rights to Ian Fleming's *Casino Royale*. Sony Pictures, who had purchased Columbia Pictures, announced its intention to make its own Bond films in 1997 (presumably *Casino Royale*) after announcing a deal with *Thunderball* producer/cocreator Kevin McClory, who owned the rights to several aspects of the James Bond character. The announcement caused Danjaq to sue Sony. As a result of the case, the *New York Times* reported,

> Under the terms of the agreement, Sony Pictures will pay MGM $5 million to settle the lawsuit, MGM said. In return, MGM said, it will pay Sony Pictures $10 million for the rights to an early James Bond spoof, *Casino Royale*, which was produced at Columbia Pictures, a Sony unit, and for all international rights to the James Bond films. (Sterngold "Sony Pictures," 11)

The film is still considered noncanonical.

MGM used the newly acquired rights and released its own *Casino Royale* in 2006. The film served as a reboot to the James Bond franchise and starred Daniel Craig.

2

THE OTHER TOP AGENTS

Derek Flint, Harry Palmer, and Matt Helm

And people with obsessions, reflected Bond, were blind to danger.

—Ian Fleming, *Moonraker*

Although James Bond brought many imitators to movie theaters and television, films featuring superspies Derek Flint, Harry Palmer, and Matt Helm were the only true contenders to James Bond's box office numbers and popularity.

DEREK FLINT

Our Man Flint **(1966)**

In November 1964 20th Century Fox released a list of sixteen films that were about to go into production; among them was *Our Man Flint*, set to be produced by *Von Ryan's Express* (1964) producer Saul David and based on a screenplay by Hal Fimberg and Ben Starr. Fimberg wrote the original story that was the basis for the movie, and Starr mostly wrote for television throughout his career, scripting various episodes of *The Guy Mitchell Show* (1957–1958),

Bachelor Father (1957–1962), and *Mr. Ed* (1961–1966) before working on *Our Man Flint* ("20th Century Fox Ending," 7).

By January 1, 1965, it was announced that James Coburn, who was coming off of breakout roles in *The Magnificent Seven* (1960), *The Great Escape* (1963), and *A High Wind in Jamaica* (1965), signed on to play the role of Derek Flint in *Our Man Flint*, which was described as a "freewheeling, big budget James Bond spoof." Flint, a former superspy for an international spy organization called Z.O.W.I.E. (Zonal Organization World Intelligence Espionage) was called out of retirement after three mad scientists for the evil organization GALAXY threatened the world with natural disasters via climate-controlling ray if the world's nations failed to give up their weapons and nuclear energy. Filming was set to begin February 2, 1965 (*"Brainstorm* Cast," 64).

Coburn was thirty-seven at the time he was cast and had been bouncing around Hollywood for the previous twelve years but had yet to have a starring role in a major motion picture. "So I moved around. I played young men, old men, heroes and villains. I've done comedy, drama, costume epics and westerns. Anything I could. And now I'm ready to play the lead," said Coburn. But when asked if the role of Flint was "make or break" for his career, Coburn responded, "I don't look at it that way. I want *Flint* to be good, of course. If it's a flop I don't think I can accept the blame. If it's a hit, the picture could be another stepping stone to more leads" (Scott "Actor James," 12).

Originally, Saul David hoped to cast former Playboy Playmate Vikki Dougan in a small role. "Vikki would be great in that," said David. "But I never have any fun. It's the second assistant directors who hire the bit players and the gorgeous girls. If I were to send word down to hire a particular girl, I'd never hear the end of it." Ultimately Dougan was not cast (Kleiner "Johnson in Hollywood," 8).

Before filming began, *BUtterfield 8* (1960) and *Who's Got the Action* (1962) director Daniel Mann took control of the director's chair, and it was reported that Coburn was doing "rigorous training" to get into shape for the role. Irving Noe of the *Van Nuys News and Valley Green Sheet* reported that "the role calls for physical feats that would frighten even Agent 007. He may have to fight off a bevy of international beauties producer Saul David is lining up for the film" (Noe "Noe News," 43). Alex Freeman, syndicated "TV Close Up" gossip columnist, reported that Coburn had been "working out in the studio gym for weeks, working on stunts he hopes will make Sean Connery flinch" (Freeman "Gotham Night," 44). Mann later indicated that he wanted the film to be more of a spoof of Douglas Fairbanks pictures like *The Prisoner of Zenda* (1937) in what he called "swashbuckling in modern dress" (Freund "Hollywood Producers," 62).

To prepare for the role, Coburn studied fencing and karate for two months. He shows off both skills within the first ten minutes of the movie (Kleiner "Burr"). It was also reported that Coburn would concede his hair to 20th Century Fox. Hollywood reporter for *Chicago's American*, Louella O. Parsons, reported that Coburn, who had been getting his hair cut by his then wife Beverly Kelly for years, would allow 20th Century Fox's chief makeup man Ben Nye to cut his hair for the film. Parsons also reported, "Mrs. Coburn isn't being a bit snippy about it" (Parsons "Ann-Margret," 13).

Also joining the cast was former Miss Israel, Gila Golan. Golan was coming off a role in Stanley Kramer's *Ship of Fools* (1965). Columnist Louella O. Parsons wrote that Golan, who would play evil agent Gila who will stop at nothing to stop Flint (a role for which Raquel Welch was reportedly originally considered), was cast for more than her acting chops. Daniel Mann said, "I've never known a girl as beautiful as Gila to be so embarrassed about showing her body." Golan quickly responded, "How would you feel doing your directing wearing a bikini?" (Parsons "Bikini Wins," 24; Hopper "Newcomer," 142).

Golan had an interesting backstory. Born in Poland, Golan was orphaned as a baby during World War II, had no known name or birthday, and may or may not have been of Jewish descent. After years of being moved around, she was finally helped by a Jewish organization that aided abandoned children, and she was settled in Israel. After winning Miss Israel in 1961, she set her sights on Hollywood (Scott "Israeli Actress").

As the more than three-million-dollar production (which later rose to approximately $4 million) began, producer David Saul took several shots at James Bond. *Los Angeles Times* motion picture editor Philip K. Scheuer reported that Saul stated, "Our basic premise is that James Bond is the perfect organization man, a dumb cop, a sucker for a pretty face, a superficial lover addicted to one-night stands and a thoroughly uninteresting human being off-duty," later adding, "Bond pictures are a steady progression of scientific high jinks and hocus-pocus. . . . Bond travels in a tawdry, mundane world of gambling casinos, cocktail lounges, and Hilton Hotels, fighting comic-book villains." But he felt that *"Our Man Flint* will be "an entirely different cup of tea—a sensitive and sensible individual, loyal to his own code instead of to an arbitrary entity which we might call 'our side.' His pleasures will be taken with verve and gusto, a la Tom Jones, and his heroics will be treated with wit and vitality, a la Douglas Fairbanks. . . . *Our Man Flint* will be free-wheeling and stylish, almost choreographed. . . . Flint's way of life will be infinitely more sophisticated and his opponent will be enormously more complex" (Freeman "Studio Betting"; Scheuer "Coburn Just Right," 65).

Our Man Flint (1966) lobby card featuring James Colburn and Gila Golan. © *1965
20th Century Fox*

At the same time, Saul David was attempting to build up his new star, comparing Coburn to the Golden Age of Hollywood's leading men. "Filmmakers are always bemoaning the passing of the leading men of yesteryear," said David. "Where, they ask, are the Garfields, the Bogarts, and the Gables of today? Yet the fact is that if an unknown Garfield or a Bogart or an Alan Ladd or a Clark Gable walked into a producer's office today he'd go without a job. . . . Producers still tend to give prime consideration to the pretty-boys, the handsome profile in casting romantic leads. . . . Although romantic leads have established that audiences react better to masculinity and style in a leading man. . . . Whatever it is that a solid leading man should have, I think James Coburn has in superlative quality and quantity" (Greenberg "Of James Coburn," 42).

Although production was originally scheduled to begin on February 4, 1965, it was put off for two months while staff "polished the script"—all while Coburn was on salary from the studio. During this time, 20th Century Fox also hired Academy Award–winner Daniel L. Fapp as the film's cinematographer. Fapp won the award for his camerawork on *West Side Story* (1960), which he shot in the widescreen format Cinemascope (Connolly "Notes from Hollywood," 19). Fapp shot *Our Man Flint* the same way.

As production finally began, 20th Century Fox released the names of two more of the film's stars, Edward Mulhare and Lee J. Cobb (Hopper "Colorful"; Scott "James Coburn Climber"). Mulhare, an Irish actor, was best known for his role in director Daniel Mann's *Von Ryan's Express* (1965) and would go on to star in the NBC series *The Ghost & Mrs. Muir* (1968–1970). Cobb was a three-time Academy Award nominee for Best Supporting Actor for *On the Waterfront* (1954), *12 Angry Men* (1957), and *The Brothers Karamazov* (1958). And although she was ultimately uncredited, 20th Century Fox announced the signing of "Sunset Strip stripteuse" Tura Satana, "whose measurements are touted as 41-25-37," as a stripper in the film. In 1965, Satana starred in Russ Meyers's gritty black-and-white exploitation-action flick *Faster Pussycat! Kill! Kill!* (Connolly "Hollywood," 35).

As production progressed, 20th Century Fox continued to announce new cast members, some of whom may or may not have appeared in the final cut of the film. It was reported that veteran character actor Lewis Charles, *His Majesty O'Keefe* (1954) and *Walk Like a Dragon* (1960) actor Benson Fong, *McHale's Navy* (1962–1966) actor Herbert Lytton, former USC All-American football standout Hal Bedsole, and stuntman Tony Eppers joined the cast ("Alec, Gina"; "Bedsole"; "Cast Grows"). Lewis Charles was known for numerous television and film appearances throughout his career. When Charles signed onto the film, it was reported he would play a "key role"; however, he only played a small role as the cabdriver who drove Derek Flint around Rome. His role was uncredited. Herbert Lytton was also uncredited in his role as a Z.O.W.I.E. Commander.

There is no record of Bedsole or Eppers playing in the film; however, Eppers may have done uncredited stunt work and Bedsole possibly can be seen in the background in the Tura Satana's striptease scene. Fong would take the largest role of the five actors, playing Dr. Schneider in a trio of evil mad scientists along with Rhys Williams as Dr. Krupov and Peter Brocco as Dr. Wu.

Although uncredited, Van Williams, who at the time was known for his role as Kenny Madison on ABC Television's *Bourbon Street Beat* (1959–1960) and its sequel, *Surfside 6* (1960–1962), provided the voice of President Lyndon B. Johnson. Later that year, Williams would provide the voice of President Johnson in *Batman: The Movie* (1966) and star in ABC's *The Green Hornet* (1966–1967). Johnson was not specifically named in the film but was referred to as "the President" and used a distinct Texas accent.

Throughout production, Coburn and producers kept distancing Derek Flint from James Bond. Coburn told Dick Kleiner, the "Hollywood Today" writer for *Newspaper Enterprise Association* (*NEA*), that he realized a comparison between Flint and Bond was inevitable but felt that Flint was a "man of more substance than Bond; he had a point of view besides being a great lady killer and a bad-man killer." Coburn also cited gimmicks and gadgets that separated his character from Bond, such as the fact that his character turned down Bond's signature gun, the Walther PPK, in favor of his multitooled cigarette lighter, which had "82 different functions, 83 if you wish to light a cigar," and, famously, his bed. Kleiner wrote, "Flint's bed is one of a kind. You see, Flint lives with four girls. Each one serves a purpose. At night, they all retire to a bed that is really five beds in one—a round, central part and five separate beds which radiate from it. . . . And you won't find that in your mail order catalog. Not this year, anyhow" (Kleiner "Hollywood Today," 4).

However, Coburn told Earl Wilson of the New York's *Herald-Sun* that he expected *Our Man Flint* to do for him what James Bond did for Sean Connery, jokingly stating that the role would "get me a better table at Sardi's."*

Director Daniel Mann also disliked the comparison to Bond. "I think Flint has more style and substance than the Bond films. It is, hopefully, humorous," stated Mann. "It has another element going for it. The story was written for the screen, not taken from a book or a play and therefore unfettered by preconceived ideas or limitations" (Scott "Ring Ding–Type," 111). Despite the distance from James Bond, the secret agent is referenced in the film. Flint rejects using Bond's signature gun and leather attaché case with a concealed knife that Bond used in *From Russia with Love*, he brings up the SPECTRE organization in a staged fight with British Secret Agent 0008, and later in the film, the villainous Gila throws down a book titled *The Adventures of 0008*.

Flint's four live-in girlfriends were described as "four international beauties of Chinese (Helen Funai), French (Sigrid Valdis), Italian (Gianna Serra), and American (Shelby Grant) origin." Flint also lives with a pair of Irish wolfhounds of the K9 variety (Greenberg "Of Stardom," 11).

During production, excitement rose among the public. Early on, in June 1965, Sigrid Valdis, Gila Golan, Helen Funai, and Shelby Grant all appeared with stars such as *Lost in Space* (1965–1968) stars Guy Williams and June Lockhart, Ed Ames from *Daniel Boone* (1964–1970) and Raquel Welch of *Fantastic Voyage* (1966) at the Century Square shopping center located in Century City, Los Angeles, California (Century City advertisement). The foursome also modeled for gossip columnist Lloyd Shearer, wearing what he called that summer's biggest fad: "Knee make-up and crew shirts." "Knee make-up" was colorful paint with pictures or slogans worn on your knees and crew shirts were simply short-sleeve, collarless shirts. The *Our Man Flint*

---

* A restaurant located in New York's Theater District.

actresses sported college crew shirts and various designs painted on their knees. Shearer's article also featured an unnamed model wearing a 007 James Bond crew shirt with 007 and a Walther PPK painted on her knees (Shearer "This Summer's Fads," 183).

Companies like McHenry Savings and Loan Associates in McHenry, Illinois, whose vice president was named John Flint, began running *Our Man Flint*-themed advertisements. They asked patrons to come in and ask for "our man Flint" to help with mortgages and loans (McHenry Savings).

Members of the press were flown to Jamaica on December 12, 1965, for a special early screening of the film. The location may or may not have been a swipe at James Bond. Jamaica was the location where Bond creator Ian Fleming wrote many of his James Bond novels, at his estate named GoldenEye. But it also did not hurt to give the people reviewing your film an island vacation (Bourke "'Our Man Flint' Invades").

While the film was in production, Coburn stated, "If it's a hit, the picture could be another stepping stone to more leads." Coburn got his wish. Even before one ticket was sold, producer Saul David and 20th Century Fox vice president in charge of production Richard D. Zanuck announced the sequel to *Our Man Flint*, which would be written by *Our Man Flint* cowriter Hal Fimberg and was set to be called *F as in Flint* (The title was later changed to *In Like Flint*). Zanuck said he was prompted to go ahead with the sequel based on "reception at preview" (Scott "Actor James," 12; "*Our Man Flint* Sequel").

After all its production delays—even minor ones, like when production was delayed for forty-five minutes when veteran stuntman Roy Jensen was supposed to "play dead" but had a case of the hiccups—the film premiered on January 16, 1966. 20th Century Fox was said to have hoped for a "Bond Bonanza" with *Our Man Flint* and British spy film *Modesty Blaise* (Scott "Maureen's"; Thomas "Movies Bet").

Theaters around the country ran special advertisements promoting the film at their theater, often comparing Flint to James Bond. The Liberty Theater in Zanesville, Ohio, asked patrons, "Did you like *Thunderball*? Come Saturday night for a special showing of a picture that 20th Century Fox said is BETTER!" The Savoy Theater in Boston called it "the *Goldfinger* of '66" (Liberty advertisement; Savoy advertisement). James Coburn was called a "Jet Press Agent" by the *Pittsburgh Post-Gazette* due to Coburn crisscrossing the country on a private jet to promote the film, which included an appearance on *The Tonight Show with Johnny Carson* (1962–1992) on Tuesday, January 18, 1966. Gina Golan also took part in a number of press junkets around the country ("Coburn, Jet Press," 9; "Tonight in Television"; "Israeli Star").

Japanese poster for *Our Man Flint* (1966). © *1966 Columbia Pictures*

Although born in the United States, Benson Fong (who also owned Los Angeles Chinese restaurant Ah Fong's) was of Chinese descent and traveled to Hong Kong and Tokyo, Japan, for leisure and, more importantly, to promote the movie. *Our Man Flint* was released in Japan under the title *Dengeki Flint GO! GO! Operations* ("Restaurateur Takes Trip").

The William Goldman Randolph Theater, located in Center City Philadelphia, reported, "7,326 Philadelphians previewed *Our Man Flint* in 6 Theaters and that's 7,326 excited people raving like the press from coast to coast!" It published a number of reviews from around the county (William Goldman Randolph Theater advertisement):

Outdoes Ian Fleming's *Doctor No* and *Goldfinger*. There's satire, gorgeous scenery, gizmos that go Zap, curvaceous dames . . . and more electronics than Cape Kennedy and Gemini 6-7!—Dwight L. Buckness, *Cincinnati Enquirer*

Flint tops James Bond. After watching James Coburn and his utterly incredible adventures as Derek Flint, whose cunning and daring saves our whole nation from destruction, we are willing to go along with the prediction that he'll be "the man of tomorrow"—Ann Marsters, *Chicago's American*

New film out-Bonds James . . . if the picture goes over as well in other countries as it did on this big island, it ought to be the hit of the year!—Gerald Ashford, *San Antonio News*

James Bond may have met his match in Derek Flint.—*Variety*

The *New York Times* published two reviews of the film: Resident film critic Bosley Crowther called the film an "inferior burlesque," writing,

Here we go again! Another James Bond! Cancel that. Another brazen travesty of the already self-burlesquing figment of the Ian Fleming super-sleuth! And if anybody in the movie audience thinks that this sort of thing has gone too far and is without sin in giving it encouragement by patronizing the Bond films, let him cast the first stone! This time the ape of 007 is a long-legged wizard name of Flint, who is played by elastic James Coburn, a spirited fellow who has already manifested his cool as a killer, both lady and lethal.

He added,

Don't look for originality in it. The trick of it is to assume that everything that is done in the Bond film is outrageous and then multiply it by at least two. That's all. Where Bond ordinarily takes his girls one by one, this fellow Flint takes his in bunches. He has four at the start to wait on him and he accumulates complaints as he goes along. Where Bond has clever bits of mechanism that do individual things, Flint has pocket gadgets that have more uses than a Boy Scout knife from Switzerland. He has a wrist watch that serves as a sleep timer, a Geiger counter, an astrolabe, a radio sender and receiver and, I believe, an acetylene torch. He has been a ballet master in Moscow and a jet pilot in the Far East. He can identify the regional derivation of a bouillabaisse by the proportions of saffron, fennel and garlic in its taste. This fellow Flint is fantastic, and when he heeds the urgent call of the Pentagon to put his sleuthing skills to the purpose of discovering the headquarters and nature of a super-gang of world subverts known as Galaxy, he goes about it in fantastic and thoroughly flamboyant ways. (Crowther "Inferior Burlesque," 23)

Journalist and activist Gloria Steinem wrote a column for New York's "newspaper of record" calling *Our Man Flint* "real boss." Steinem called the film a

breezy James Bond spoof only a few notches above *Batman* level . . . Coburn starts out with four girls and acquired a fifth. . . . The film is hardly a showcase for acting ability, but box office success has pointed up Coburn's qualifications for leading man, circa 1966; he's handsome enough to be a convincing romantic lead, off-beat enough for the Beatles generation (and photographs 10 years younger than his current 38), brainy enough to make master-spy feats convincing, and villainous enough to be anti-establishment at all times. (Steinem "Our Man Is 'Real Boss,'" 109)

Henry T. Murdock of the *Philadelphia Inquirer* called *Our Man Flint* a "comic-strip film" that is "played for absurdities, burlesquing its predecessors, enhancing all the gimmicks." Murdock also saw *Our Man Flint* as the end of the spy spoof craze. "We are beginning to feel like one who has been left too long near a box of candy. It's fine to sample, distressing to gorge. We are running out of description where the current spy cycle is concerned" (Murdock "James Coburn Plays Hero," 12).

A special 4:00 a.m. premiere was held at New York's Forum Theatre to a crowd of eight hundred dressed in "tuxedos and long dresses, in paint-splattered jeans and bell-bottom slacks, defying the early morning hour, the bitter cold, long lines, and the prospect of a full day's work ahead." The admission was free if patrons wore formal clothes. A number of film and Broadway stars attended the event, most notably a party led by Andy Warhol, who "arrived in outfits best described as vintage Salvation Army." It was reported the postpremiere party included "a live band, discotheque dancers and Manhattan night clubs and, of course, champagne and breakfast." The breakfast ended around 7:00 a.m. ("Film Fans Flock," 11).

The movie score was conducted and composed by Jerry Goldsmith. Goldsmith previously composed the scores for series *The Man from U.N.C.L.E.* (1964–1968) and movies *The Satan Bug* (1965) and *Von Ryan's Express* (1965). Throughout the 1960s, the composer would score films such as *Stagecoach* (1966), *In Like Flint* (1967), *Planet of the Apes* (1968), and *The Chairman* (1969). Over a career spanning six decades, he would score hundreds of films and series, be nominated for eighteen Academy Awards, and win once for *The Omen* (1977). The album was released as a vinyl LP by 20th Century Fox Records.

Our Man Flint was the ninth highest grossing film of 1966 in North America, grossing $6,500,000, and would go on to make over $15 million worldwide. However, the James Bond adventure *Thunderball* (1965), which was released in the United States toward the end of 1965, on December 22, took the top spot in 1966 earning $26,000,000 in North America, four times more than *Our Man Flint* ("Big Rental Pictures 1966"; "*Flint* Sparks").

James Coburn returned to theaters the next year with the sequel, *In Like Flint*.

In Like Flint (1967)

When *Our Man Flint* was still in production, producer Saul David and 20th Century Fox vice president in charge of production, Richard D. Zanuck, announced the sequel to *Our Man Flint,* which was set to be called *F as in Flint.* The follow-up would be written by *Our Man Flint* cowriter Hal Fimberg and would begin production in early 1966 ("*Our Man Flint* Sequel").

In March 1966 producers began scouting locations for the film, still scheduled to be titled *F as in Flint,* in Cape Kennedy, Cypress Gardens, Puerto Rico, Virgin Islands, Jamaica, Barbados, and Martinique. Ultimately, producers chose to shoot in Jamaica ("Show 'Nuf"). By April 1966 it was announced that James Coburn and Lee J. Cobb would return, and Gordon Douglas, whose directing credits included a number of *Our Gang* comedy shorts, *Zombies on Broadway* (1945), *Dick Tracy vs. Cueball* (1946), *Them!* (1954), and *Stagecoach* (1966), would be directing the sequel ("Bit Parts"; "Movie Men").

Elston Brooks of the *Fort Worth Star-Telegram* broke the news on April 27, 1966, that the title of the film would be changed from *F as in Flint* to *In Like Flint* (Brooks "Movie Critic"). It was later revealed that Coburn hated the new title, stating, "It's a cheap, tasteless title—a connotation of the old cliché 'in like Flynn.' Most of us on the film are fighting it, but a couple of executives at 20th are insisting on keeping the silly tag." Although there is some dispute, the phrase "in like Flynn" is one that goes back to the 1940s and presumably refers to the legendary sexual prowess of actor Errol Flynn (Manners "Ladies Love," 53).

Between making *Our Man Flint* and *In Like Flint,* James Coburn made the film *Dead Heat on a Merry-Go-Round* (1966), a film that was originally titled *Eli Kotch,* with future *Murderers' Row* (1966) and *Assignment K* (1968) star Camilla Sparv (Brooks "Movie Critic"). Coburn also used his *In Like Flint* earnings on a house that he described as an "old Spanish hacienda-type with eighteen major rooms and uncounted tiny rooms on three acres of Beverly Hillside" (Ibid., 10).

Cobb worked on the Western television show *The Virginian* (1962–1971) between films, playing the role of Judge Garth. Reports also indicated that E. G. Marshall, star of CBS Television's *The Defenders* (1961–1965) and *12 Angry Men* (1957) as juror number four was also cast. Marshall did not appear in *In Like Flint*; reports may have confused Marshall with fellow *12 Angry Men* star Cobb, who played juror number three in the celebrated picture (Muir "Fess Takes Daniel").

There was talk that Geraldine Brooks, a character actress who appeared on *The Virginian* (1962–1971), *Combat!* (1962–1967), and *The Outer Limits*

(1963–1965), would join the production. Ultimately, Brooks was not cast. However, Jean Hale, known for her appearances on *McHale's Navy* (1962–1966), *My Favorite Martian* (1963–1966), and *Batman* (1966–1968), was cast as the female lead (Freeman "Robert Preston"; Muir "Looking at Hollywood").

The cast added television Western actor Andrew Duggan. Known for his work on *Wagon Train* (1957–1962), *Maverick* (1957–1962), and *The Big Valley* (1965–1969), Duggan was cast as US president Trent. No word what happened to the President Johnson soundalike (voiced by Van Williams) in *Our Man Flint* (Swaebly "Duggan Happy").

Notable casting also included Steve Ihant, whom the *Charlotte Observer*'s Emery Wister called "such a good bad man," Hollywood Golden Age character actress and television staple Anna Lee, and future Batgirl Yvonne Craig (Wister "Squeaky Don's," 28).

Production began in May 1966 in Jamaica, and the cast stayed at Montego Bay's Round Hill Hotel. Hollywood reporter Mike Connolly wrote that he received a postcard from Montego Bay from James Coburn, who said, "Jamaica's great. Am stranded with 60 bikini-clad beauties." But he noted that Coburn did not mention his then wife, Beverly Kelly, among the "bikini-clad beauties" (Connolly "Taylor Joins," 29). "Bikini-clad beauties" would also become one of the biggest publicity tools for the picture—and Flint's biggest onscreen enemy.

Earl Wilson, a New York–based gossip columnist, reported a wacky story that ran in a number of national newspapers, "The tall 'Amazon' girls [played by Erin O'Brien, Ginny Gan, Eve Bruce, Inge Jaklyn, Kay Farrington, Thordis Brandt, Inga Neilsen, and Marilyn Hanold] filming *In Like Flint* in Jamaica have their problems—the local hotels don't have beds long enough for 'em" (Wilson "Midnight Earl," 36). Eight "bikini-clad gals" were spotted walking on the sidewalk of Los Angeles on a 100-degree day to publicize the film ("Even with the Temperature," 7). All eight "Amazon girls" were photographed in leopard bikinis learning football plays with UCLA football coach Tommy Prothro ("Pointers," 31; "Beauties Receive," 19). "Amazon" Thordis Brandt was spotted with Pittsburgh Pirates infielders Gene Alley and Bill Mazeroski, urging the pair to try California orange juice ("For What Ails Them," 152). James Coburn began appearing in press photos with the "Amazon girls" as well—perhaps the same photos he sent in a postcard to Earl Wilson ("Bikini Plot Foiled," 279).

Much like during the production of *Our Man Flint*, Producer Saul David was reportedly "annoyed" by the continued comparisons between Derek Flint and James Bond. Once again, David stated his case that he believed that Flint was closer to Douglas Fairbanks than to James Bond. "I shouldn't get angry about it," said David, adding, "People always get angry when they are accused of trying to make a better banana when all they're trying to do is make an apple" (Kleiner "Flint's Not a Bond," 32).

On July 10, 1966, Carol Bjorkman of *Women's Wear Daily* wrote the first real preview into the upcoming film: "All the hair dryers all over the world have conditioners inside that condition women—they say mankind has destroyed the world so let's get together and really love. The plot deals with women taking over the world" (Bjorkman "'In' Mr. Flint," 124). Bosley Crowther of the *New York Times* later laid out a more detailed plot:

> It seems that a conspiracy of women, master-minded by a beauty-cream tycoon, is out to take over the Government and, through control of the nuclear bomb, control the world. . . . So this mischievous Mafia of women arranges to kidnap the President and put in his place an actor who has been made to look exactly like him by plastic surgery. Only they haven't counted on being detected by the miraculous Flint, who is called in to fathom the mystery by his old Pentagon friend, Lee J. Cobb. That's the gist of the nonsense, and the trouble with it is that there are simply more girls and gadgets than there are jokes in Hal Fimberg's script. A female health-farm located in the Virgin Islands is the principal locale, and next door to it is a super-science-fiction rocket-launching base. Between the two, Mr. Coburn shuttles casually in his slapdash efforts to solve the mystery and prevent the destruction of the world. Under Gordon Douglas's direction, Anna Lee and Jean Hale play the most powerful females in a decidedly sluggish way, and Andrew Duggan, not that other fellow you may be thinking about, plays the President. (Crowther "*In Like Flint* Opens," 53)

Although at the end of *Our Man Flint*, Flint added a fifth girl to his stable of girlfriends, adding the once villainous Gila (Gila Golan), at the beginning of *In Like Flint*, he reduced the number to a more manageable three. When asked about Flint's arrangement, Coburn admitted, "I don't believe it myself" ("*Flint Sparks*," 17).

Excitement for the new Flint adventure was apparent. Theaters began advertising for *In Like Flint*, and Dell books released the novelization of the film, *In Like Flint* ("Dell Best Seller List"). Right before the film was released, it was reported that 20th Century Fox had signed Coburn to another *Flint* picture. But soon afterward, Coburn seemingly threw cold water on the report and on *In Like Flint*: "In Like Flint is already out of date, even before it's released, because of advances in technology—such films as *Blow Up* (1966) and *A Man for All Seasons* (1966) have moved the industry way ahead of us" ("More Flint"; Kleiner "Carol Channing," 21).

Originally scheduled to be released for Christmas 1966, *In Like Flint* was finally released to theaters on March 15, 1967, but sneak previews of the film were shown as early as February 3. The Capitol Theater in New York held a special invitational premiere on March 14, 1967. The first two hundred people wearing bathing suits were admitted for "a swim party" ("*Flint* Is In," 331). Roger Ebert of the *Chicago Sun-Times* wrote, "The sexiest thing in the new Derek Flint misadventure, 'In Like Flint,' is Flint's cigarette lighter, which is supposed to know 82 tricks but actually delivers only five, of which one is the not extraordinary ability to clip Lee J. Cobb's mustache. . . . Second place goes to a preposterous scene in which 51 Amazons run through the surf in their Catalina swimsuits, looking like the opening scene of 'Hawaii' re-shot as a missionary training film." Ebert added, "The beauty of the James Bond films has always been their quick pace, the sense of breathless events taking place. But *In Like Flint*, alas, lingers over every tired joke and every special effect as if they were the last of their kind in the world. One wishes it were so" (Ebert "In Like Flint Review," n.p.).

The *New York Times*' Bosley Crowther echoed Ebert's sentiment, writing, "Although the film crawls with dime-store beauties, there is a noticeable lack of sexiness in it. Women bent on being tyrants evidently haven't much time for anything else" (Crowther "*In Like Flint* Opens," 53).

Kathleen Carroll of the *New York Daily News* felt that although *In Like Flint* had "gals" and "action," the film was weak on plot. She called it "another less-than-potent dose of James Bond American-style" (Carroll "In Like Flint— Gals," 516).

Once again, Coburn took to the skies and flew across the country following the release of the film in the states and later to European capital cities in mid-May 1966 to promote the film. One report stated that Bill Lear of Learjets flew Coburn personally from Los Angeles to Puerto Rico for a showing of the film. The film was later released in Japan as well, under the title *Dengeki Flint Attack Operation* ("Bill Lear"; Bradford "Notes from Hollywood").

A $4 million production, *In Like Flint*, like *Our Man Flint*, was shot in the widescreen format known as Cinemascope. *In Like Flint* and the Doris Day spy spoof *Caprice* (1967) were the final films that 20th Century Fox produced using that film format ("*Flint* Sparks"). Jerry Goldsmith was brought back to compose the original score, which was released as a vinyl LP in 1967. The soundtrack included the "In Like Flint Theme," which was now called "Where the Bad Guys Are Gals." It also included the song "Your Zowie Face," with lyrics by Leslie Bricusse.

Despite its lukewarm reviews, *In Like Flint* earned $5,000,000 at the box office in North America, making it the eighteenth highest grossing film of 1967. But once again, Derek Flint was beat out by James Bond. That year, *You Only Live Twice* was the second highest grossing film of the year, earning $10,200,000 ("Big Rental Films of 1967").

No other Flint movie was ever made by James Coburn or 20th Century Fox. However a made-for-television movie, *Our Man Flint: Dead on Target*, starring Ray Danton as Derek Flint, aired on ABC on March 17, 1967. The production was made in the hope of making it into a series, but the movie was not picked up by the network.

HARRY PALMER

The Ipcress File (1965)

After top British scientist Radcliffe (Aubrey Richards) is kidnapped from a train, Harry Palmer (Michael Caine), of the Ministry of Defense, is tasked by Colonel Ross (Guy Doleman) with connecting Radcliffe's disappearance to the apparent "brain drain" of fourteen other scientists, who all quit their profession at the peak of their careers. The Ministry of Defense believes Eric Grantby (Oliver MacGreevy), codenamed "Housemartin," is a prime suspect. But after Housemartin is arrested and later found dead in his jail cell, it is believed a larger conspiracy was behind the kidnapped scientist. After a botched rescue attempt of Radcliffe, Palmer discovers a strip of microfilm titled IPCRESS. IPCRESS is later found to stand for "Induction of Psychoneurosis by Conditioned Reflex under Stress." It is soon believed IPCRESS may have something to do with the missing scientists, which is confirmed after Radcliffe is exchanged for ransom and it is discovered his memory has been completely wiped.

Based on a 1962 novel of the same name by Len Deighton and written by Bill Canaway and James Doran, *The Ipcress File*, like many spy films of the era, could easily be compared to a James Bond story. However, *The Ipcress File* was produced by James Bond coproducer Harry Saltzman via his production company, Lowndes Productions.

Saltzman also brought on John Barry, who wrote the iconic "James Bond Theme," to write "A Man Alone" for *The Ipcress File*. This theme has a similar sultry spy-fi sound and feel. Although certainly not as popular as the "James Bond Theme," it was recorded by a number of orchestras in the mid-1960s.

Poster for *The Ipcress File* (1965) that makes Harry Palmer's signature eyeglasses look more like sunglasses. © *1965 Universal Pictures Co.*

The Ipcress File was shot in downtown London, England—in near-complete secrecy. A year prior, Michael Caine made a name for himself in the British war epic *Zulu* (1964), the film in which Saltzman first saw Caine, and 1965 was nearing the height of the 1960s spy craze, so producers did not want interruptions while shooting. Despite having a cast and crew of one hundred people and shooting within two large Victorian-style homes, the film's executive producer Charles Kasher stated, "It was an operation almost as secretive as something out of a film on espionage." He went on to say, "It was essential that no one knew about the filming for fear of the production being held up by sight-seers and autograph hunters. Thousands of dollars could be wasted if the filming had been delayed for even minutes" (Oppenheimer "Failure," 62; "*Ipcress File* Is Mystery," 29).

Other stars of the film would have notable spy film roles as well. Guy Doleman would play Count Lippe in *Thunderball* (1965), appear on British television's *The Prisoner* (1967–1968), and reprise his role as Colonel Ross in *Funeral for Berlin* (1966) and *Billion Dollar Brain* (1968). Oliver MacGreevy could be found in Euro-spy Bond spoof *The 2nd Best Secret Agent in the Whole Wide World* (1965), British spy comedy *Modesty Blaise* (1966), and *Salt and Pepper*

(1968), an American spy spoof starring Sammy Davis Jr. and Peter Lawford. Also appearing in the film is Nigel Green. Green made appearances on the shows *Danger Man* (1960–1962 and 1964–1968) and *The Avengers* (1961–1969) and in spoofs such as *Deadlier Than the Male* (1967) and *The Wrecking Crew* (1968).

Although made by the same producer and unlike many spy films of the era, Harry Palmer is not a James Bond clone. It is often noted that Harry Palmer is notably more of a "blue-collar" figure than James Bond is. Palmer has a working-class Cockney accent, wears National Health Service (NHS) eyeglasses, does his own grocery shopping, owns a modest working-class apartment, makes his own coffee in the morning, gets the newspaper strictly for the horse-racing forms, works in a dreary office, wears an ill-fitting suit, and is *very* concerned about his wages. In addition, Palmer is far from a "superspy." He has bad eyesight (without his signature glasses)—at one point he shoots the wrong person—does not get involved in high-speed chases, and does not have an unlimited expense account or expensive cars and gadgets to complete his mission.

The *Newspaper Enterprise Association* (NEA) declared, "Bond uses gimmicks, but Harry uses brains." Caine himself was quoted as saying, "Our pictures are unlike the Bond pictures in that we don't require man-eating sharks to create excitement. My whole thing is empathy." Caine also believed Harry Palmer was different from the spy films that were being produced in the United States, stating, "The English spy heroes also differ from your American heroes. We're a bit subtle. American spies are 6-feet-5 for a start. They have fantastic bodies, marvelous sun tan, and their teeth are just right. Hollywood would have given the Harry Palmer part to Rock Hudson and would have Brigit Bardot- and Elizabeth Taylor–type girls falling for him. With me, there is no image to follow. Just good performance from an actor working to the top of his ability" ("Bond Uses Gimmicks," 30; Lewis "Caine Cases," 32).

At a time when Sean Connery was already looking to step away from playing James Bond because of the fear of being typecast, Michael Caine did not have the same fears. "If they are successful, I may be Palmer for the rest of my life," he said in an interview with Newspaper Enterprise Association's Joan Crosby. "I don't fear being typed as Palmer. I know the Bond image hit Sean Connery pretty hard, but he is now making half a million for outside pictures, so that's not too bad. Besides, the Bond image was presold because of the popularity of the books." Caine also believed that Harry Palmer's signature glasses may help. "I normally wear glasses and when Harry Saltzman saw me, he suggested I wear them," he told London reporter Harold Stern. "I'd know how to handle them where a lot of actors wouldn't. I like the idea of glasses. They may help me from being trapped like Sean Connery. This way, when I wear glasses on the screen,

I'm Harry Palmer. When I don't, I can be everything else" (Crosby "Raising Caine," 10; Stern "Anti-Hero," 10).

Although *Dr. No* (1962) and *From Russia with Love* (1963) were generally praised by critics, by the time *Goldfinger* (1964) was released, the genre was filled with parody and copycat "superspy" films, and critics were falling over each other to declare James Bond and spy films dead despite record box office numbers. *The Ipcress File*, which opened on March 18, 1965, in the United Kingdom and on August 2, 1965, in the United States was different.

Variety wrote, "Harry Saltzman and Albert R. Broccoli, who produce the Bond razzmatazz, diversified by bringing to the screen a kind of 'anti-Bond' spy in the character of Harry Palmer." But it criticized the film's cinematography: "Sidney J. Furie's direction, allied with Otto Heller's camera, provides some striking effects. But sometimes he gets carried away into arty-crafty fields with low-angle shots and symbolism adding to the confusion of the screenplay" ("Ipcress File").

Newsweek called *The Ipcress File* "a thinking man's *Goldfinger*"; *McCall's* wrote that it was "A taut, tingling film"; *Time* called it "a tingling, no nonsense suspense yard"; *Saturday Review* believed *The Ipcress File* was "the very model of suspense entertainment," while the *New Yorker* stated that it was an "admirable thriller in every respect!" (6 Mile Theater advertisement; "*Ipcress File* Shows," 13).

The Ipcress File had positive reviews and box office numbers, and it inspired two sequels starring Michael Caine as Harry Palmer: *Funeral in Berlin* (1966) and *Billion Dollar Brain* (1967). In 1999 it was named number fifty-nine on the British Film Institute's (BFI) Top 100 British Films.

After *The Ipcress File*, director Sidney J. Furie would go on to direct the influential horror film *The Entity* (1982), and *Superman IV: The Quest for Peace* (1987), starring Christopher Reeve. Furie would also cocreate the *Iron Eagle* action franchise. Cinematographer Otto Heller, who previously helped create the first-person point-of-view aesthetic for slasher horror films in *Peeping Tom* (1960), would also do the cinematography for the two sequels of *The Ipcress File*.

Although it certainly did not reach James Bond levels of merchandising, an *Ipcress File* board game was released by Milton Bradley in 1966.

Funeral in Berlin (1966)

Based on a 1964 novel of the same name by Len Deighton that in 1965 the *New York Times* called "even better than 'The Spy Who Came In from the Cold' and was on the *New York Herald*'s best-seller list throughout early 1965,

Funeral in Berlin marks the second of three Harry Palmer films starring Michael Caine" (*Funeral in Berlin* advertisement; "Best Sellers," 20). Harry Saltzman, producer of *The Ipcress File*, acquired the rights to the property reportedly for "more than $100,000" ("Ferocious Fable," 89).

Between shooting *The Ipcress File* and *Funeral in Berlin*, which began production in Germany in the fall of 1965, Michael Caine starred in the comedies *Alfie* (1966) alongside Millicent Martin, Shelley Winters, and Jane Asher, and *Gambit* (1966) with Shirley MacLaine (Graham "Hollywood Everywhere"; "Michael Caine Proves"; "Actor Caine," 59).

While on the set of *Alfie*, Caine talked about his character, Harry Palmer. "I thought I'd be an unconventional hero, because I wanted to be like ordinary people. . . . I didn't want the audience to look up to me," said Caine. "I wanted them to identify with me. I play the ordinary man, the gray man who blends into the scenery. I'm the exact opposite for the flamboyant James Bond" (Graham "Michael Caine," 8).

Despite being an anti-Bond, Michael Caine, at the time a bachelor, was enjoying his newfound wealth and notoriety and was spotted with a number of women, including actresses Edina Ronay and Luciana Paluzzi. "It's not difficult getting birds," Caine said. "After all, girls will go out with a short fat man with money, so wouldn't they go out with a tall, thin one? And it helps being well known, I reckon someone like Marlon Brando could date any bird once. I bet he does, come to that" (Man "Poor Boy," 24).

Shot on location with returning cinematographer Otto Heller, in the still-war-torn and divided Berlin, *Funeral in Berlin* cost $2.5 million to produce, $150,000 of which went to Caine (Graham "Can Ava Gardner," 10).

British MI5's Colonel Ross (Guy Doleman) sends agent Harry Palmer (Michael Caine) to help a Soviet intelligence officer, Colonel Stok (Oskar Homolka), defect to the West. Palmer conceives of a plan to bring Colonel Stok into West Germany via a coffin, with fellow agent Johnny Vulkan (Paul Hubschmid) and an escape artist Otto Kreutzmann (Günter Meisner). Along the way, Palmer joins a hunt for Nazi gold and is involved romantically with Israeli model-turned-agent Samantha Steel (Eva Renzi). Palmer soon learns he's been double-crossed by most everyone involved in the operation, including Colonel Ross, and now must evade Israeli agents who desperately want documents in Palmer's possession.

Hungarian actor Oskar Homolka was best known for his portrayal of a Communist heavy, as in Alfred Hitchcock's thriller *Sabotage* (1936), or that of an evil lackey, as seen in William Castle's horror flick *Mr. Sardonicus* (1961). German Günter Meisner, often cast as a Nazi, also played in *The Quiller Memorandum* in 1966 but would later best be known as Arthur Slugworth in *Willy Wonka & the Chocolate Factory* (1971).

Funeral in Berlin marked Eva Renzi's first English-language film. She would go on to appear in Delbert Mann's *The Pink Jungle* (1968) and Dario Argento's *The Bird with the Crystal Plumage* (1970). Paul Hubschmid mostly made films throughout Europe, notably starring in the Euro spy flick *The Spy with Ten Faces* (1966).

Although reports of the *Funeral in Berlin*'s production repeatedly called Harry Palmer the "newest of the James Bond-type characters" or "the thinking man's James Bond," Michael Caine was beginning to be seen as "very hot property" in Hollywood (Greenberg "Shirley MacLaine," 27; "From Sloop," 16). "It's amazing to think that one could put on glasses and an ill-fitting suit and become a star," said Caine. He added, "I'd like to get a good 20 years as an actor. If you can make a career last that long, you're pretty lucky" (Thomas "Michael Caine Treated," 1).

At the conclusion of production, it was announced that the next Harry Palmer film would be *Billion Dollar Brain* and would be presumably followed up by *Horse on the Water* (Scheuer "Hit Raises").

Aside from being produced by Harry Saltzman, *Funeral in Berlin* had another link to the James Bond films. Director Guy Hamilton had directed *Goldfinger* (1964) for producer Harry Saltzman. Hamilton would direct three more Bond films: *Diamonds Are Forever* (1971), *Live and Let Die* (1973), and *The Man with the Golden Gun* (1974).

Funeral in Berlin first premiered in the United States on December 22, 1966, and in the United Kingdom on February 23, 1967. Not all critics were keen on Palmer's second adventure. *The New York Times* critic Bosley Crowther wrote, "It's so overloaded with plot, so studiously crowded with people who are double-crossing and triple-crossing their associates, that it all becomes very confusing, and gentle Harry Palmer soon seems but a cipher in the midst of a complex intrigue that the viewer finds hard to understand." He added, "Thus, all of his bland maneuvers, his dry impulses and his casual tricks whereby he confronts his opponents, seem arbitrarily and mechanically engineered by a scriptwriter [Evan Jones] picking from what I am told is a good Len Deighton book" (Crowther "Funeral in Berlin," 17).

However, *Variety* called the film an "excellent Cold War suspenser full of surprises and adroit humor." And Nadine M. Edwards of the *Los Angeles Evening Citizen News* said the film had "all the overtones of sex and sophistication, as well as considerable wit and down-to-earth taut suspense" (*Variety Film Reviews*, 425; Edwards "Exciting Vehicle," 14).

Billion Dollar Brain (1967)

In the third Harry Palmer film, Palmer (Michael Caine) leaves his government job as a spy to join the private sector and becomes a private eye. But Palmer is soon pressed back into service by his former MI5 chief, Colonel Ross (Guy Doleman), with the help of a little blackmail, and he's tasked to retrieve six virus-laden eggs that have been stolen from a British research facility.

While caught in a love triangle between ex–CIA agent Leo Newbegin (Karl Malden) and the beautiful Anya (Françoise Dorléac), Palmer infiltrates an organization fronted by an American, General Midwinter (Ed Begley), who plans to use a computer network called "The Brain" to start a war with Latvia and other Communist Bloc nations. Harry must now join forces with his Soviet rival, Colonel Stok (Oskar Homolka), to stop General Midwinter.

Caine, Doleman, and Homolka all reprised their roles from earlier in the series. Academy Award–winning actor Karl Malden was best known for his roles in *A Streetcar Named Desire* (1951) and *On the Waterfront* (1954). Françoise Dorléac could also be found in spy films *That Man from Rio* (1964) and *Where the Spies Are* (1966). Character actor Ed Begley made his one and only spy film appearance in *Billion Dollar Brain* but had notable roles in the films *12 Angry Men* (1957) and *The Unsinkable Molly Brown* (1964).

Billion Dollar Brain also marked the first onscreen appearance of Michael Caine's twenty-five-year-old (younger) brother Stanley Caine. Stanley Caine made only two other film appearances, *Play Dirty* (1969) and *The Italian Job* (1969), in his short film career, also with his older brother ("Stanley Caine").

Prior to the release of *Billion Dollar Brain*, Michael Caine was asked if he was afraid of being typecast. Caine responded, "I love the character and no matter how many times I play Harry Palmer, he's my safety valve. He KEEPS me from being typecast. Connery played James Bond in his regular style, without special make-up or costuming, and that's who he is off screen too. He had to grow a Clark Gable mustache and to do *The Hill* (1965) to get away from the Bond image. It's different with me. I put on eyeglasses and a rumpled suit and I'm Harry Palmer. I take 'em off and I'm Michael Caine" (Howard "3 Marquees," 38).

Producer Harry Saltzman assigned Ken Russell to direct. Russell was considered one of the "young lions of British TV," directing a number of made-for-television biographies, but *Billion Dollar Brain* would mark his major feature debut. He would go on to direct science fiction classic *Altered States* (1980) and musicals *Tommy* (1975) and *Lisztomania* (1975) both with featured members of the rock band the Who ("Billion Dollar Brain," 10).

The rights to produce the film were originally purchased by Harry Saltzman in November 1965 for $250,000, and production began in England in February 1967. In March, filming moved to Helsinki, Finland. While shooting in Helsinki, reportedly five thousand citizens filled the city's Ice Palace for a filmed hockey game, and "two top Finnish teams also participated." It was reported that "the ice hockey match was chosen as the setting for the meeting because the game, one of the fastest and most aggressive of sports, symbolized and emphasizes the dangerous, devious, exciting relationship between the cockney spy, Harry Palmer, played by Caine, and the beautiful Finn, Anya, portrayed by Miss Dorleac." Production moved back to England after several weeks in Finland (Weiler "Shooting for 'Sixpence'"; "Billion Dollar Brain"; "Five Thousand Finns," 27).

While the film was in production in Finland, Caine lamented about how he did not act simply for the money, stating that although at the time he made about $500,000 a picture, he acted because he liked it and that he was "an actor for 10 years and wound up $11,200 in debt" (Brown "Michael Caine Returns," 62). Also while shooting in Finland, again Caine talked about the differences between his character Harry Palmer and James Bond. "Bond is a Superman and Palmer is not," said Caine. "Bond with all his gadgets and a girl in every bedroom, is the type a young guy can look up at and say 'Gee, I wish that was me.' And he's the type a bird can look up at and say 'Gee, I wish that was my man.' Palmer's not like that. He's an everyday guy like you and me—someone you can identify with" (Brown "Michael Caine Returns," 62).

Billion Dollar Brain was released on December 20, 1967. Critics had differing opinions on the film. Reed Porter of the West Hollywood *Valley Times* called it a "million-volt thrill" and said that Michael Caine, "smoother and more polished in every appearance, . . . makes every incredible situation believable with his deft styling and aureate delivering of smart dialogue" (Porter *"Billion Dollar Brain* Million-Volt," 8). Wanda Hale of New York's *Daily News* believed *Billion Dollar Brain* "lacks two important factors that the two preceding spy thrillers had, suspense and a certain amount of reason." She also felt that the billion dollar "brain" supercomputer found in the film began to emulate the ever-growing cache of over-the-top gadgets of James Bond films (Hale *"Billion Dollar Brain Lacking,"* 74).

Billion Dollar Brain did not succeed at the box office. It was only the sixtieth highest grossing film of 1968, earning approximately $1,500,000 in North America, and it was the last Harry Palmer film of the era ("Big Rental Films of 1969"). Although the film did not succeed at the box office, the book *Billion Dollar Brain* by Len Deighton succeeded at bookstores and was one of the best-selling books by Dell Books in 1967 ("Dell Best Seller List").

A year after *Billion Dollar Brain* was released, Michael Caine, was rumored to be in the running to take on the role of James Bond in *On Her Majesty's Secret Service* (1969) despite having played Harry Palmer, the near antithesis of James Bond, in three films for Harry Saltzman. George Lazenby was ultimately cast as Bond, but Michael Caine had a parting shot at Lazenby and was quoted as saying, "The difference between Sean [Connery] and George [Lazenby], Sean can act" (Graham "New James Bond," 28; Graham "Saturday Sit-In," 9).

MATT HELM

The Silencers (1966)

At the height of the 1960s spy craze, American producers were looking for a new American spy franchise to capitalize on the success of James Bond. In July 1964 Philip K. Scheuer, the *Los Angeles Times* motion picture editor, announced that a film, *The Silencers*, featuring fictitious American secret agent Matt Helm, who was featured in (at the time) eight books written by Donald Hamilton that sold over five million copies, would be produced by Irving Allen and released by Columbia Pictures. Allen was noted for having produced the epic *Genghis Khan* (1965), shot on 70mm film, a year prior. The studio did not have a name attached to the project to play Matt Helm but were confident the film would succeed. Columbia had secured the rights to eight of Hamilton's Matt Helm books (Scheuer "Pair Acquire"; "Martin Returns"; "Columbia to Film").

Eight months later, the studio made a decision. Hollywood reporter Hedda Hopper reported that Columbia cast Dean Martin, Las Vegas "Rat Pack" crooner, host of his own NBC variety show, one half of former comedy team Martin & Lewis (with Jerry Lewis), and film star. "Columbia ended its long search for a rugged, virile, suave, ruthless man to play Matt Helm, the American James Bond, and guess whom they got? Dean Martin." Hopper added, "Can't you see Dean in trench coat surrounded by a dozen beautiful dolls? He could stand at the corner of Hollywood and Vine and give a moose call and they'd come running." Martin reportedly signed a five-picture deal (four of which were produced), and his casting marked the first time he worked for Columbia since *Who Was That Lady?* (1960) (Hopper "Horton," 31).

The Silencers, based on two of Donald Hamilton's Matt Helm novels—*Death of a Citizen* and *The Silencers*—was filmed in Santa Fe, New Mexico, and Hollywood, California. When director Phil Karlson, producer Sergei Petschnikoff, and production designer Joe Wright were touring shooting locations in the

Santa Fe area in May 1965, director Phil Karlson said, "We feel Matt Helm is our answer to James Bond because he is the American secret agent and we are going to top *Goldfinger.*" Karlson was no stranger to the action genre, having previously directing the two-part pilot episode of *The Untouchables* (1964–1969), and movies including Robert Mitchum jungle adventure *Rampage* (1963), Guy Madison/Kim Novak heist movie *5 against the House* (1955), and gritty film noir *Kansas City Confidential* (1952) ("Columbia to Film," 1).

There was another link to James Bond. Warwick Productions, the production company co-owned by *The Silencers* producer Irving Allen, was also owned by James Bond producer Albert "Cubby" Broccoli. Although the studio had not put out a picture since 1962 (Broccoli obviously focusing on producing James Bond films via Eon Productions with Harry Saltzman), Irving Allen told Hollywood reporter Herb Stein that Warwick Productions offices in Audley Square, London were being redecorated to the tune of $30,000. "[Warwick Productions] can't decide if the decor should be Helm or Bond," said Allen. "Maybe Dean [Martin] and Sean Connery will have to arbitrate it for us." Warwick Productions' films were released by Columbia Pictures, hence the connection between Allen and Columbia (Stein "Best of," 18).

Elmer Bernstein was brought in to conduct the jazzy big band soundtrack, *The Silencers.* Lyrics on the album were written by Mack David, and although most of the songs were sung by Dean Martin, the title track was performed by Vikki Carr.

At the time, Bernstein was best known for having composed themes for *The Ten Commandments* (1956), *The Magnificent Seven* (1960), and *The Great Escape* (1963) and would go on to notably compose themes for *True Grit* (1969), *Animal House* (1978), *The Blues Brothers* (1980), *Ghostbusters* (1984), and *Three Amigos!* (1986).

Mack David was an Academy Award–nominated songwriter perhaps best known for having written "Bibbidi-Bobbidi-Boo" with Jerry Livingston and Al Hoffman for Disney's *Cinderella* (1950), among others. In addition, David composed a number of pop hits and Broadway tunes.

Vocalist Vikki Carr was best known for her 1965 album *Anatomy of Love* and as the original vocalist of the song "He's a Rebel," which was later recorded and made famous by the Crystals. Carr later had success with her album, *It Must Be Him,* which was nominated for three Grammys and would earn a place on the Hollywood Walk of Fame. *The Silencers* star Dean Martin reportedly believed Carr to be "the best girl singer in the business" (Keely "Nevada Scene," 243).

The twelve-week shoot began in July 1965, and soon it was announced that more star power was added to the cast in the form of three beautiful costars: Stella Stevens, Daliah Lavi, and Beverly Adams ("Stella Stevens," 14). Blond-haired, blue-eyed costar Stella Stevens (who dyed her hair red for the picture) was a former *Playboy* Playmate and January 1960 Playmate of the Month, had notably starred in *Girls! Girls! Girls!* (1962) alongside Elvis Presley and in *The Nutty Professor* (1963) with Jerry Lewis, had appeared on television shows *Alfred Hitchcock Presents* (1955–1965), *Hawaiian Eye* (1959–1963), and *Bonanza* (1959–1973), and had just come off a stint on *Ben Casey* (1961–1966).

Interestingly, Stevens noted that *The Silencers* was indeed America's answer to James Bond—at least one of them. "Helm is the American James Bond. . . . I guess I should say an American James Bond," said Stevens (Stern "This Star," 19).

The Silencers marked Daliah Lavi's second American film, the first being *Two Weeks in Another Town* (1962), with Gregory Peck. The Israeli actress with long, dark hair was featured in a number of European films, including Mario Bava's *The Whip and the Body* (1963) and British mystery thriller *Ten Little Indians* (1965).

On the set, Hollywood correspondent Dick Kleiner reported that while Lavi and Martin were filming a love scene, they kissed after walking through a door: "And they kissed and then she lay down on the bed and he knelt beside her and kissed her again. And when director Phil Karlson said, 'Let's do it one more time,' Martin looked at the crew and quipped, 'What a life. They keep asking me to do things I don't want to do but I have to do this, you understand.' And he kissed her again. She giggled" (Kleiner "Dino," 15).

Beverly Adams had previously starred as red-headed, bikini-clad beauty Cassandra in American International Pictures *How to Stuff a Wild Bikini* (1965). In *The Silencers*, she played Lovey Kravezit and was the first of the many women featured in the film.

Villains were also announced. Despite not being of Chinese or East Asian descent, the rotund character actor Victor Buono, best known at the time for his role in *What Ever Happened to Baby Jane?* (1962), was cast as Chinese villain Tung-Tze and put in stereotypical East Asian makeup (Marth "Buono"; Sar "Buono's Current").

When cast, Buono had a weight problem. The six-foot-three Buono weighed 350 pounds but wanted to *gain* 25 more pounds for the role because he felt that "villains are fat and since I'm a super villain, I guess I'll have to be super fat." When asked how he would manage to put on the extra weight Buono answered, "Will power. Sheer willpower. I have to lay off those low-calorie foods and eat lots of starches. It's tough, but I'm strong. I'll do it" (Estes "Actor Weighs,"

124). Buono would famously go on to play villain King Tut on television's *Batman* (1966–1968).

Two character actors were added to the cast to play henchmen for Buono's Tung-Tze: Roger C. Carmel and Richard Devon. Armed with his trademark handlebar mustache, Roger C. Carmel made notable appearances on episodes of *Route 66* (1960–1964), *Car 54, Where Are You?* (1961–1963), and *The Man from U.N.C.L.E* (1964–1968), among others. Like Buono, Carmel would go on to portray a villain on *Batman*, taking on the role of Colonel Gumm in episodes "A Piece of the Action" and "Batman's Satisfaction," which were crossover episodes with *The Green Hornet* (1966–1967), and interstellar con man Harry Mudd on *Star Trek* (1966–1969) in the episodes "Mudd's Women" and "I, Mudd."

Richard Devon was mostly seen under a cowboy hat in television Westerns like *The Rifleman* (1958–1962), *Tales of Wells Fargo* (1957–1962), *The Life and Legend of Wyatt Earp* (1959–1961), and *Johnny Ringo* (1959–1960), but he also appeared in a number of science fiction/horror films such as *Teenage Doll* (1957), *Blood of Dracula* (1957), and *War of the Satellites* (1958). Like his villainous compadres, Devon also had a link to Batman. Devon voiced the character of Batman on the radio series *The Adventures of Superman* (1940–1951).

A poster for *The Silencers* promised "Girls, Gags, & Gadgets! The Best Spy Thriller of Nineteen Sexty-Sex!" And there were plenty of all three.

Matt Helm (Dean Martin), who thought his days as a secret agent for ICE (Intelligence and Counter-Espionage) were over and spent his time photographing beautiful women, particularly his assistant Lovey Kravezit (Beverly Adams), was convinced to return to action to save the world from double entendre evil organization Big O and villain Tung-Tze (Victor Buono), who planned on using a missile in an underground atomic bomb test. Helm is joined by agent Tina (Daliah Lavi) and eventually by Gail Hendricks (Stella Stevens), a clumsy bystander who Helm believes is possibly an agent for Big O.

The film's "World Premiere" was held at the Balaban & Katz and State-Randolph Theaters in Chicago on February 18, 1966. Stars Stella Stevens, Beverly Adams, and "The Slay-Girls" were in attendance and appeared onstage with Chicago area disc jockeys Jim Runyon, Herb Kent, Don Phillips, Bud Kelly, and Bob Larson. The first four thousand filmgoers received a recording of Vikki Carr's "The Silencers" (*Silencers* World Premiere advertisement). The film opened everywhere else a month later but most notably at the Sands Hotel in Las Vegas, which was for charity. The event, which cost $250 a ticket, included a stage show hosted by Dean Martin and was produced by Jack Entratter, manager of the Sands Hotel who famously brought "The

Promo photo of Dean Martin with the "Slay-Girls" on the set of *The Silencers*.
Author's collection

Rat Pack" (Frank Sinatra, Dean Martin, Sammy Davis Jr., Peter Lawford, and Joey Bishop) to Las Vegas casinos and hotels a decade earlier. Attendees were also treated to the "Slay-Girl Review," which Hollywood reporter Herb Stein said was "the new name given to Dino's [Dean Martin's] numerous companions in the picture." Stein also noted the Slay-Girls were originally called "Slaymates," but Columbia became "cautious" and decided against using that tag because of a possible "holler" from men's magazine *Playboy* (Stein "Best of," 18).

New York Times writer A. H. Weiler wrote, "As another inevitable parody of James Bond, spies, sex and popular tunes, *The Silencers* . . . never lives up to its title, but it is loud, fast, obvious and occasionally funny." He later added, "Dean Martin is about as charmingly lackadaisical and flip about the favors [Beverly Adams, Stella Stevens, and Daliah Lavi] throw at him as he is about stopping the atomic threat to the United States. He can't be blamed. *The Silencers* is proof, in vivid, living colors, that you can get too much of a good thing" (Weiler "Dean Martin and [Shapely]," 35).

The Silencers also marked what is believed to be the first postcredit sequence. Although in the postcredits in James Bond movies, it was often announced that "James Bond Will Return . . . ," there was never any additional action. *The Silencers* not only announced the next Matt Helm adventure, stating, "Coming up next: Matt Helm Meets Lovey Kravezit in *Murderers' Row*," the sequence also included a shirtless Dean Martin surrounded by (and kissing two) attractive women in bras and panties on a spinning round bed (Brayson "When Did Post-Credits").

According to *Variety*, *The Silencers* was the seventh highest grossing film of 1966, earning approximately $7 million in North America, and the Associated Press reported the number to be as high as $9 million. However, the film failed to "top" *Goldfinger* (1964) at the box office as director Phil Karlson had hoped. Nor did the film outperform the newest James Bond adventure *Thunderball* (1965), which was the highest-grossing movie in 1966, earning $26,000,000 in North America alone ("Bond Films"; "Big Rental Pictures of 1966"; "Columbia to Film," 1).

Murderers' Row (1966)

Released on December 20, 1966, in time for the Christmas holiday and in the same year as *The Silencers*, Dean Martin returned as Matt Helm in his second film of the series (the film was even released in Japan as *Silencer Vol. 2: Murder Squad*). In the film, based on Donald Hamilton's book *Murderers' Row*, Helm once again took on the evil organization The Big O. This time Helm fakes his own death in the bathtub (six months before 007 faked *his* own death in the James Bond adventure *You Only Live Twice*) to better take on enemy agent Julian Wall (Karl Malden). Big O agent Wall was the mastermind behind stealing the deadly "Helio Beam," which was located at a secret island base in the French Riviera. Helm must prevent The Big O and Julian Wall from using the "helio beam," which is pointed at Washington, DC. In addition, he must save the kidnapped inventor of the beam, Dr. Norman Solaris (Richard Eastham).

Poster for a Matt Helm double feature: *The Silencers* (1966) and *Murderers' Row*
(1966). © *1967 Columbia Pictures*

Despite what *The Silencers'* postcredit sequence implied, Beverly Adams's character Lovey Kravezit, Helm's assistant, did not have a larger role (The sequence read: "Coming up next: Matt Helm Meets Lovey Kravezit in *Murderers' Row*"). Instead the female lead was given to Ann-Margret. Ann-Margret was a top recording artist of the early 1960s, was featured on numerous television appearances, and rose to movie stardom, starting with musicals *State Fair* (1962), *Bye, Bye, Birdie* (1963) and *Viva Las Vegas* (1964). She went on to star in *Made in Paris*, *Stagecoach*, and *The Swinger*, all of which were released in 1966.

The film's actors' clothing seemed to be on everyone's mind. Ann-Margret appeared in promotional photos for *The Silencers* wearing a "the latest from Paris": a cover-up wet suit made from a combination of silk and rubber. She was quoted as saying, "It's more comfortable than a bikini." And it was announced that Dean Martin would wear $20,000 worth of Sy Devore men's wear brand clothing for the film. Devore dressed a number of stars of the era, including the other members of the Rat Pack, Elvis Presley, President John F. Kennedy, and Nat King Cole ("Comfortably Chic," 32; Muir "Looking at Hollywood," 27).

Also appearing was Swedish born actress Camilla Sparv. Sparv costarred in *Dead Heat on a Merry-Go-Round* (1966) with *In Like Flint* star James Coburn and would stick with the spy genre, appearing in British spy film *Assignment K* (1968) two years later. At the time, Sparv was married to producer Robert Evans and told celebrity gossip communist Lloyd Shearer she intended to continue to work in both Europe and Hollywood, stating, "My husband is very understanding. I am really the luckiest girl in the world. At 23 I seem to have it made." However, Shearer questioned Shearer's longevity in Hollywood, writing, "Hollywood realists, conceding Camilla is endowed with 'the perfect face,' have some doubt about her overall sex appeal. Unfortunately they point out, many Scandinavian girls tend to be 'too thin on top.'" He added, "Makeup and wardrobe experts can certainly fill her out" (Shearer "She Claims," 83).

Although Shearer's comments may have been insensitive, Sparv's career, which later included movies such as *Nobody Runs Forever* (1968), *Mackenna's Gold* (1969), *The Greek Tycoon* (1978), and *Survival Zone* (1983), *did* seemingly stall after her divorce from Robert Evans in 1968. Evans went on to produce films such as *Chinatown* (1974), *Marathon Man* (1976), and *Urban Cowboy* (1980).

Also appearing in *Murderers' Row* were Dean Paul ("Dino") Martin Jr. (Dean Martin's son) and Desi Arnaz Jr. (son of Desi Arnaz and Lucille Ball) in a nightclub scene. Of course, the film included Matt Helm's scantily clad "Slay-Girls," a detail that was widely used in publicity for the film. The Slay-Girls appeared at the Robert Treat Hotel in Newark, New Jersey. "Everyone with a camera" was admitted to photograph the Slay-Girls, and pictures were sent to Columbia for judging and prizes ("Slaygirls," 64).

Fort Worth Star Telegram in Fort Worth, Texas, columnist Elston Brooks had this to say when the Slay-Girls made an appearance at the Press Club next to the historic Worth Hotel to promote the film: "Movie columnists were taking nitroglycerine pills as Columbia's nine Slay-Girls stepped into the Press Club, dressed in the calendar girl costumes they wear in *Murderers' Row*." He added, "There was more skin showing than in a Noxzema commercial" (Brooks "Girls," 16).

Henry Levin replaced Phil Karlson as the director for *Murderers' Row*. Levin previously directed the epic *Genghis Khan* (1965) for producer Irving Allen, and spy flick *Kiss the Girls and Make Them Die* (1966) for producer Dino De Laurentiis. The soundtrack was composed by Lalo Schifrin. Schifrin also composed "The Theme to *Mission: Impossible*" and would notably later compose soundtrack albums for films *Cool Hand Luke* (1967), *Bullitt* (1968), *Dirty Harry* (1971), and *Enter the Dragon* (1973). The soundtrack was released on Columbia's Colgems label.

Critic Bosley Crowther for the *New York Times* felt that *Murderers' Row* was simply a James Bond knockoff, writing, "Culled from the Donald Hamilton novel, [the film] simply latches on to bits and pieces of predecessors, notably *Thunderball* and *Doctor No*; stirs in a succession of cuties and stale wisecracks, and tacks on a tired finale of meandering confusion. The picture bumps along uncertainly, pegged on Mr. Martin's wisecracks, which are neither as blue nor as funny as before; Ann-Margret's octopus cuteness, and some random roughing-up." He also said, "Dean Martin, Ann-Margret and scads of luscious dolls, all of them loosely packaged in a feeble serving of James Bond left-overs . . . sputtered into the Victoria* and local showcases," in reference to the film opening on December 20, 1966, and added, "As a sequel to last season's *The Silencers*, when Mr. Martin amusingly invaded the super-sleuth game, this Columbia offering is a disappointing clinker. . . . This time, and no wonder, Dino hardly stays awake" (Crowther "Flag Is Down," 39).

But John Bustin, amusements editor for the *Austin American-Statesman* in Austin, Texas, felt the film aided the genre. "Cinematic secret agents have lately become an almost dreary lot, each trying to outdo the other—and all trying to outdo pace-setting James Bond—in matters of gimmicky weapons, bizarre villains and sexy playgirls. In *Murderers' Row*, however, Dean Martin somehow

---

* The Victoria was a Louis XV–style theater located at Broadway and West Forty-Sixth Street in New York City.

manages to put a little color and freshness into the rapidly deteriorating spy-spoof genre, mainly by not trying at all." Bustin expanded on this stating, "For this outing, which is now on display at the Paramount, old Dino simply cools it in his customary fashion, playing espionage agent Matt Helm with the same sort of easy aplomb that he shows on his weekly TV variety show"* (Bustin "Show World," 13).

Syndicated columnist Earl Wilson believed *Murderers' Row* was going to be a "big hit in Hollywood"—and he was not wrong (Wilson "Nancy," 14).

Ann-Margret in a predicament in *Murderers' Row* (1966). *Author's collection*

* Dean Martin hosted *The Dean Martin Show* (1965–1974) on NBC.

Reports from *Variety* indicated *Murderers' Row*'s box office numbers stayed on par with *The Silencers*, earning $6,240,000, and was the eleventh highest grossing film of the year ("Big Rental Films of 1967").

The end of *Murderers' Row* features Helm once again being dropped into his pool from his bed while making out with Suzie, while Dean Martin's "Not the Marrying Kind" played in the background. Soon the pool is surrounded by lingerie-wearing beauties, one of whom is armed with a machine gun. Helm exclaims, "Let's get out of here. It's an ambush!"—foreshadowing the name of the next Matt Helm adventure.

The Ambushers (1967)

Twelve years before James Bond went to outer space in Bond's first science fiction–based adventure, *Moonraker* (1979), Matt Helm (Dean Martin) tracked down a flying saucer in the third Matt Helm spy spoof, *The Ambushers*. Helm takes time off from training at a school for female spies (who are all attractive) to track down a stolen government-built UFO from an exiled South American dictator, Jose Ortega (Albert Salmi). Although the saucer was lost, the pilot, Sheila Sommars (Janice Rule), who has no memory of the flight, was found.

Dean Martin's spy-fi thrills on full display on the lobby card for *The Ambushers* (1967). © *1967 Columbia Pictures*

It is explained that only women can fly the saucer due to men not being able to handle the electromagnetic force. Helm and Sommars are sent to Acapulco, Mexico, to find the saucer, under the guise of Helm being a fashion photographer, where they get caught up with beautiful girls, one being enemy agent Francesca Madeiros (Senta Berger). Matt Helm's assistant Lovey Kravezit (Beverly Adams) and dozens of Matt Helm's signature "Slay-Girls" make an appearance in the film as well.

Mostly a television actor, Albert Salmi was commonly seen as the heavy or as an authority figure in shows from the 1950s through the 1980s and made his first and only spy film appearance in *The Ambushers*. Janice Rule was also new to the genre and notably played in *Bell, Book and Candle* (1958) and *Invitation to a Gunfighter* (1964). Senta Berger appeared in spy flick *The Quiller Memorandum* (1966) and on television on *The Man from U.N.C.L.E.* episode "The Double Affair" (1964). That episode was included in *The Man from U.N.C.L.E.* movie, *The Spy with My Face* (1964), which stitched together episodes of the show to make a feature-length film.

"The Slay-Girls" were outfitted by Oleg Cassini, who dressed them all in the latest fad—miniskirts. When asked how short skirts can get, Cassini responded, "Well, once a girl shows her knees, it depends on how much of her thighs she is willing to reveal. In most cases it depends on how good her figure is." He added, "Young girls want freedom in their clothes just as they do in other things. And short skirts allow them to have freedom of movement. And frankly, I think they look good in them." Cassini also believed that both Bond and Helm helped push the boundaries of the fashion trend (Scott "Mini-Skirts," 9).

Despite *The Ambushers* title being foreshadowed at the conclusion of *Murderers' Row*, it was reported by Betty Martin of the *Los Angeles Times* that the original title for the film was *The Devastators* (Martin "Third Matt Helm"). Based on two Matt Helm books by Donald Hamilton, *The Menacers* and *The Ambushers*, the film was once again directed by Henry Levin but this time was written by Herbert Baker, who wrote parts of *The Silencers* and all of *Murderers' Row*. Baker, the son of vaudevillian actor Belle Baker, said that he thought Dean Martin was an excellent comedic actor and liked him personally. "So many comics when they become stars start taking themselves very seriously. They think the world should care what they eat, how they think, even how they worship," said Baker. "That's one thing about Dean. He doesn't take himself seriously. He takes his work seriously, sure, but that's all. His philosophy is you lead your life and I'll lead my life" (Kleiner "Hedy Shuffles," 8).

During production of *The Ambushers,* Dean Martin was number one on television. *The Dean Martin Show* spiked in the ratings in early March 1967, making the NBC variety show the highest-rated show on television. The sign on the NBC studio door read, "Dean Is Number One." Dean Martin quipped, "You know what it says on the back of that sign? It says, 'this week.' At least I'm number one this week." *The Dean Martin Show* was the fourteenth highest rated show that season ("Dean Martin Looks," 87; Brooks and Marsh 1979).

The movie was filmed on location in Acapulco, Mexico. Very few reports came from the set other than Martin reportedly stating that he was getting into the "Mexican spirit," and when producer Irving Allen phoned him, a secretary reportedly said, "Mr. Martin can't speak to you now. He's taking his siesta lesson." When the cast returned to Hollywood to complete the interior scenes, Martin said he "left the flies and lizards behind" ("Joshua Logan," 18; Wilson "It Happened," 6; Mason "Planet of Apes," 22).

Released on December 22, 1967, *The Ambushers* was given awful reviews:

Variety felt that the Matt Helm films were diminishing in quality. "The warnings are clear from *The Ambushers*: if the Dean Martin gumshoe series is to merit uppercase continuation, it had better shape up better in the script and direction departments . . . while production values remain strong, acting, writing and direction are pedestrian." (*Variety Film Reviews*, 586)

Echoing *Variety*'s sentiment was *New York Times* critic Howard Thompson. "There's absolutely nothing special about Dean Martin's new vehicle, *The Ambushers*, except its air of tired stupidity and professional staleness. This completely lusterless super-agent vehicle for the star—the third in the Matt Helm series . . . trailing a lot of hand-me-down gags, some third-rate, suggestive dialogue and leftovers from the James Bond bonanza." Thompson added, "One thing this Columbia presentation does have, eye-filling color backgrounds in and around Acapulco. Otherwise, its seasonal junk, with Mr. Martin racing down below the border to squelch a power-mad villain who has stolen a flying saucer belonging to the government—our government." (Thompson "Super-Agent Martin," 24)

Despite the poor reviews, *The Ambushers* was the twenty-second highest grossing film in North America in 1968, according to *Variety*, earning $4,700,000 at the box office, and Helm would return in *The Wrecking Crew* ("Big Rental Films of 1968").

The Wrecking Crew (1968)

Following the release of *The Ambushers,* Dean Martin talked about his desire to continue to play the role of Matt Helm because the part was "up his alley."

Martin said, "Matt Helm is a very demanding part. I have to drink and smoke and chase pretty girls. But at least I understand the part" ("Martin's Happy," 19).

The Wrecking Crew, based on the Donald Hamilton book of the same name, went into production in June 1968 with director Phil Karlson. Karlson returned to the Matt Helm franchise for Columbia, having previously directed *The Silencers* (1966), the first film in the franchise (Gardiner "Television," 34).

The film had a number of notable members of the cast and crew. Nigel Green, who may be best known for his role in *Jason and the Argonauts* (1963) and previously played in franchise spy flicks *The Ipcress File* (1965) and *Deadlier Than the Male* (1967), was cast as Count Contini, who was attempting to crash the world's economy by stealing a billion dollars in gold. Of course, Matt Helm was tasked by ICE (Intelligence and Counter-Espionage) to bring down the evil Count ("Green in 'Wrecking'"). German-born actress Elke Sommer would portray Count Contini's evil accomplice Linka Karensky. Sommer, a former Playboy Playmate, appeared in *Deadlier Than the Male* (1967) with Nigel Green and made frequent appearances on *The Dean Martin Show* (1965–1974). In 1968, following the abandonment of the Hays Code, nudity in American films became commonplace. Sommer said she was "bored with the current state of nudity on the screen" and as a result would wear eighteen different dresses for her role but still painted in the nude at home ("Camera Angles," 25; Graham "Hollywood Move," 5).

In late May 1968, columnist Vernon Scott announced "sexy" Sharon Tate had joined the cast. At the time, Tate was best known for her roles in *The Fearless Vampire Killers* (1967), which was directed by her future husband Roman Polanski, and *Valley of the Dolls* (1967). In the *Valley of the Dolls,* Tate was nominated for a Golden Globe Award for Most Promising Female Newcomer. Tate would play Freya Carlson, believed to be a spectacled, bumbling tour guide from the Danish tourism bureau but in reality a British secret agent and karateka (Scott "Song of Norway").

Hollywood columnist Jack Bradford reported that Nancy Kwan, star of *The World of Suzie Wong* (1960) would be joining the cast as well, playing Linka Karensky's evil counterpart, Wen Yurang (Bradford "Hollywood Highlights"). Tina Louise, who played castaway Ginger "The Movie Star" Grant on *Gilligan's Island* (1964–1967), also joined the cast as Lola Medina.

Sweet Smell of Success (1957) and *The Defiant Ones* (1958) star Tony Curtis did not appear in the film, but his house did. Tony Curtis lent his Holmby Hills estate in Los Angeles for exterior scenes and interior scenes, which included Sharon Tate dodging bullets in Curtis's garden and Elke Sommer being thrown in the indoor swimming pool. Tony Curtis's house was one of only two homes on his street which were next door to blond bombshell Jayne Mansfield's residence, which had an infamous heart-shaped pool ("Curtis Helps Out"; Kleiner "Actress Is Gung Ho").

Also appearing in uncredited roles were boxers Wilhelm von Homburg and Joe Gray, professional wrestler Pepper Martin, and karate experts Joe Lewis, Ed Parker, and a young Chuck Norris. Coming off his role as Kato on *The Green Hornet* (1966–1967), Bruce Lee is credited as a "karate advisor" on *The Wrecking Crew* but does not appear. Lee taught Sharon Tate his own brand of martial arts known as Gung Fu (Kleiner "Actress is Gung Ho").

After shooting commenced, Nancy Kwan talked about her onscreen martial arts battle with Sharon Tate. "Naturally, I lost," said Kwan. "Nowadays, Orientals always lose and I'm Oriental. Every part I get these days, the Oriental is the heavy, the Communist, the bad person. It is very hard for me to find a sympathetic part anymore." Tate later commented about her fight with Kwan stating, "I had to kick Nancy and I practiced—and I broke a heavy board with my foot. I'm going to put one of the pictures of that scene up at home, to show Roman [Polanski] so he'll be afraid of me" (Kleiner "Actress is Gung Ho," 18).

Tate, who before *The Wrecking Crew* mostly appeared in what columnist Dick Kleiner called "heavy dramatic films," also talked about her love of appearing in action and comedic roles. "All this physical stuff is so unfeminine but bloody good fun. It seems to get the adrenaline going." She added, "Comedy is new for me, too. I never thought I could do it but Phil [Karlson] said I could. I don't know if it's working but I'm enjoying it" (Kleiner "Actress Is Gung Ho," 18).

Not returning to the franchise was Beverly Adams. At the time of the film's production, Adams was expecting a baby with her husband, hair stylist Vidal Sassoon (Cohen "Brief Encounter").

The film's score was provided by Hugo Montenegro. Montenegro scored a number of other spy adventures, including television's The *Man from U.N.C.L.E* (1964–1968) and the previous Matt Helm film, *The Ambushers* (1967). He also released an album titled *Come Spy with Me* on RCA Victor, which covered a number of famous spy film and television themes.

The Wrecking Crew held its world premiere on Christmas Day 1968 at twenty theaters throughout Canada. Lois Miller of the *Kingston Whig-Standard* in Kingston, Ontario, Canada, reported, "If first-day response is an indication, the show should be a success. Even for the early evening show, crowds lined the sidewalk and packed the theatre" (Miller "Beautiful Girls," 18). The film had a number of sneak previews around the United States in late 1968 and in January 1969 but officially premiered in theaters throughout the states on February 5, 1969. The film's poster promised "The Big Gold Train Heist! The

Poster for the last Matt Helm film produced, *The Wrecking Crew* **(1968).** © *1968 Columbia Pictures Corp.*

Minicopter Getaway and Most of All Those Danish Dames" (*Wrecking Crew* advertisement).

Although critics were never fond of the Matt Helm films, Vincent Canby of the *New York Times* seemed to feel that spy spoofs as a whole were on their last gasp. "Everything in *The Wrecking Crew* . . . seems to contain a booby-trap. Whisky bottles, beds, girls, ceilings, automobiles—they all explode, ignite, collapse or turn over with such regularity that the effect of the movie is to equate human beings (and, what's worse, movies) with disposable drinking cups," wrote Canby. He added,

> *The Wrecking Crew* . . . doesn't even have the virtue of contemporaneousness. It's the last faint wheeze of the old spy cycle, out of gas and imagination and, apparently, low on budget. Its gadgets look as if they had been inspired by the ones in Buster Crabbe's old *Flash Gordon* serials omnipresent TV cameras feeding back to omnipotent TV monitors, Kodaks that discharge a lazy green smoke that is supposed to have paralytic effect, helicopters that are practically pocket-sized, and the like.

Canby also criticized the film's cinematography: "Aside from a couple of second unit shots of Copenhagen, the movie was photographed in a southern California whose Beverly Hills mansions, vast, arid valleys and mountain ranges bear little resemblance to small, flat Denmark, where most of the story takes place" (Canby "Matt Helm Back," 32).

The Wrecking Crew was the forty-second highest grossing film of 1969 in North America, earning $2,400,000 at the box office that year ("Big Rental Films of 1969").

Eight months after the release of *The Wrecking Crew*, Sharon Tate was murdered by members of the Manson Family at her Hollywood residence. *The Wrecking Crew* was the last of Tate's films released before her death. Her film *The Thirteen Chairs* (1969) was released posthumously. Her role in *The Wrecking Crew* and her training with Bruce Lee was re-created and immortalized in Quentin Tarantino's *Once upon a Time in Hollywood* (2019) with Margot Robbie playing Tate and Mike Moh as Bruce Lee

Although the postcredits sequence of *The Wrecking Crew* announced that Matt Helm would return for the fifth film in the franchise, *The Ravagers*, which would be based on *The Ravagers* novel by Donald Hamilton, the film was never made despite all four Matt Helm films being financially successful for the three equal partners in the franchise—producer Irving Allen, Columbia Pictures, and Dean Martin (Graham "Producer Allen").

Reports surfaced in October 1969 that Dean Martin would be heading to Miami to begin production and that Martin planned on playing golf and going to local drinking establishments with Jackie Gleason while in town. But Martin never showed up for shooting, and production never began. An unnamed Columbia executive was quoted by syndicated columnist Marilyn Beck as saying, "We were all set to roll. A crew had been assigned, a production date set. Now the script's resting on a shelf and *The Ravagers* will probably never be made" (Beck "Dean Martin's Pout, 19")

There are conflicting reports on why Martin refused to make the fifth movie in the series. A number of reports stated that Martin was too overcome with grief over the death of *The Wrecking Crew* costar Sharon Tate to make another Matt Helm film. Other reports stated that Martin was upset when his choice of leading lady was not available (the common belief being he wanted Goldie Hawn to costar in the picture). Martin possibly was looking to take on more serious roles after appearing in the disaster thriller *Airport* (1970). Or there is a possibility Martin was just getting tired of taking many roles, looking to slow down, and planning to focus on his NBC variety show, *The Dean Martin Show* (1965–1974) (Graham "Producer Allen"; Beck "Dean Martin's Pout"; Manners "Behind the Scenes"; "Dino Hits").

The Wrecking Crew played at theaters and drive-ins throughout 1969 and the early 1970s, occasionally with other Matt Helm adventures in what one Raleigh, North Carolina, drive-in theater, Tower Drive-In, called a "Dean Martin Festival of Fems, Fun & Guns" (Tower Drive-In Theater advertisement).

Although another Matt Helm film was never produced, Tony Franciosa would play the titular secret agent on the ABC television series *Matt Helm* (1975–1976).

3

AMERICAN CLOAK-
AND-DAGGER
OPERATIONS

*Bond reflected that good Americans were fine people and that
most of them seemed to come from Texas.*

—Ian Fleming, *Casino Royale*

Hollywood studios were eager to exploit the James Bond craze and brought many different American secret agents to movie theaters, with varying degrees of quality and success.

13 Frightened Girls (1963; a.k.a. *The Candy Web*)

Released by Columbia Pictures, *13 Frightened Girls* was produced and directed by William Castle, an infamous showman known as "King of the Gimmick" who directed a string of horror films throughout the 1950s and early 1960s. Living up to his nickname, Castle famously swung a skeleton through the rafters of theaters during the conclusion of *House of Haunted Hill* (1959), attached electrodes to seats for his film *The Tingler* (1960), and allowed audiences to vote on which ending they wanted to see in *Mr. Sardonicus* (1961).

In 1963 Castle was one of the first producers to realize that *Dr. No* (1962) would create a new trend of films and was one of the first to jump on the bandwagon. As in his previous films, Castle also included a gimmick for his new spy film. But the gimmick used to promote *13 Frightened Girls* did not take place during screenings. Instead, it took place even before filming began. Castle and

Columbia's International Department organized a worldwide talent search for teenage girls to represent "the ideal teenager of her respective county, and [to be] designated as a 'Miss Teenage Diplomat.'" The press release for the contest made sure to note "this competition guaranteed a role in the picture and was definitely not a beauty search." Despite the film's title, fifteen girls were selected, and several were certainly not from the countries they represented in the film. American Judy Pace played a Liberian and British actress of Chinese descent Lynne Sue Moon represented China ("Teen Diplomats").

The contest (which may or may not have been predetermined) was eaten up by the press. Seemingly every day, entertainment articles were published about the film, most notably, and often about Castle's "Miss Teenage Diplomats."

"Attractive, green-eyed, platinum blonde" Jackie Benson from Aurora, Colorado, traveled to Salt Lake City in order to stow away on a B-17 "movie publicity bomber" in order to get William Castle's attention in hopes of being cast in *13 Frightened Girls*, which in production was known as *The Candy Web*. She was given an interview with Castle and although she was not cast as a teenage diplomat as she had hoped, she was given a small role in the film. "Millions of girls write letters or use the telephone. I wanted to do something different so I would get a chance," said Benson ("Plane Stowaway," 40).

Los Angeles Angels starting pitcher and 1962 rookie sensation Bo Belinsky, who was reported to be having a love affair with actress Ann-Margret, was rumored to be in talks to star in *13 Frightened Girls*. United Press International (UPI) reporter Louella O. Parsons wrote that "Bo should jump at the chance

Teenage diplomats learning about espionage in *13 Frightened Girls* (1963). *Author's collection*

because *Candy's Web* is being sweetened up by [William] Castle," in reference to the girls being cast in the film from around the world. Parsons added, "But 'till they get here, Bo stopped to visit Ann-Margret. That's playing it safe." Belinsky had to pass on the role after injuring himself while riding a horse. Although Belinsky was rumored to also have been linked to a number of other Hollywood stars, such as Connie Stevens, Tina Louise, and Mamie Van Doren, and was even married to 1964 *Playboy* Playmate of the Year Jo Collins, Belinsky never was cast in roles in film or television (Parsons "Human Bondage," 16; Bacon "Belinsky Shuns," 14).

The film's sixteen-year-old star Kathy Dunn, as the teen diplomat representing the United States, who took a leave of absence from her role as Louisa Von Trapp on Broadway in *The Sound of Music* and was nominated for Best Actress in a Musical for her role two years prior, reportedly wowed Columbia Executives with her work while the film was still in production and was even offered a contract. "Columbia Executives are so thrilled with the rushes (of *The Candy Web*) that they've offered me a fabulous 40-week per year guaranteed salary," said Dunn. "However we'd have to move out there [Dunn's family lived in Passaic, New Jersey] and we don't want to do that until the whole family can move out together" ("Kathy Dunn Wows," 47). Although Dunn turned down the contract, she agreed to make two pictures a year for Columbia and hoped to still appear in films and television shows for other studios as well. Despite the agreement, Dunn never made another film for Columbia or any other studio for that matter. She only has four credits to her name following the release of *13 Frightened Girls*, television series *The DuPont Show of the Week* in the TV-movie *Ride with Terror* (1963) and daytime soap operas *The Doctors* in 1963, *Our Private World* in 1965, and *Days of Our Lives* in 1967.

Photos of different teenage diplomats arriving in Hollywood filled entertainment pages across the country, and press coverage was given whenever a new actor signed onto the picture. Production was even given attention when Castle moved the cast to Lake Arrowhead for exterior scenes to mimic the teenage diplomats' boarding school set in Switzerland ("Europe's Teen-Age"; "Teenage Latin"; Winchell "Broadway"; "Marlowe"; "Filming Begins"; "Candy Web").

Van Alexander signed on to compose and conduct the original score. Alexander had previously composed the score of films such as *The Atomic Kid* (1954), *Andy Hardy Comes Home* (1958), and *The Private Lives of Adam and Eve* (1960) ("Alexander Signed").

As noted earlier, William Castle was not one to release a film without a theatrical gimmick. Castle installed safety belts in select theater's chairs so audience members "won't hit the roof with shock."

Advertisements for *13 Frightened Girls*, released internationally under the original title *The Candy Web*, exclaimed, "13 Frightened Girls Trapped in a Web of TERROR." Other advertisements urged audiences to see the film because it would be "presenting an international cast of young screen beauties," with the tagline using the film's original title: "A trap was laid for each lovely deb caught in the grip of *The Candy Web*" (*Candy Web* advertisement).

The film was first released in Australia in March 1963. The cinema critic for the Melbourne, Australia, newspaper *The Age* wrote,

> This proves a really juvenile thriller worth neither its publicity nor its safety belts. Kathy Dunn is almost sickeningly cute as the pigtailed daughter of an American charge d'affaires in London, who tries her hand at master-spying against a bunch of huge bald Red Chinese. She wriggles in and out of embassy basements faster than James Bond, uncovering knifed bodies and priceless microfilm in every cupboard. The picture also boasts Mr. Castle's latest gimmick, "12 [*sic*] international teenage diplomats" who appear to have been picked not so much for their pettiness as for their total inability to act. (Bennett "Another Williams," 19)

When *13 Frightened Girls* was released in the United States in July 1963, *New York Times* critic Bosley Crowther wrote a very similar review. "Precocious 16-year-old daughter of an American chargé d'affaires . . . has a crush on a member of the 'Counter-Intelligence Agency.' . . . [L]earning that he may be dismissed if he fails to gather information about a mysterious Red agent, the young woman singlehandedly runs down the dastard, ferrets out several important documents, uncovers the activities of a spy ring and saves the American Government from some compromising situations." Crowther added, "The young Mata Hari is vigorously played by pretty Kathy Dunn. . . . If only young Kathy could have raised her voice in song instead of playing detective, things might have been different at the United States Embassy" (Crowther "Romantic," 32).

The official film industry review bulletin published by the Motion Picture Association of America, *The Green Sheet*, called the film "both merry and hair-raising. . . . The cloak and dagger touches add excitement to other diverging elements in the lively mystery" ("'Teen Diplomats' Star," 12). Whereas *Variety* wrote, "The incredibly contrived goings-on that occur in *13 Frightened Girls* and dramatic absurdities of the production are more than can be tolerated by any but the more puerile audiences. . . . The picture fluctuates between comedy and suspense melodrama. Incidents are built up, then dropped like hot political potatoes whenever explanations and resolutions are in order" (cited in Wilson "North Carolinian Acts," 26).

13 Frightened Girls was often paired up with British musical comedy *Just for Fun* (1963) and occasionally with the Rory Calhoun/William Bendix war film *The Young and the Brave* (1963) or the Columbia comedy *Gidget Goes to Rome* (1963) on the drive-in circuit. The film played regularly throughout the country throughout the rest of 1963 into 1964.

Dr. Goldfoot and the Bikini Machine (1965)

In 1963 exploitation studio American International Pictures (AIP) released the immensely popular *Beach Party* (1963) starring young stars Frankie Avalon and Annette Funicello. The studio followed the success of *Beach Party* with sequels *Muscle Beach Party* (1964) and *Bikini Beach* (1964) which created a "beach party" genre of film in the mid-1960s. In 1965 the studio decided to capitalize on the popularity of the beach party *and* emerging popularity of the spy film genre.

Originally titled *Dr. Goldfoot and the Sex Machine*, AIP announced the production of what would become titled *Dr. Goldfoot and the Bikini Machine* in March 1965, along with another beach themed film—Tommy Kirk vehicle *Girl in the Glass Bikini,* which also starred Annette Funicello. *Girl in the Glass Bikini* got a name change as well. The title was changed to *The Ghost in the Invisible Bikini* which was released in 1966 ("Spiegel to Film").

Producers cast *Beach Party* movie star and teen idol Frankie Avalon, as secret agent 00 ½ Craig Gamble, alongside horror movie veteran Vincent Price in the title role. It was the first and only time the pair worked together. Jack Mullaney, who played on CBS sitcom *My Living Doll* (1964–1966), a show about a sexy female robot starring Julie Newmar, was cast as Dr. Goldfoot's assistant Igor; he joked, "I don't even have to memorize lines any more, I know all the technical jargon by heart" ("Knows the Lingo," 28).

The cast included seventeen gold bikini–wearing female robots, described by Dick Kleiner, Hollywood correspondent for the Newspaper Enterprise Association, as "reformed Playboy Playmates, a scattering of starlets who needed money, a few AIP's regulars and a few dewy-eyed just-in-from-the-sticks rookies" (Kleiner "Hiding," 3). William Asher, who directed television's *Bewitched* (1964–1972) and beach party movies *Beach Party* (1963), *Muscle Beach Party* (1964), *Bikini Beach* (1964), *Beach Blanket Bingo* (1965), and *How to Stuff a Wild Bikini* (1965), was originally scheduled to direct *Dr. Goldfoot and the Bikini Machine,* but the job was later given to Norman Taurog (Russell "Passing Show"). Taurog added Dwayne Hickman to the cast as Todd Armstrong. The pair had worked together twenty-five years earlier, when Hickman at five years of age was an extra in the Spencer Tracy film *Men of Boys Town* (1941), which Taurog directed ("Hickman Back").

There were even reports from Walter Winchell, noted newspaper gossip columnist, about Dr. Goldfoot's cat, Rasputin. Winchell reported that "the talented cat seen in Dr. Goldfoot and the Bikini Machine enriched its owner by $100 a day" (Winchell "It Takes," 4).

The film also included a cameo by Frankie Avalon's *Beach Party* partner, Annette Funicello; Harvey Lembeck, best known for *The Phil Silvers Show* (1955–1959) and for playing biker gang leader Eric Von Zipper in several *Beach Party* movies; Deborah Walley, who played the title role in *Gidget Goes Hawaiian* (1961); and a performance by "prehistoric" San Francisco rock and roll act, Sam and the Ape Men, who were regional favorites at the time.

In the film, Dr. Goldfoot and Igor invent a machine that produces gold bikini–clad female robots who are programmed to seduce and marry wealthy men in order to get them to sign over their bank accounts and power of attorney. Their plan is thwarted by secret agent 00½ Craig Gamble and wealthy Todd Armstrong, who were both seduced by and fell for the robot Diane (Susan Hart). Although the film was billed as a spy movie, and the film's poster gave the impression the film was a secret agent adventure, other than Frankie Avalon's character being a spy by occupation, any similarities to the spy genre is purely coincidental.

Hollywood columnists followed the film's production closely throughout the spring and summer of 1965. Bill Fiset of the *Oakland Tribune* reported on the film's production in Southern California writing, "You're aware of the bikini movie formula, where teen-agers flock to any picture with adolescent stars and bikini bathing suits? Well, the wildest one yet will be filmed soon, partly on location in the Bay Area—called *Dr. Goldfoot and the Bikini Machine*" (Fiset "Misadventures in Paradox," 15). Celebrity columnist Dorothy Kilgallen declared, "Everybody in Hollywood wants to get into the American International set to view the wild machine they've constructed for the Bikini Machine," but she did not specify who "everybody in Hollywood" was. After production wrapped, AIP even brought the bikini machine and girls in gold bikinis along for previews shown to theater owners at a banquet sponsored by the production company aimed at getting more AIP pictures in more theaters across the country (Kilgallen "Connery Marriage," 24; Monahan "Existentialism").

For American International Pictures, a notoriously low-budget studio, *Dr. Goldfoot and the Bikini Machine* was reportedly the most expensive film to produce. It cost the studio $1,500,000, which was fifteen times the budget of *Beach Party* two years earlier, in 1963 (Kilgallen "Voice," 6). The budget was

Scene from *Dr. Goldfoot and the Bikini Machine* featuring Frankie Avalon as Craig Gamble, Dwayne Hickman as Todd Armstrong, Vincent Price as Dr. Goldfoot, Marianne Gaba as a robot, and Jack Mullaney as Igor. *ZUMA Press, Inc./Alamy Stock Photo*

due in part to the film's haunted palace, pit, and pendulum, electronic devices that were erected at Producers Studio in Hollywood. The set reportedly cost American International approximately $150,000. In addition, the film included a Claymation title sequence animated by Art Clokey, who also animated *The Gumby Show* (1957–1968) and *Davey and Goliath* (1961–1964, 1971–1975); a theme song by the Supremes; and music scoring by lounge exotica composer Les Baxter ("Palace Haunts").

Even before it was released to theaters, a sequel to *Dr. Goldfoot and the Bikini Machine* was announced: *Dr. Goldfoot for President*. At the same time, the sequel to another yet-to-be-released Frankie Avalon project, *Sergeant Deadhead* (1965), was announced by American International Pictures: *Sergeant Deadhead Goes to Mars*. The latter was never produced ("Sequel").

The premiere of *Dr. Goldfoot and the Bikini Machine* was held at the Golden Gate Theater in San Francisco where, ten years prior, AIP producer Jim Nicholson was the theater manager (Dunne "What Happened"). To promote the film, Frankie Avalon toured eighteen cities in thirteen countries. Avalon brought famous New York vocal coach Carlo Menotti in tow to help maintain his voice during performances. Promotional shots of the film's stars, most notably Vincent Price learning to do "the Swim" with Diane DeMarco, ran in papers throughout the country to promote the upcoming film in September 1965 (Kilgallen "Off Stage"; "Dr. Who?").

Reviews were mixed. The *New York Times* wrote, "Occasionally it's diverting to see just how bad or unfunny a supposed laugh-package of a movie can be. Meet *Dr. Goldfoot and the Bikini Machine* . . . this new American International goody is pure, dull junk. . . . What a mess and what a waste!" But the *Los Angeles Times* writer Margaret Harford felt it was a "sparkling comedy [with] enough fresh, amusing gags to make it entertaining" and that "Price is splendid" ("Designing Parisians," 29; Harford "*Goldfoot* Sparkling," 19).

Although *Dr. Goldfoot and the Bikini Machine* was not a musical like the other *Beach Party* movies, two weeks after the premiere, on November 18, 1965, ABC's popular dance show *Shindig!* (1964–1966) aired an episode "The Wild Weird World of Dr. Goldfoot." The program, sponsored by AIP producers James H. Nicholson and Samuel Z. Arkoff, included a number of song-and-dance numbers featuring *Dr. Goldfoot and the Bikini Machine* stars Vincent Price, Aron Kincaid, Harvey Lembeck, and Susan Hart. The episode also includes an appearance by Tommy Kirk, star of AIPs *The Ghost in the Invisible Bikini.*

Variety reported that *Dr. Goldfoot and the Bikini Machine,* which cost $1.5 million to produce, grossed $1.9 million in North America. The film may have been more popular and profitable in Europe, which led to the sequel, *Dr. Goldfoot and the Girl Bombs* (1966), which was originally scheduled to be titled *Dr. Goldfoot for President,* to be made in Italy by both Italian International Film and American International Pictures ("Big Rental Pictures of 1966").

After the film's completion, Frankie Avalon said that he was through with the beach party movie genre: "Even a sea gull leaves the beach from time to time, and I'm getting a little sick of sand." Avalon did not return for *Dr. Goldfoot and the Girl Bombs.* He traded his surfboard for a hot rod, opting to star in AIP's teen stock car racing film *Fireball 500* (1966), pairing up with fellow teen idol Fabian and reuniting with Annette Funicello (Scott "Hollywood Calendar," 473).

Operation CIA (1965)

Following his stint as Native American blacksmith Quint Asper on fabled Western television show *Gunsmoke* (1955–1975), Burt Reynolds was cast in 1965 in the ultra-low-budget, black-and-white action spy film *Operation CIA*. Reynolds had previously played in films *Angel Baby* (1961) and *Armored Command* (1961); however, *Operation CIA*, released by United Artists, was Reynolds's first starring role.

Operation CIA's director Christian Nyby had previously directed Howard Hawks's influential science fiction thriller *The Thing from Another World* (1951). The film's score was provided by Paul Dunlap. Dunlap scored mostly Westerns throughout his career but his resume included a number of horror films for American International Pictures (AIP) and four 1960s feature-length films starring the Three Stooges.

Made at a time when American involvement in the conflict in Vietnam was beginning to escalate, Burt Reynolds plays CIA Agent Mark Andrews, who travels to Saigon after a fellow agent is killed in an explosion before he can deliver an important message to the United States and complete his mission. Of course, Andrews must outsmart and elude the Viet Cong throughout and even uncovers and thwarts a plot to kill an American ambassador.

Although the film was low-budget, it was shot on location in Bangkok, Thailand. In addition, Burt Reynolds received attention and comparisons to the most successful spy, James Bond. The film's producer and cowriter Peer J. Oppenheimer called Burt Reynolds "Hollywood's answer to James Bond," stating, "He hunts international spies, swims crocodile-infested rivers, embraces beautiful women, dodges poisonous snakes." He added that the twenty-nine-year-old Reynolds was "swarthy, ruggedly handsome" and that "many in Hollywood predict he has the same kind of magic that Sean Connery had when he took on the 007 role" (Oppenheimer "Hollywood's Answer," 63).

Write-ups for the film often also compared Burt Reynolds to fellow actor Marlon Brando in both his appearance and his performance—specifically due to Brando's performance in *The Ugly American* (1963), which had a similar theme (McGrotha "Big Season"). A year following *Operation CIA*'s release, Reynolds would return to television and star in the very short-lived police procedural *Hawk* (1966) about a Native American New York City detective. He would also travel to Italy to star in the spaghetti Western *Navajo Joe* (1966).

Although it is unclear whether Reynolds was being facetious, while he was promoting the film that solidified his fame—*Deliverance* (1972)—he recalled that *Operation CIA* was produced for $70,000 (a number cited when the film's budget was listed) and won the "Polish Film Festival." He added, "I got to fight a boa constrictor in it, and he gave the best performance of the movie" (Prelutsky "Two Centerfolds," 228).

The Satan Bug (1965)

Also released as *Operation: Satan Bug*, *The Satan Bug* tells the story of Lee Barrett (George Maharis), a former, disobedient secret agent turned private eye who is tasked to recover a lost vial of a bioweapon from Dr. Gregor Hoffman (Richard Basehart). Hoffman, a pacifist, plans on using a virus, which had been nicknamed "The Satan Bug," to depopulate Earth, thus ending all wars. Barrett is joined by old flame Ann Williams (Anne Francis) who is assigned to be his partner on his mission to retrieve the virus.

George Maharis was coming off a starring role on a popular adventure drama anthology series *Route 66* (1960–1964), while Richard Basehart was enjoying success on the science fiction series *Voyage to the Bottom of the Sea* (1964–1968). Anne Francis, best known for her roles in *Blackboard Jungle* (1955) and *Forbidden Planet* (1956), at the time was guest starring on a number of television shows such as *Alfred Hitchcock Presents* (1962–1965), *The Twilight Zone* (1959–1964), *The Virginian* (1962–1972), *The Man from U.N.C.L.E.* (1964–1968), and even *Route 66* with *The Satan Bug*'s star, George Maharis.

The Satan Bug also featured a number of notable character actors: James Hong, James Doohan, and Ed Asner who were relatively unknown to audiences at the time. Hong would make a name for himself in movies *Blade Runner* (1982) and *Big Trouble in Little China* (1986). Asner rose to prominence playing Lou Grant on *The Mary Tyler Moore Show* (1970–1977). James Doohan would take on the role of Montgomery "Scotty" Scott on *Star Trek* (1966–1969).

Two established television stars appeared as well: Richard Bull and Frank Sutton. Richard Bull costarred with Richard Basehart on *Voyage to the Bottom of the Sea*, and Frank Sutton was best known as Gunnery Sergeant Carter from *Gomer Pyle, U.S.M.C.* (1964–1969).

Although the film's trailer called *The Satan Bug* "the Ultimate Suspense!," it received harsh reviews from critics around the country. Similar to criticisms of James Bond at the time, critics felt that Maharis's character was too invulnerable and unreliable and was more of a Superman-type character that is seemingly invulnerable to bullets and can get out of any situation. A critic for the *Buffalo News* wrote, "I feel obligated to say that the movie gives us the perfect solution to the super-weapon of germs: The super hero. Maharis isn't merely intrepid; he's a walking immunity. So when two agents clutch their throats and fall writhing to the ground under the same exposure to a lethal germ, Mr. Maharis loosens his tie and goes about his business" ("*Satan Bug* Will Get," 54). Dan Lewis, of Hackensack, New Jersey's *The Record*, noted, "Bullets bounce off him. A deadly gas is tossed into a room where George and two others are captive. George survives, the other two die, of course. He takes on two antagonists in a helicopter, high above Los Angeles and you just know the others will get tossed out, not Superman George" (Lewis "Maharis," 41).

Long Island, New York, newspaper *Newsday* writer Joseph Gelmis made the obvious comparison to James Bond when he quipped, "Here he comes, James Bond Jr., Secret Agent 003½." He proceeded to call the film "low-budget, low-velocity James Bond stuff" and to pan Maharis as miscast and "unconvincing, with his lip-pursing, finger pointing, finger-pointing, indecisive . . . and eyes downcast like a teenage with a deputy James Bond badge" (Gelmis "Bugs," 106).

Van Nuys News and Valley Green Sheet's Ali Sar compared *The Satan Bug* to director John Sturges's other films *The Magnificent Seven* (1960), *The Old Man and the Sea* (1958), and *The Great Escape* (1963), writing that "as soon as one starts recalling the suspense, action and highly charged drama created in *Great Escape*, one quickly will discover *Satan Bug* never can generate such a reaction." Interestingly, moviegoers in Van Nuys, California, would have been able to watch both *The Satan Bug* and *The Great Escape* at the Americana Theatre, which played them as a double feature upon *The Satan Bug*'s release (Sar "Sturges'," 38).

Akron, Ohio, newspaper the *Akron Beacon Journal* writer Dick Shippy simply said the film had "clumsy construction" and panned the acting from both Maharas and Basehart (Shippy "The Suspense," 12). Stephen Palmer of the *Lexington Herald-Leader* in Lexington, Kentucky, found that *The Satan Bug* was "provocative." Palmer also noted that it was "extremely well done. There is plenty of fast action, as many murders as any James Bond story but far fewer women" (Palmer "*Satan Bug* Found," 62).

A Man Could Get Killed (1966)

Originally given the strange title of *Welcome, Mr. Beddoes*, Universal Studios announced the production of *A Man Could Get Killed* in June 1965. The film, based on the book *Diamond for Danger* by David E. Walker, would star James Garner, Melina Mercouri, Sandra Dee, and Tony Franciosa. The film's producer, Robert Arthur, stated that the four actors were cast in the $3.5 million project "because it was felt that these actors would draw a lot of people to see the picture" ("Universal Changes," 23; Anderson "Producer," 10). It was also announced that Cliff Owen was directing the film, which had already begun production in Lisbon, Portugal ("Universal Changes").

Garner plays reluctant and oblivious spy William Beddoes (hence the original title), an American banker who is mistaken for a British secret agent on the hunt for stolen diamonds. Everyone ranging from criminal organizations to governments think that Beddoes is a spy, except for Beddoes, who unwillingly gets caught up in the diamond hunt. At the time, Garner was best known as the title character on the ABC Western *Maverick* (1957–1961) and would go on to star in the NBC detective series *The Rockford Files* (1974–1980).

Melina Mercouri was best known for her award-winning film *Never on Sunday* (1960), and Sandra Dee for her role as the titular star of *Gidget* (1959). Tony Franciosa, a year later, would star alongside Raquel Welch in *Fathom* (1967) and in 1975–1976 would portray Matt Helm, a character Dean Martin made famous in four 1960s spy spoofs, on the short-lived ABC television series of the same name.

Shooting on location in Lisbon reportedly came with problems with permits and dealing with local officials. But producer Robert Arthur was able to work the problems out, and he believed he "paved the way" for other films to shoot in the city (Cameron "Gem Robbery," 23). Arthur, traditionally a Florida filmmaker, was asked by *Miami Herald* "Nightlife" columnist George Bourke why *A Man Could Get Killed* was shot in Europe and not Florida. Arthur cited the "romantic freedom required of the plot" and that the film needed the "perfect emotional climate" provided by Lisbon and Rome (Bourke "Producer," 49). Bourke also made it a point to mention that Arthur had been planning to bring the project to the screen since 1962—"That's pre-James Bond" (Ibid.). While *A Man Could Get Killed* was in production, syndicated Hollywood columnist Sheilah Graham was quick to point out that it "is one of the 137 secret-agent adventure stories filmed in Europe" (Graham "James Garner," 46).

In July 1965 it was officially announced that director Cliff Owen was being replaced by Ronald Neame, director of the 1956 spy film *The Man Who Never Was*. "Difference of opinion concerning interpretation of the script" was the reason given, and the parting was called amicable. Owen had already concluded shooting exterior scenes in Lisbon and London, and production was heading to Rome for interior sequences. It was resumed after a brief shutdown that allowed Neame to review the footage already shot by Owen ("Owen Resigns," 15; "Movie Filming," 7).

Sandra Dee reportedly did not like the delay in filming; in fact Dee did not want to make the film at all. Dee stated that she "begged (producers) not to make me do the picture. So I spent a miserable four months in Lisbon, little fishing villages and in Rome, making a picture that should have taken eight weeks" (Thomas "Hollywood Highlights," 15).

A Man Could Get Killed finally premiered in six Greater Miami, Florida, area theaters on March 25, 1966, and opened nationwide that May. A review in the *New York Times* called the film "neither affecting nor funny" and "not even coherent." In addition: "When Jack Valenti, the former White House aide, was appointed president of the Motion Picture Association of America, he allowed that he had never seen a bad movie come out of Hollywood. Now is his chance to begin his education" ("Unrewarding Spy," 51). William Mootz, critic for the *Courier-Journal* in Louisville, Kentucky, believed the film "should have got killed on the cutting-room floor. All of it." And he called the film a "crashing bore" (Mootz "Killed," 32).

A flop at the box office, the most notable thing to come out of *A Man Could Get Killed* is the song originally recorded for the film: "Strangers in the Night," composed by Bert Kaempfert. Later in the year, the song was given lyrics by Charles Singleton and Eddie Snyder and recorded by Frank Sinatra. "Strangers in the Night" became a number-one hit on the *Billboard* charts, Sinatra's first number-one hit in eleven years, in the United States and United Kingdom. And in both the United States and the United Kingdom, the song replaced the Beatles' "Paperback Writer" in the top spot. "Strangers in the Night" spent one week at number one and then was replaced by the Tommy James & the Shondells' song "Hanky Panky."

Agent from H.A.R.M (1966)

Lobby cards for *Agent from H.A.R.M* promised "electrifying excitement. . . . Terrifying thrills. The most exciting secret agent of them all." Others stated it was "a blast of blood curdling terror from outer space!"

However, nothing from the film was from outer space, as the posters promised. Adam Chance (Mark Richman) was an agent for H.A.R.M. (Human Aetiological Relations Machine), a top-secret American spy organization. Chance is assigned to protect a former Soviet biochemist, Professor Janos Steffanic (Carl Esmond). Professor Steffanic defected after learning of a Soviet plot to unleash a spore that turns humans into a fungus. Barbara Bouchet played Ava Vestok, Professor Steffanic's niece, eventual love interest of Chance, and double agent for the Soviets.

The film's star, Mark Richman, could be spotted making appearances on numerous television shows of the era, including *The Outer Limits* (1963–1965), *Combat!* (1962–1967), and *Voyage to the Bottom of the Sea* (1964–1968). Austrian-born Carl Esmond made a living playing villainous German characters in an era when the horrors of World War II were still fresh in Americans' minds.

Esmond was seen on television shows such as *77 Sunset Strip* (1958–1964), *Hawaiian Eye* (1959–1963), *Run for Your Life* (1965–1968), and later, *The Man from U.N.C.L.E.* (1964–1968), *Garrison's Gorilla* (1964–1968), and made-for-TV movie *My Wicked, Wicked Ways: The Legend of Errol Flynn* (1985).

Model-turned-actress Barbara Bouchet had previously played in the war epic *In Harm's Way* (1964), with John Wayne, Kirk Douglas, and Henry Fonda, where she famously appeared seminude. Photos of Bouchet later appeared in the pages of *Playboy*. To play up on Bouchet's inherent sex appeal, promotional ads for *Agent from H.A.R.M.* called Barbara Bouchet "a treacherous, bikini-clad menace" (Miller "Another Secret Agent," 23).

A year after her appearance in *Agent from H.A.R.M.*, Bouchet would stick with the spy genre and take on the role of Miss Moneypenny in the noncanon Bond film *Casino Royale* (1967) and in the British spy film *Danger Route* (1967). After appearing in *Playboy* once again in a "Girls of *Casino Royale*" feature in February 1967, the actress starred in a number of Italian-made psychological thrillers, known as *giallo* films, throughout the 1970s.

Film critics in 1966 were clearly growing tired of spies and James Bond imitations. Howard Thompson of the *New York Times* called *Agent from H.A.R.M.* a "pale Bond copy" and said that "even the jaunty angularity of the photography and a thumping Bond-type musical score can't camouflage a bony sham made for a fast buck" (Thompson "Pale Bond," 20). Clearly fatigued by the flood of spy films hitting cinemas, Jeanne Miller of the *San Francisco Examiner* noted that the film "contains the familiar blend of sex, Steve Canyon*–heroics and plenty of violence, it takes itself so seriously that it becomes a science fiction bore, rescued only occasionally by mildly suspenseful moments that are all too rare." She concluded, "*Agent from H.A.R.M.* was palpably designed, with little wit, grace or suspense, to capitalize on the current craze. Who will invent an antidote for this epidemic?" (Miller "Another Secret Agent," 23).

The Sydney Morning Herald in Sydney, Australia, published a review stating, "The trouble with spy thrillers is that the James Bond films and their ilk make it hard for one to take them seriously. One keeps looking for laughs." In addition, "*Agent from H.A.R.M.* is not a send-up; it is a reasonably competent piece of drama overshadowed, through no particular fault of its own, by the welter of bigger, brighter and better films around" (Victory "Agent from H.A.R.M.," 87). The Catholic Church's Legion of Decency even called *Agent from H.A.R.M.* "objectionable in part for everyone" ("Legion," 10).

---

* Steve Canyon was an action-adventure comic strip that ran from 1947 to 1988.

Agent from H.A.R.M., released by Universal Pictures on January 5, 1966, played alongside teen rock and roll ski film *Wild Winter* (1966). It was still making the rounds at drive-ins and second-run theaters in late 1967. It was being shown on television by early 1968, making it perfect late-night filler for local television stations ("TV Program Listings").

Dimension 5 (1966)

Time-traveling secret agent Justin Power (Jeffrey Hunter) was featured in the ultralow-budget "spy-fi" film *Dimension 5*. Agent Power works for a top-secret government organization, Espionage, Inc., and is sent back in time using a belt capable of time travel to save Los Angeles from atomic destruction. Power is paired with an agent "from the Far East section," Kitty (France Nuyen) to take on crime lord "Big Buddha," who plans on smuggling the bomb into the country.

Today, *Dimension 5* star Jeffrey Hunter may be best known as Captain Pike in the pilot episode of *Star Trek* (1966–1969): "The Cage." The episode was famously rejected by NBC, and William Shatner was brought in to take the helm of the *Enterprise* as Captain Kirk. Although the show's creator Gene Roddenberry regularly showed the episode at *Star Trek* conventions and scenes from "The Cage" were used in a later episode, "The Menagerie," it was unavailable in its original form for the average viewer until 1986. By that time, Hunter was best known for his roles in movies *The Searchers* (1956) and *The Longest Day* (1962). In 1966 Hunter appeared on television shows *The Legend of Jesse James* (1965–1966), *Daniel Boone* (1964–1970), and *The Green Hornet* (1966–1967).

French-born actress France Nuyen was of East Asian descent and was often cast in stereotypical Asian roles, appearing in films such as the musical *South Pacific* (1958), *The Last Time I Saw Archie* (1961), and *Satan Never Sleeps* (1962). A year after *Dimension 5*'s release, Nuyen would marry television spy Robert Culp, the star of NBC's *I Spy* (1965–1968). The marriage lasted until 1970.

Perhaps most notably, the film also featured Harold Sakata. Sakata was known to fans of professional wrestling at the time as Tosh Togo, but spy fans would recognize Sakata from his role as Goldfinger's henchman Oddjob in the third James Bond movie, *Goldfinger* (1964). Sakata was prominently featured on the film's poster, where he was even billed as Harold "Oddjob" Sakata.

Dimension 5 was directed by Franklin Adreon. In the 1930s and 1940s, Adreon specialized in writing movie serials for Republic Studios. His writing credits include *S.O.S. Coast Guard* (1937), *Zorro's Fighting Legion* (1939), and

Jesse James Rides Again (1947). Adreon later moved to direction and production at Republic, producing *Zombies of the Stratosphere* (1952), a serial that marked one of the first screen appearances for *Star Trek*'s Leonard Nimoy. Adreon served as both director and producer on the serial *Canadian Mounties vs. Atomic Invaders* (1953), *Trader Tom of the China Seas* (1954), and *King of the Carnival* (1955) and later directed the low-budget, science fiction thriller *Cyborg 2087* (1966).

Writing credit went to Arthur C. Pierce. Pierce is best known for writing a number of shlock science fiction films throughout the era, most notably *Cosmic Man* (1959), *Beyond the Time Barrier* (1959), *Women of the Prehistoric Planet* (1966), *Destination Inner Space* (1966), and *Cyborg 2087* (1966).

United Pictures Corporation (UPC), the company who earlier that year released *Castle of Evil* (1966) and *Destination Inner Space* (1966), released *Dimension 5* alongside its aforementioned time-travel film *Cyborg 2087* (1966) ("Theater Schedule").

Despite playing top markets like Los Angeles and Philadelphia (the film never played in New York, Chicago or Detroit), *Dimension 5* was ignored by critics. It was rarely given more than a listing in newspapers around the country.

The Fat Spy (1966)

Rotund Friars Club "Roast Master" and infamous insult comic Jack E. Leonard, film noir staple Brian Donlevy, and rising comic Phyllis Diller star alongside "40-21-35" blond bombshell Jayne Mansfield in a film that sees teens doing a new dance called "the Turtle" and having a scavenger hunt on a seemingly deserted island off the coast of Florida, led by the rock band the Wild Ones. The teens soon find themselves caught in the middle of a race by island's eccentric residents to find the Fountain of Youth.

Based on the title alone, *The Fat Spy* may be the most egregious attempt to cash in on the spy genre. Despite the film's title and what is suggested on the poster, *The Fat Spy* has very little to do with spies. And unlike American International Pictures' films, such as *Dr. Goldfoot and the Bikini Machine* (1965), the film did not attempt to include an element of espionage or a secret agent character in the script. In addition, the film does not have much in terms of conflict. The teens are never challenged or confronted by the residents nor do the teens interrupt the search for the fountain of youth.

Filmed in June 1965 over the course of twenty-seven days in Cape Coral, Florida, area newspapers were buzzing about the production and the film's stars

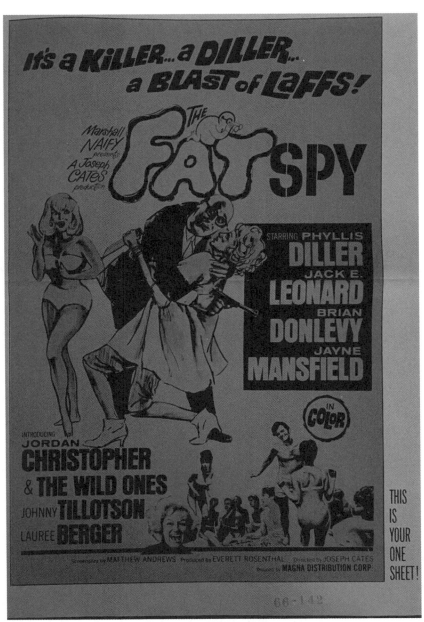

Promotional one-sheet for *The Fat Spy* **(1966).** *Courtesy of Owen Klein*

coming to town. Florida papers lauded the film's producers for taking advantage of the sunny Florida weather and updated readers with pictures on the whereabouts of the cast and crew. One of the film's stars, Phyllis Diller, had members of the press over to her motel room for what she called "garbage soup" while fielding questions about her career and the film. There were even reports of Jack E. Leonard's affinity for bread and gravy, and stories about Jayne Mansfield's daily beauty routine (Runnells "Worst"; "Feature Page"; "Shooting Starts"; Ketridege "Give Me"; "Pert, Blonde"; "Fat Spy"; "Phyllis Diller Arrives"; Head "Diller Serves"; Rasor "Just Plain"; "Film Make at Cape").

Released in the spring of 1966, *The Fat Spy* was the last scripted film to be released to American theaters to feature actress Jayne Mansfield, who died in an infamous and horrific car accident in 1967. Country Western musical comedy *The Las Vegas Hillbillies* (1966), which featured Mansfield, was released one month prior. *The Wild, Wild World of Jayne Mansfield* (1968), the mondo documentary featuring the life of Mansfield that was released a year after her death failed to even mention *The Fat Spy*.

Dale Stevens of the *Cincinnati Post* called *The Fat Spy* "another takeoff on the current James Bond trend [with] . . . overtones of the rash of beach pictures aimed at young ticket buyers" (Stevens "Phyllis Diller's," 22). The *Los Angeles Times* staff writer Kevin Thomas stated that the film was "lean fare," called the film's plot "confused," and classified the film a "Florida-made quickie" (Thomas "*Fat Spy* Lean," 71).

Edwin Howard, amusements editor for the *Memphis Press-Scimitar*, was thankful the film was "not another spy film" and was one of the only critics to point out that "the title, in fact, has nothing to do with the story." He added that "though there is no real spy in the film, there is quite a lot of fat . . . there is also a lot of pointless repetitious footage which might better have wound up on the cutting room floor. All those shapely girls wiggling about in Bikinis get so dull after a while" (Howard "State's *Fat Spy*" 22).

The film's director, Joseph Cates, is known for helping create *The $64,000 Question* game show, producing a number of television specials throughout his career, and directing the Sal Mineo crime thriller *Who Killed Teddy Bear?* (1965). Cates is also the father of *Fast Times at Ridgemont High* (1982) star Phoebe Cates and grandfather of Owen Kline, director of the comedy *Funny Pages* (2022).

The Fat Spy marked Phyllis Diller's first starring film role. After the release of the film, Phyllis Diller would star in *Boy, Did I Get a Wrong Number!* (1966), with Bob Hope, and her own short-lived sitcom in the fall of 1966: *The Pruitts of Southampton*, which was later renamed *The Phyllis Diller Show* (1966–1967).

New York–based rock and roll band the Wild Ones were featured throughout the film. The group is best known for being the first to record "Wild Thing," about a year before the Troggs made it a hit in 1966. The Wild Ones did not perform "Wild Thing" in the film.

Although *The Fat Spy* is considered by many to be one of the worst films ever made, it is often praised by Cape Coral historians and elected officials for its historical footage. What amusements editor Howard called "pointless repetitious footage which might better have wound up on the cutting room floor" showed many of the town's now demolished and forgotten landmarks. In 2018 the *News-Press* in Cape Coral, Florida, wrote that the film was a "publicity stunt orchestrated by Cape Coral developers Gulf American Land Corp. That's why the city's name is mentioned often in the film and why scenes are shot at tourist-friendly spots like the Cape Coral Yacht Club, the beach, the Iwo Jima memorial and former tourist attraction Cape Coral Gardens, including shots of its rose garden, fountains and popular porpoise show" (Runnells "Worst Movie"; Howard "State's *Fat Spy*," 22).

Last of the Secret Agents? (1966)

In their film debut as a comedy team, Marty Allen (best known for his catchphrase "Hello Dere!") and Steve Rossi, collectively known as Allen & Rossi, star as two Americans in Paris who had been inexplicably recruited by the Good Guys Institute (GGI), a "worldwide police force dedicated to recovering stolen works of art." They are led by J. Frederick Duval (John Williams) after the two unwillingly helped an organization of archcriminals, code-named "THEM," who had stolen a sizable portion of the world's art and were plotting to steal the Venus De Milo.

Allen & Rossi formed in 1957, performed on Broadway, had a highly successful nightclub act, and were television staples. Most notably, Allen & Rossi performed on *The Ed Sullivan Show* (1948–1971) forty-four times throughout their career, even appearing on the show the night the Beatles made their second appearance on the show on February 16, 1964. That night Allen & Rossi performed a skit with Allen as a punch-drunk boxer who is scheduled to fight the winner of the upcoming Sonny Liston versus then Cassius Clay (Muhammad Ali) fight. Allen & Rossi had a tough act to follow after the Beatles performed their first set of songs: "She Loves You," "This Boy," and "All My Loving." The biggest reaction the duo got from the crowd (who clearly were only interested in seeing John, Paul, George, and Ringo) was when Allen exclaimed that he was the "mother of the Beatles."

Marty Allen's signature line—"Hello Dere"—featured prominently on the poster for
The Last of the Secret Agents **(1966).** © 1966 Paramount Pictures Corporation

Ed Sullivan is featured in a cameo role in *Last of the Secret Agents?* Also featured is Nancy Sinatra, a year before she belted out the theme for the James Bond film *You Only Live Twice* (1967). Sinatra not only appeared in *Last of the Secret Agents?* but she also sang the theme. Character actors John Williams, best known for his role as Chief Inspector Hubbard in Alfred Hitchcock's *Dial M for Murder* (1954), and Lou Jacobi, who would go on to appear in *Everything You Always Wanted to Know about Sex* (*But Were Afraid to Ask)* (1972) and *My Favorite Year* (1982), also made appearances.

Last of the Secret Agents? was directed by Norman Abbott (nephew of Bud Abbott of Abbott and Costello fame). Norman Abbott was mostly known for directing episodes of *Get Smart* (1965–1970), *Leave It to Beaver* (1957–1963), *The Jack Benny Program* (1950–1965), and *The Munsters* (1964–1966). The film was written by Mel Tolkin, former head writer of the seminal Sid Caesar sketch comedy show *Your Show of Shows* (1950–1954).

Advertisements asked, "Will Spying Ever Be the Same Again?" Press releases for the film called it "side splitting." But the film was not well received by critics (*Last of the Secret Agents?* advertisement; "Allen and Rossi Team," 34). Marjoy Adams of the *Boston Globe* believed Allen & Rossi had "neither a clever nor a very entertaining debut." Adams added that Allen & Rossi were not in the "same class" as other comedy duos like Dean Martin and Jerry Lewis (Adams "Allen, Rossi," 10). The *Los Angeles Times* motion picture editor Philip K. Scheuer believed that Allen & Rossi were unable to save the film and that although the opening sequence was "one of the most hilarious ever to break in a spy film," it lasted too long, much like the film. Scheuer added that "after a giggle-filled 45 minutes or so the picture runs steadily downhill" (Scheuer "Even Allen and Rossi," 79).

Allen & Rossi made fourteen personal appearances throughout the United States to promote the film. Appearances often included a special master of ceremonies (often local disc jockeys or television personalities), appearances by local politicians, brass bands, autograph signings, and special comedy routines by the duo (Monahan "Recalling"; "Allen, Rossi in Person," 24).

The film displayed a number of 1966 styles and trends. On top of capitalizing on the spy craze, *Last of the Secret Agents?* included a brassy, swinging 1960s soundtrack, exotic belly dancers (by which many films and television shows at the time were infatuated), parodies of commercials for the era, and topless go-go dancers (although no nudity was shown).

Despite its bad critical reception, the film was a success with moviegoers in 1966. According to *Variety* the film made $1,250,000 at the box office ("Big Rental Pictures of 1966").

The Man Called Flintstone (1966)

Television's favorite modern Stone Age family, *The Flintstones* even got into the spy game. On January 21, 1966, syndicated gossip newspaper columnist Hedda Hopper wrote that television's popular Hanna-Barbera animated prehistoric sitcom, which at the time was being translated into seventeen languages and broadcast in forty-seven foreign countries, *The Flintstones* (1960–1966), would be joining the spy fad with a feature-length animated feature film: *The Man Called Flintstone*. Hopper noted, "The pen and ink stars travel to Eurock where they'll meet agents of the dreaded spy organization S.M.I.S.H." (Hopper "Flintstones," 60).

The film, a musical based on an original story by R. S. Allen and Harvey Bullock, would be released by Columbia Pictures and produced and directed by William Hanna and Joseph Barbera of animation production company Hanna-Barbera. *The Man Called Flintstone* featured the voices of Alan Reed as Fred Flintstone, Mel Blanc as Barney Rubble, Jean Vander Pyl as Wilma Flintstone, and Gerry Johnson as Betty Rubble. Legendary voice actor Paul Frees would be added to the cast to play "the fiendish Green Goose" and to do the voices of several other characters, such as master of disguise Agent XXX and superspy (who looks just like Fred Flintstone) Rock Slag.

Character actor Henry Corden, who appeared in bit roles in numerous television shows and movies throughout his career, provided Fred Flintstone's singing voice for the film. Cordon would go on to voice Fred Flintstone full-time after Alan Reed's death in 1977. *The Danny Kaye Show* (1963–1967) regular and future *Carol Burnett Show* (1967–1978) cast member, Harvey Korman, provided the voice of Rock Slag's superior officer, Chief Boulder. Korman also provided the voice of the Great Gazoo on the last season of *The Flintstones* ("'Flintstones'"; Connolly "Mike Connolly").

Syndicated Hollywood columnist Charles Witbeck remarked that *The Man Called Flintstone* would be *The Flintstones* "swan song" since the show was "given the TV ax" by ABC and would be leaving the airwaves April 1966. He noted that prime-time cartoons were "obsolete" but the show would be hitting the "softer syndicated market." Witbeck also saw the film as the Flintstones' "one more stab at stardom" (Witbeck "Flintstones," 40).

The Man Called Flintstone was not Hanna-Barbera's first animated feature. *Hey There, Yogi Bear* was released to theaters in 1964; it was a film that Charles Witbeck indicated did not make money and was the studio's experiment with the feature film. Producer Bill Hanna stated that *The Man Called Flintstone* was different because, unlike *Hey There, Yogi Bear*, *The Man Called Flintstone* was geared toward both adults and children. "We have slanted this picture to get the adult audience," said Hanna. "And if the idea works we'll make others." He also observed that cartoons that air weekly on Saturday mornings or once a week at kiddie matinee shows take years to make money, but feature-length films have the ability to make a profit in a much shorter amount of time (Witbeck "Flint-stones," 40). Although *Hey There, Yogi Bear* may have been an experiment for Hanna-Barbera, the studio invested $1,500,000 in the production of *The Man Called Flintstone*, using 120 animators who created three hundred thousand drawings that took more than a year to complete (Willey "TV to Become"; Bladen "Fred Flintstone").

In the film, which spoofs the James Bond, Matt Helm, and Euro-spy films of the era, Fred Flintstone is discovered by Secret Intelligence's Chief Boulder to be an exact double for a Bondesque playboy, supersecret agent named Rock Slag. Slag has been hospitalized in the Flintstone family's town of Bedrock, and Fred is asked to replace Slag. Fred is sent on a secret mission to "Eurock"; he travels to Paris and Rome with his family, wife Wilma and daughter Pebbles, and their best friends and neighbors, Betty and Barney Rubble and their son Bamm-Bamm, in tow. Fred's mission is to track down Green Goose, the leader of the evil organization S.M.I.S.H, while keeping his supersecret mission from his travel companions and even his wife.

While many articles about *The Man Called Flintstone* wrote about the obvious comparison to James Bond, teen newspaper column "The Swinging Set," by Sylvie Reice, noted the fact that the Beatles, who starred in their own adventure musicals *A Hard Day's Night* (1964) and *Help!* (1965), "are now on TV in an animated cartoon," and *The Flintstones* "made an adventure musical comedy movie" (Bladen "Fred Flintstone," 15; "Teen-Talizers," 19).

Throughout their time on television, *The Flintstones* took jabs at modern living and lampooned the latest fads. *The Man Called Flintstone* was no different, satirizing air travel, modern marriage, 1960s technology, and even the ease James Bond had in attracting women in his adventures on screen. William Hanna noted, "There is a return to caricature and satire as opposed to reality in the entertainment field and it's best portrayed through animation" (Bladen "Fred Flintstone," 15).

The film's poster parodies that of *Our Man Flint* (1966), which was released January 1966. But *The Man Called Flintstone* is more similar in storyline to Alfred Hitchcock's reluctant spy thriller *North by Northwest* (1959), about an advertising executive who is mistaken for a secret agent and is pursued by enemy agents. *The Man Called Flintstone* also shared similarities with two short-lived ABC (the same network *The Flintstones* aired on) television

The Man Called Flintstone **(1966) lampooned both James Bond and Derek Flint films.**
Everett Collection, Inc./Alamy Stock Photo

shows *The Man Who Never Was* and *The Double Life of Henry Phyfe*. Spy drama *The Man Who Never Was* (1966–1967) debuted on television in September 1966 and was about Peter Murphy (Robert Lansing), an American spy in Europe who assumed the identity of millionaire Mark Wainwright (also played by Lansing), after Wainwright is assassinated by killers sent to kill Murphy. *The Double Life of Henry Phyfe* (1966), a spy spoof starring Red Buttons, debuted in January 1966 but only lasted half a season. The show was about a mild-mannered accountant Henry Phyfe (Red Buttons) who could double for an enemy agent and is tasked to learn new skills to infiltrate an enemy organization each week.

The soundtrack *The Man Called Flintstone: Music from the Original Motion Picture* was released by Hanna-Barbera Records and included songs and instrumental tracks from the film. However "Pensate Amore (Think Love)" by Louis Prima, which was featured in the film, was not included on the LP. The same year famed dance instructor Arthur Murray incorporated the Batusi from *Batman* (1966–1968) in his lessons, he also taught his students the dance seen in *The Man Called Flintstone*: "The Rock Age."

Early test market screenings of *The Man Called Flintstone* were positive and were reported to have done better in those test screenings than Dean Martin's Matt Helm spy spoof *The Silencers* (1966) and Lee Marvin's Western comedy *Cat Ballou* (1966) ("Next at the Movies").

The Man Called Flintstone had a nationwide release on August 3, 1966, and played regularly throughout late 1966 and even into 1967 at theaters and drive-ins throughout the United States. However, it was reported by the Associated Press that the film had "middling results" at the box office ("TV Provides," 19).

Phyllis Funke, Louisville, Kentucky, *Courier-Journal* movie critic questioned "whether all of this is worth more than the half-hour allotted to it on television." But she added, "This problem, though, did not seem to bother the younger youngsters in the audience" (Funke "Flintstones Try Hand," 28).

In November 1967 the *New York Times* reported that the film would soon be playing "matinees at neighborhood showcases" aimed at the kids and that plans were in place to "repeat this three-day matinee program at other theaters." The paper noted, "Columbia Pictures has done a workmanlike job of stretching the half-hour animated cartoon show into a feature-length. . . . The trick, of course, was to keep the Flintstones bouncing across the screen with the same good-natured naiveté that they exude on the home set. . . . And bounce they do until the last quarter, when the picture simply runs out of gas—and gags. The kids and kids at heart shouldn't mind too much because the Flintstones are at home more or less as usual, with some nice pastel color backgrounds and batch of perky tunes added." The film played kiddie matinees regularly throughout the rest of the 1960s ("Man," 42).

Dr. Goldfoot and the Girl Bombs (1966) (Italian: *Le spie vengono dal semifreddo/ The Spies Who Came In from the Cool*)

Originally set to be titled *Dr. Goldfoot for President*, *Dr. Goldfoot and the Girl Bombs* served as a sequel to two films: American International Pictures (AIP)–produced *Dr. Goodfoot and the Bikini Machine* (1965) and the Italian– produced *Two Mafiosi against Goldginger* (1965) (Wilson "Boyer Thinks").

Unlike *Dr. Goodfoot and the Bikini Machine,* released in Italy as *Dr. Goldfoot and Our Agent 00¼, Dr. Goldfoot and the Girl Bombs* was not solely produced by AIP. Instead AIP coproduced the film with Italian production company, Italian International Film. So *Dr. Goldfoot and the Girl Bombs could* just as easily be classified as a Euro-spy. The film was shot and released in Italy under the title *Le spie vengono dal semifreddo,* which literally translates to *The Spies Who Came in from the Cool,* a takeoff on the popular 1965 spy novel *The Spy Who Came In from the Cold* and the 1965 film of the same name.

Vincent Price returned as mad scientist Dr. Goodfoot, who has been hired by the Chinese government to provoke a war between the United States and the USSR by building his patented sexy, gold bikini–clad female robots that are "programmed for love and destruction" and set to explode and kill Western generals during a NATO war game. To make matters worse, Goldfoot also planned on setting off an atomic bomb in Moscow.

Frankie Avalon did not return for *Dr. Goldfoot and the Girl Bombs* to reprise his role as Secret Agent 00¼ Craig Gamble from *Dr. Goodfoot and the Bikini Machine.* Avalon claimed that he was through with the "beach party" genre. Instead of traveling to Italy, Avalon starred in AIP's teen stock car–racing film *Fireball 500.* However, one of Avalon's *Fireball 500* costars, Fabian, did make the trip to Italy in Avalon's place (Scott "Hollywood Calendar"). Teen idol singer-turned-actor Fabian played womanizing secret agent Bill Dexter, who is set to take down Dr. Goldfoot and save the world by any means necessary with the help of two Italian doormen/wannabe spies Franco & Ciccio (Franco Franchi and Ciccio Ingrassia).

The film's director, Mario Bava was coming off a string of directing very successful and influential Italian-produced horror films *Black Sunday* (1960), *The Girl Who Knew Too Much* (1963), *Black Sabbath* (1963), *The Whip and the*

Body (1963), *Blood and Black Lace* (1964), *Planet of the Vampires* (1965), and *Kill, Baby, Kill* (1966). It has been reported that Bava was originally not interested in directing *Dr. Goldfoot and the Girl Bombs*, his only rendezvous into both the spy and comedy genres as a director, but was contractually obligated due to an agreement with the film's producer Fulvio Lucisano, who produced Bava's *Planet of the Vampires* (Pisoni "Kill Baby Kill").

Dr. Goldfoot and the Girl Bombs' cinematographer, Antonio Rinaldi, worked exclusively for Bava and had previously worked with him on three pictures: *Planet of the Vampires* (1965), *Knives of the Avenger* (1966), and *Kill, Baby, Kill!* (1966). Rinaldi would go on to do the cinematography for Bava on *Danger: Diabolik* (1968), *Five Dolls for an August Moon* (1970), *Roy Colt and Winchester Jack* (1970), *Four Times That Night* (1971), and *Baron Blood* (1972).

Because *Two Mafiosi against Goldginger* was not seen in the United States until 1969, when it was dubbed and released by AIP under the title of *The Amazing Dr. G* for AIP Television, the Italian- and English-language cuts were much different from one another. The Italian version focused on Italian comic duo Franco & Ciccio, who were featured in *Two Mafiosi against Goldginger*. The English-language version focused more on Fabian's character, Secret Agent Bill Dexter.

Even the scores differed. The Italian version of the film was scored by Lallo Gori. Gori composed the score for a number of Italian giallo, sword-and-sandal (peplum), and spaghetti Westerns. The English-language cut was by lounge/exotica composer Les Baxter. At the time, Baxter was scoring a number of AIP-produced pictures such as *Beach Party* (1963), *Muscle Beach Party* (1964), *Bikini Beach* (1964), *Pajama Party* (1964), *Beach Blanket Bingo* (1965), *How to Stuff a Wild Bikini* (1965), *Sergeant Deadhead* (1965), the film's predecessor *Dr. Goldfoot and the Bikini Machine* (1965), *The Ghost in the Invisible Bikini* (1966), and *Fireball 500* (1966).

As noted earlier, the Italian title *Le spie vengono dal semifreddo* is a mockery of the 1963 Cold War spy novel by author John le Carré and the 1965 movie starring Richard Burton: *The Spy Who Came In from the Cold*. Much like *Dr. Goldfoot and the Bikini Machine*, the movie seemed to be a favorite among drive-in theatergoers and played alongside a myriad of cofeatures that included Woody Allen's spoof *What's Up, Tiger Lily?* (1966), sex comedy *The Swinger* (1966), Japanese giant monster movie *Godzilla vs. The Thing* (1964), fellow spy spoof *Bang! Bang! You're Dead!* (1966), the Peter Fonda and Nancy Sinatra motorcycle exploitation flick *Wild Angels* (1966), drama *An Eye for an Eye* (1966), and Elvis Presley's *Tickle Me* (1965).

Dr. Goldfoot and the Girl Bombs (1966) album, featuring a theme by The Sloopys. The Sloopys' only other music credit is the single "Gonna Give You Back Your Diamond Ring/Wait Johnny For Me." © *1966 Allied Artists*

Los Angeles Times staff writer Kevin Thomas observed at the time that "each week brings a new James Bond takeoff that is even worse than the last." Thomas wondered "how a science fiction-spy spoof could be lousier staggers the imagination" and noted that "the color was glum, the sets cheap, the dubbing dreadful and the direction resolutely pedestrian"—despite Mario Bava being "well-respected for his stylish horror pictures" (Thomas "Second 'Dr. Goldfoot,'" 92).

The Glass Bottom Boat (1966)

Doris Day, best known throughout her career for quirky romantic comedies and one of America's most popular film stars, also got into the spy game in 1966 with the MGM–produced comedy *The Glass Bottom Boat.*

Widow Jennifer Nelson (Doris Day) works in public relations at an aerospace company that is working on a top-secret gravitational device known as GISMO. She also works part-time for her father Axel Nordstrom's (Arthur Godfrey) glass bottom boat tour company as a costumed mermaid. While playing her role as a mermaid, Jennifer Nelson's fishtail costume bottoms get caught in the fishing reel of Bruce Templeton (Rod Taylor), who happens to be her boss at the aerospace company, leaving her bottomless with only her bikini top on in the water. As this is a romantic comedy, of course, the duo eventually fall in love.

At a time when people were seeing Soviet spies behind every corner, security guard Homer Cripps (Paul Lynde) overhears Ms. Nelson making a phone call to someone named "Vladimir" and obviously assumes she is making a clandestine call to give GISMO state secrets to a Soviet agent. In reality, Vladimir is her dog, who is home alone. To give Vladimir exercise while she is at work, she calls home so Vladimir will run toward the phone. In the meantime, *actual* spies attempt to obtain the secrets of GISMO, and hilarity ensues.

New York Times critic Vincent Canby was less than kind to the film and its director, writing, "Frank Tashlin, one of the few Hollywood directors to pursue the slapstick muse, may someday make a really funny film, full of outrageous sight gags, mistaken identities and lunatic chases. In the meantime, you can chalk up as another frantic failure *The Glass Bottom Boat*, the new Doris Day vehicle that chugged into the Music Hall* yesterday, and promptly sank." He added that the screenplay was "predictable when it shows any inner logic, and simply absurd when it doesn't" (Canby "The Glass Bottom Boat," 54).

However, *Los Angeles Times* motion picture editor Philip K. Scheuer felt that although reviewers "sneered at the film," he felt that "*The Glass Bottom Boat* is

---

* A New York City theater.

one of those inane comedies that won't amuse anybody but us lowbrows" and went on to compliment Doris Day's acting alongside comedic talents such as Paul Lynde, Dom De Luise, John McGiver, Dick Martin (of Rowan and Martin), Edward Andrews, and Arthur Godfrey (Scheuer "Glass Boat," 68).

Stanley Eichelbaum of the *San Francisco Examiner* felt that Doris Day's "innocence" and "purity," a character trait of almost every character she has

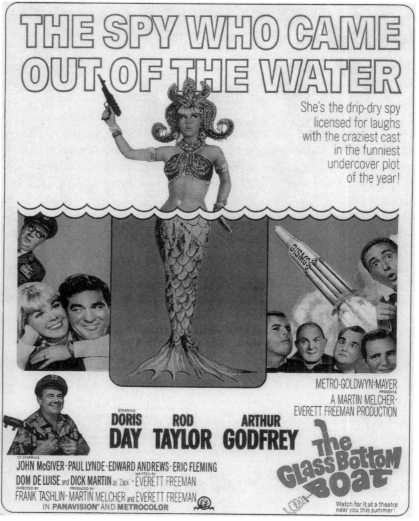

Poster for *The Glass Bottom Boat* (1966) drawn in the style of a James Bond film.
Cinematic Collection/Alamy Stock Photo

played, helped make the movie worth seeing, adding, "Nothing in the movie puts Miss Day in 007's league. Her antics are flat and stale. But I will admit that an occasional pratfall made me smile, maybe because Doris worked so punishingly hard at it" (Eichelbaum "Doris Flirts," 26).

The film's title sequence was created by Chuck Jones. Jones was best known for his animation work on *Looney Tunes*, and *The Glass Bottom Boat* was Jones's first assignment as director of MGM's Animation/Visual Arts Division. Frank DeVol, composer for other Doris Day films *Pillow Talk* (1959), *Lover Come Back* (1961), and *Send Me No Flowers* (1964), along with many other films and television shows, provided the film's score ("Making Debut"). The film's poster mimicked a typical 1960s James Bond film poster and included the tag line "The Spy Who Came Out of Water," a parody of *The Spy Who Came In from the Cold*.

In the Australian continent, *The Glass Bottom Boat* was marketed as a much more risqué film than "girl next door Doris Day" (as the film's trailer refers to her) could ever be. In that market, *The Glass Bottom Boat* was released as *The Spy in Lace Panties* and referred to Doris Day as the "Oh Oh-Sex Girl." In Japan the film was released as *Operation Mermaid* (Kleiner "U.S. Idols"; *Spy in Lace Panties* advertisement).

The Glass Bottom Boat also leaned into the spy craze by including a cameo by Robert Vaughn as Napoleon Solo, his character on the television show *The Man from U.N.C.L.E.* (1964–1968). *The Man from U.N.C.L.E.* was also produced by MGM. The theme from *The Man from U.N.C.L.E.* plays when he appears.

Although critics were not a fan of *The Glass Bottom Boat*, the film successfully rode the spy wave and was a financial venture for MGM. It was the twentieth highest grossing film of the year in North America, earning $4,320,000 at the box office ("Big Rental Pictures of 1966").

What's Up, Tiger Lily? (1966)

Following the release of *What's New Pussycat?* (1965), the film's writer, Woody Allen, who had made a name for himself as a New York Greenwich Village standup comic (called by *Esquire* magazine the "hot comedian" of 1966), through numerous television talk show appearances, and with his self-titled comedy album, wanted more creative control over his future projects. The future auteur's first project would be *What's Up, Tiger Lily?* Released on November 2, 1966, by American International Pictures, *What's Up, Tiger Lily?* took the existing James Bond–inspired Toho studio's Japanese spy film *International Secret Police: Key of Keys* (1965), directed by Akiko Wakabayashi, redubbed the dialogue, and changed the plot, turning the film into the search for the world's best egg salad recipe (Borsch "You Must Be").

Woody Allen does appear in the film to explain the premise to the audience:

> Hollywood wanted to make the definitive spy picture . . . so we took a Japanese film, made in Japan by Japanese actors and actresses. We bought it and it's a great film, beautiful color, and there is raping and looting and killing in it. And I took out all the soundtrack, I knocked out all their voices and I wrote a comedy. And I got together with some actors and actresses and we put our comedy in where they were formerly raping and looting and the result is where people are running around killing one another and doing all those James Bondian things but what is coming out of their mouth is something wholly other.

The film also featured the music of 1960s folk rock band, the Lovin' Spoonful. The Spoonful performed the movie's theme, "Pow," and the rest of the soundtrack. The film's star, Tatsuya Mihashi, who did his best James Bond for the film, previously appeared in the Toho horror film *Human Vapor* (1960) and would later appear in the American World War II film *Tora, Tora, Tora* (1970). Two actresses who appear in the film, Akiko Wakabayashi and Mie Hama, both appear in the James Bond film *You Only Live Twice* (1967).

The *New York Times* wrote, "The idea for this satirical adventure is so bright, it's a real pity that the picture doesn't hold up, even with some truly hilarious moments, specifically wisecracks, courtesy of Woody Allen and a battery of six comedy writers." In addition: "What happened was this. Mr. Allen, as he explains in a disarming prologue, was hired to spruce up, with editing and dubbed English, a mess of color footage from the Orient with some Japanese performers slam-banging away at James Bond" ("Woody-Allenized," 33).

Kevin Thomas of the *Los Angeles Times* wrote, "Take one lousy imitation Japanese James Bond, give it to Woody Allen, who erases the soundtrack and substitutes his one wild dialogue, add a groovy Lovin' Spoonful score and you have *What's Up, Tiger Lily?*—the funniest spy spoof of them all." However, Thomas concedes, "Even though *What's Up, Tiger Lily?* runs but eighty minutes, its one joke wears a bit at the end. Still, Allen does satisfactorily answer the question of how to spoof a spoof of a spoof" (Thomas "Tiger Lily," 84).

Although Allen would appear in the James Bond spy spoof *Casino Royale* (1967) a year later, *What's Up, Tiger Lily?* was the one and only spy spoof he would direct. Allen would go on to direct a number of critically acclaimed movies, such as *Everything You Always Wanted to Know about Sex* (1972), *Annie Hall* (1977), and *Manhattan* (1979).

A similar production that involved dubbing over old movies to make an entirely different plot was tried in 1985 with the syndicated television show *Mad Movies with the L.A. Connection* by a comedy group who would perform live over old films in theaters (Brass "L.A. Comedy Group").

Caprice (1967)

In 1966, Doris Day released the successful spy comedy *The Glass Bottom Boat*, directed by Frank Tashlin. The next year, Day starred in yet another Tashlin-directed spy comedy, *Caprice*, written by John Kohn and Frank Tashlin. In February 1966, it was announced that cowriter John Kohn, who also cowrote the original story "Caprice," with Martin Hale, took on the role of the film's producer (Martin "Warner to Film," C9).

Rather than a story of international intrigue dealing with nuclear secrets and political assassinations, *Caprice,* which is the name of a water-repellent hair spray, is a story of two competing spies in the cosmetics industry, played by Doris Day and Richard Harris, who inevitably fall for each other. Day was known for starring in a string of successful romantic comedies throughout the 1950s and 1960s, and Harris was nominated for Best Supporting Actor at the Academy Awards four years earlier, for his role in *This Sporting Life* (1963).

Production began in May 1966, and the film was released by 20th Century Fox to theaters on April 18, 1967. It was occasionally seen in double features with spy thriller *Fathom* (1967), starring Raquel Welch (Scheuer "Paris Film").

Edgar J. Driscoll Jr., of the *Boston Globe*, wrote that Doris Day fans would "probably eat this one up" but added, "From where we sat you could sniff all those other spy spoof formulas from which *Caprice* was made in almost overwhelming bouquet. . . . While such nonsense ever really come off as pure nonsense, *Caprice* does offer some mighty lush sets and settings" (Driscoll Jr. "*Caprice* Pits," 59).

Chicago Sun-Times critic Roger Ebert wrote in his review of the film, "When everything has been said and done, you really have to stand back and admire the sheer professional competence of the people who make Doris Day movies. They take the screen's most narcissistic teenager; cast her opposite the Great Balding Stone Face, Richard Harris; limit their emotional range to blank stares (his) and fluttering false eyelashes (hers), and lower them both to be boiled alive in a story about counter-spies in the cosmetics industry. Maybe they get a kickback on the makeup necessary to make Miss Day look just as young and fresh and dewy eyed as she did" (Ebert "Caprice," n.p.).

But Ebert still felt that *Caprice* was a fun and well-made picture, writing, "Faced with this situation, Miss Day's director, the set designer, her clothes designer and the camera crew fight back with skill and cunning. If her movies never go anywhere, at least they don't take all day about it. They're directed with a light touch, skillfully edited, and get it over with in no time. And they're beautiful to look at. Miss Day has about two dozen outfits in *Caprice*, and the great thing is, all of the sets are in coordinated colors. She wears a black-and-white checked dress in a black-and-white checked room and a blue-on-blue in a blue-on-blue room, and sometimes only her voice lets you know she's there" (Ibid.).

However, it would not be a spy film without a mention of 007. "When James Bond sneaks in a double entendre, you feel safe in rolling your eyes, nudging your date with an elbow and snickering. But when Richard Harris tries to push Doris Day onto a swinging bed suspended from the ceiling by chains, and she says, 'Oh, no, I never do anything until an hour after dinner,' you don't know whether to snicker. So Miss Day winks and giggles, and Harris smiles gamely and stands around while the camera glorifies her as just the cutest, prettiest, brightest little bundle of joy in the world, and it's all done so cleverly that it seems like it's in a flash. What fun" (Ibid.).

Frank De Vol, who provided the music for *Glass Bottom Boat*, was brought back to score *Caprice*. An actor from *Glass Bottom Boat* was brought back as well: comedian Arthur Godfrey, who played Doris Day's character's father in *The Glass Bottom Boat*, plays her father again, but this time he is only seen in a photograph.

Caprice and fellow spy spoof *In Like Flint* (1967), with James Coburn, were the last two pictures 20th Century Fox made in the widescreen format known as Cinemascope. Characters in the film can be seen watching the animated opening sequence of ABC's *Batman* (1966–1968). The end credits mention Batman creator Bob Kane and notes, "Batman television sequence based on characters created by, appearing in Batman and Detective comics magazines published by Periodical Publications, Inc."

Ultimately the film was not a success. After *Caprice*, Day only made three more films, *The Ballad of Josie* (1967), *Where Were You When the Lights Went Out?* (1968), and *With Six You Get Eggroll* (1968). Then she transitioned to television with her own CBS situation comedy, *The Doris Day Show* (1968–1973).

The Double Man (1967)

Based on the 1958 novel *Legacy of a Spy*, by Henry S. Maxfield, and directed by Franklin J. Schaffner, Yul Brynner stars as CIA agent Dan Slater, who, soon after learning of a Soviet plan to infiltrate the CIA, is informed of his son's death. Suspicious of the report, Slater travels to the Alps, where his son was on a ski trip, to investigate the claim. While in Austria, Slater encounters Gina (Britt Ekland), a supposed witness to his son's death. During Slater's investigation, he discovers the Soviets' plan on killing him and replacing him with a body double who has been given plastic surgery to look exactly like Slater (hence the title).

Write-ups about *The Double Man* did not focus on actor Yul Brynner of *The King and I* (1956) and *The Ten Commandments* (1956) fame. Instead the focus was on twenty-four-year-old, Swedish actress Britt Ekland, and not on her acting skills. Vernon Scott of United Press International compared Ekland to Greta Garbo and Ingrid Bergman, stating that Ekland is "one of those rare ones among contemporary actresses; the kind whose physical appearance alone stops a scene stone cold. . . . Britt is the universal image of what a Swedish girl should be. Blonde hair tumbles below her shoulders, her skin is as clear as a Scandinavian sky. Her blue eyes are wide-set, her nose tip-tilter and her figure absolutely perfect." And *The Record* in Hackensack, New Jersey, called her "pert, sexy and charming" (Scott "Glamor Gal," 11; "Britt," 50).

At the time, Ekland was married to actor/comedian Peter Sellers, who, the same year *The Double Man* was released, starred in Columbia Pictures' non-canon Bond film *Casino Royale* (1967). The couple divorced a year later.

Although the film debuted in the United Kingdom on April 25, 1967, it did not make its premiere in the United States until more than a year later, May 1, 1968.

The *New York Times* called *The Double Man* "a modest third-rate film," calling attention to the film's cinematography: "The color of the movie is not good, some covering scenes that were shot on fake snow in England in summer look fake, and real ski scenes are done more effectively each year in television's sports coverage." But the article conceded that "the plotting is tight and Mr. Brynner looks exotic and stony enough to keep one's mind off the title; when the denouement[*] comes it is a moderate surprise" ("Spy with a Mission," 57).

On the other hand, *Los Angeles Times*'s Kevin Thomas felt the movie was "action-packed," "well-acted," and "set in colorful locales." Contradictory to the *New York Times*, Thomas noted what he believed to be "superb color photography" and called the film's cinematographer Denys N. Coop "one of

* Finale.

Britain's best cameramen." But he believed that both *The Double Man* and the film it often was paired with, the Richard Boone drama *Kona Coast* (1968), were "perhaps not quite strong enough to stand alone; but together they make a thoroughly satisfying double bill" (Thomas "Kona," 16).

Critic for the *Boston Globe,* Edgar Driscoll Jr., called the film "a better-than-average work in the genre" thanks to Yul Brynner's acting but felt there were "implausibilities" in the plot. But, Driscoll continued, "by and large, if its modest entertainment you're after you'll find it here" (Driscoll "Yul Brynner Scores," 69). Surprisingly, the film was approved for general patronage and given an A-1 rating by the National Catholic Office for Motion Pictures (NCOMP) ("Recent Movie Ratings," 10).

A year after directing *The Double Man*, Franklin J. Schaffner would direct *Planet of the Apes* (1968) and go on to direct films such as *Patton* (1970) and *The Boys from Brazil* (1978).

Fathom (1967)

A year after Raquel Welch starred in her breakout role as Loana in Hammer Films' prehistoric adventure film *One Million Years B.C.* (where she famously wore a fur bikini that Welch called "mankind's first bikini," she took on the role of Fathom, a dental assistant/professional skydiver on a tour of Europe ("Filmfacts 1967").

The plot of the film feels like an unmade *The Man from U.N.C.L.E.* (1964–1968) episode in which, as often happened, an average person got caught up in international espionage and intrigue. Fathom Harvill, a skydiver for the US parachute team and dental assistant by trade, is recruited by NATO to skydive into the Mediterranean to find the triggering mechanism for a missing nuclear weapon hidden in a Chinese dragon figurine. Once in the Mediterranean, Fathom is confronted with the fact that she may not be on a mission for NATO but, instead, for a private collector in search of the figurine.

Strangely, 20th Century Fox acquired the film rights to *Fathom* from author Larry Forrester, based on the Fathom character he introduced in his first book *A Girl Called Fathom*, but the film is based on his unpublished novel *Fathom Heavensent*. Reports at the time stated that *Fathom Heavensent* was "still in the draft stage" and that the film series started with the second book anyway because the story "involves the dangerous and spectacular sport of skydiving, which is rapidly gaining popularity throughout the world, and particularly in the USA and Britain" ("Sensational," 23).

Raquel Welch in *Fathom* **(1967), wearing a much different bikini than she did in** *One Million Years B.C.* **(1966).** *Author's collection*

The film's director, Leslie H. Martinson, and writer, Lorenzo Semple Jr., had a connection to an iconic 1960s movie made a year prior. Martinson directed and Semple wrote the screenplay for *Batman: The Movie* (1966), released in July 1966. *Batman: The Movie* was released following the debut of *Batman* (1966–1968) on ABC television in January 1966, which brought about the pop-culture phenomenon known as Bat-Mania.

Chicago Sun-Times critic Roger Ebert wrote, "Nobody expects *Fathom* to be a masterpiece. But that doesn't mean it shouldn't be made. Why not have a skydiving movie, with lots of great footage of skydivers floating through the air, and lots of great footage of Raquel Welch? It could be fun. You can only be ponderous so long, and then you need to look at someone like Raquel Welch for a while. It's good for you." Yet he conceded, "But when Raquel Welch speaks, she sounds like every drive-in waitress and every beauty queen and every female high school class president and every not-very-bright good sport you ever heard. She stands there in that bikini, with her hair flowing in the breeze, and her face looking haughty and beautiful, and then she opens her mouth and says, 'Gollee, you fellows have got yourself the wrong gal. I didn't kill him, honest. I mean, really'" (Ebert "Fathom," n.p.).

Alan Ward of the *Oakland Tribune* criticized Raquel Welch's acting chops but praised her looks, writing, "It is fortunate for Raquel she has a face and figure worth noting, because her acting ability is somewhat less than shattering." He later noted that "as might be expected, Miss Welch consistently appears in various stages of approximate undress, and it would be ungallant indeed to suggest the sight is either unpleasant or cloying" (Ward "*Fathom* a Spy Film," 47).

A review of the film by Bill Dial of the *Atlanta Constitution* called the film "nothing more than an exploitation vehicle for Raquel Welch" (Dial "*Fathom* Really Hard," 12). The *Miami Herald* described *Fathom* as "breezy" but said that "at times confused plotting offers very little opportunity for her to look anything more than seductive, suspicious, angry, seductive, alarmed, seductive and healthy." The paper also made sure to note that Welch "changes from mini-skirt to bikini and back again more than a dozen times" ("Easy to *Fathom*," 36). The *Pittsburgh Press* called the film "a silly episode" that was "a la James Bond" with foreign agents, precious jewels, speeding auto, motorboats, helicopters and planes" ("Current Movies," 42).

Producers hoped to make *Fathom* an entire series of films, as with James Bond or Matt Helm, but failed to capture audiences. The film was a losing venture at the box office, only taking in around a million dollars and failing to make a profit ("Sensational"; "Big Rental Films of 1967").

Thigh Spy (1967)

Not to be confused with the R&B group the Persuaders' 1971 song of the same name, *Thigh Spy* is a takeoff on the title of the popular television show *I Spy*. However, the title is the only correlation between the two.

The ultra-low-budget, black-and-white sexploitation "Adults Only" film's poster promises, "The screen reveals the Secrets of the Secret Agents," "A Shocking Undercover Affair," "A Spy's Eye View of Sin!" It says the film contains "the Women . . . Who Know More Than One Way to Skin a Spy. The Men . . . Who Know What They . . . Want and How to Take It." The film does not deliver on the poster's promises.

The film revolves around Bartholomew, a starving artist hired to kill a secret agent (because he must "kill for his art"), who proceeds to attempt to hunt the secret agent down throughout the streets of New York City. Of course the hunt includes orgies and a lot of nude women, including Bartholomew's girlfriend Chrissy. One of the only highlights of the meandering plot of *Thigh Spy* are the New York winter street scenes (presumably shot without a permit), which gives viewers a time capsule of the city in the 1960s.

An advertisement in the *Philadelphia Inquirer* for a showing of the film at a theater that began showing pornographic films in the 1960s, the Walton Art Theater, located in the Germantown section of Philadelphia, exclaimed, "There's cold blooded murder and hot blooded lust that would make James Bond blush in this shocking undercover affair where everything is uncovered!" ("*Thigh Spy* Ad").

Director William K. Hennigar also directed other low-budget nudie films such as *See How They Come* (1968), *The Wicked Die Slow* (1968), and another naughty take on a 1960s television show title, *Surfside Sex* (1968). *Thigh Spy* played throughout the United States in the late 1960s along with other low-budget, nudie sexploitation flicks such as *The Alley Cats* (1966), *The Bed and How to Make It* (1966), *Sex and the Single Sailor* (1967), and *The Touch of Her Flesh* (1967; a.k.a. *Spoiled Flesh*).

Come Spy with Me (1967)

Filmed on location in Jamaica and armed with perhaps the most obvious title for a 1960s spy flick (a takeoff on "Come Fly with Me," by Frank Sinatra) *Come Spy with Me* stars Andrea Dromm as Agent Jill Parsons. Agent Parsons is sent to Jamaica to investigate kidnappings in the Caribbean. While on her mission, she uncovers a plot by a reclusive enemy agent, Walter Ludeker (Albert Dekker), to assassinate world leaders via an underwater bomb. To aid in her mission, Jill Parsons conscripts a civilian, Pete Barker (Troy Donahue), who owns a boat charter business.

In 1967 Troy Donahue was most famous for his work on television's *77 Sunset Strip* (1960–1961), *Surfside 6* (1960–1962), and *Hawaiian Eye* (1962–1963). At that time, Andrea Dromm was best known for having starred in a 1963 National Airlines commercial, her prominent role in the second pilot episode of *Star Trek*, "Where No Man Has Gone Before," in 1965, and playing a babysitter who fell in love with a Soviet sailor in the film *The Russians Are Coming, the Russians Are Coming* (1966).

Donahue and Dromm are supported by character actor Albert Dekker. Dekker starred as the optically challenged title character of Paramount's science fiction film *Dr. Cyclops* (1940). However, Dekker also notably starred in noir films *The Killers* (1946) and *Kiss Me Deadly* (1955); more recently to 1967, he played the heavy on episodes of television shows including *The Man from U.N.C.L.E.* (1964–1968), *Mission: Impossible* (1966–1972), *and I Spy* (1965–1968). Five months after the release of *Come Spy with Me*, Albert Dekker died an infamous and rather gruesome death but not before portraying corrupt railroad agent Pat Harrigan in *The Wild Bunch*, which was released in 1969.

Also featured are a number of thrilling underwater sequences, musical interludes, and twisting dance numbers, most notably introducing a new dance called "The Shark."

The film's theme, *Come Spy with Me*, was written by Smokey Robinson and performed by Smokey Robinson and the Miracles. The song was released as a B side to "The Love I Saw in You Was Just a Mirage" by Motown Records.

The *New York Times* called the film "Mr. Donahue's pathetic little spy romp" that was "chock full of rock 'n' roll youngsters and juiced up by a jazzy photographer who must have had St. Vitus Dance."* The article added that *Come Spy with Me* "has a sunny, blue-watered Jamaican locale in its favor—and that alone" ("One Million Years," 21).

Wanda Hale of New York's *Daily News* asked, "Is this any way to make a movie? You bet it isn't," which was in reference to Andrea Dromm's National Airlines commercial, where she asked, "Is this any way to run an airline? You bet it is!" (Hale "2 Gals," 20).

Come Spy with Me was directed by Marshal Stone, who until that point had only directed and produced television and commercials and only directed one other film afterward, the television movie *Flying without Fear* (1985). Writing

---

* According to the American Heart Association, St. Vitus Dance is a rheumatic fever that causes "frequent rapid, irregular, and aimless involuntary movements of all four limbs."

credits go to Cherney Berg and Erven Jourdan. Erven Jourdan had three other credits to his name, writing and producing forgettable films *The Half Pint* (1960), *Money in My Pocket* (1960), and *The Great Hitch-Hike Race* (1972). Cherney Berg, on the other hand, was a longtime writer and producer on the early sit-com *The Goldbergs* (1949–1957) and wrote spoken-word albums *Famous Monsters Speak* and *King Kong (The Original 20th Century Fox Motion Picture Classic)*. Both albums were found for sale in the back pages of seminal monster movie magazine *Famous Monsters of Filmland*.

Throughout the country, *Come Spy with Me* was most often seen as the second half of a double feature with Hammer Films' *One Million Years B.C.* (1966) starring Raquel Welch and John Richardson. The *New York Times* noted, "It's not every double-bill that runs the gamut from dinosaurs to Troy Donahue." ("One Million Years," 21).

Salt and Pepper (1968)

Dean Martin was not the only member of the Rat Pack (Frank Sinatra, Dean Martin, Sammy Davis Jr., Peter Lawford, and Joey Bishop) making spy films in the 1960s. In 1968, Peter Lawford and Sammy Davis Jr. made their first onscreen appearance as a pair in the spy spoof *Salt and Pepper*.

Salt and Pepper was directed by Richard Donner, who at the time was coming off a string of directing a number of episodes of popular television shows such as spy shows *Get Smart* (1965–1970), *The Man from U.N.C.L.E.* (1964–1968), and *The Wild Wild West* (1965–1968). It was written by Michael Pertwee, who wrote numerous British-produced comedy films and for television shows *The Saint* (1962–1969) and *Danger Man* (1960–1962 and 1964–1968), among others. The film follows Soho London nightclub owners Charles Salt (Sammy Davis Jr.) and Christopher Pepper (Peter Lawford), who find a beautiful woman in the club, Ma Ling (Jeanne Roland), believe her to be drunk, and send her home in a taxicab. The next morning, Ling is found murdered, and although the nightclub owners are prime suspects in the murder investigation led by Inspector Crabbe (Michael Bates), the two become amateur investigators to find the killer and uncover an international plot to overthrow the British government.

Throughout the film the characters' races and names are a running gag that is a one-note joke beaten into the ground (Sammy Davis Jr., who was Black, plays Salt, and Peter Lawford, who was white, plays Pepper). The gag does not hold up to more modern sensibilities or even the sensibilities of 1968 audiences, as seen in several of the film's reviews.

Critics often made the obvious comparison with *Salt and Pepper* and James Bond and occasionally with slapstick comedians of the silent-film era, such as Mack Sennett and the Keystone Cops (Kelly "Movie 'Censorship'"; Weiler "*Salt and Pepper* Opens"). Famed *Chicago Sun-Times* critic Roger Ebert wrote that "*Salt and Pepper* is at least nominally a comedy. But it contains scenes too violent to be absorbed by the comedy form and becomes a weird exercise in inconsistency: We're never quite sure whether to expect a pratfall or an immolation. In any event, we get too many of both" (Ebert "Salt," n.p.).

A. H. Weiler of the *New York Times* said, "Now that screen spoofs of intrigue in high places are as common as fish and chips in London, *Salt and Pepper*, which was added to moviegoers' menus yesterday . . . is not likely to change consumer habits to any great extent." Weiler added that the film is "merely nice spice on a familiar dish of comedy-melodrama" (Weiler "*Salt and Pepper* Opens," 62).

Perhaps the highest compliment paid to the team of Peter Lawford and Sammy Davis Jr. was by Joan Deppa of the *Pittsburgh Press*, who believed that if the movie clicked with audiences and made money at the box office, Lawford and Davis could be the next Abbott & Costello. Deppa quoted director Richard Donner as saying, "In most scenes I kept them as close together as possible. If they're not together they're panicky. Sammy will yell 'Pe-ep-per' which sounds a lot like the way Costello used to yell 'A-ab-bott.'" In addition, "in some ways they're a lot like an updated Abbott and Costello, only much more sophisticated" (Deppa "Davis, Lawford," 99).

Around the time *Salt and Pepper* was released in 1968, movie studios abandoned what was known as the Hays Code. The Hays Code had been adopted in 1934 to avoid government intervention and censorship. The code outright banned studio films from including adult themes such as nudity, sex, and graphic violence. Studios now favored the Motion Picture Association of America (MPAA) rating system (Rated G: Suggested for general audiences; Rated M: Suggested for mature audiences—Parental discretion advised; Rated R: Restricted—Persons under 16 not admitted unless accompanied by parent or adult guardian; Rated X: Persons under 16 not admitted).

Herb Kelly of the *Miami News* saw *Salt and Pepper* as a test of the new rating system: "The new system sounds encouraging but how can it be enforced? Can a parent who wants to expose his children to an 'X' film be refused admittance? Can a 15-year-old boy or girl be barred from seeing an 'X'? Remember, this censorship is voluntary, not law," said Kelly. He claimed he witnessed a father buy tickets for his family with three small children to see *Salt and Pepper*, despite the film including partial nudity and the theater's cashier telling him that "this

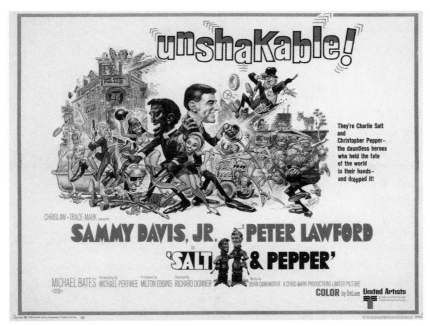

Cartoonist Jack Davis illustrated the poster for *Salt and Pepper* (1968). Davis also famously drew for *Mad* magazine and created the posters for *It's a Mad, Mad, Mad, Mad World* (1963) and *The Bad News Bears* (1974). *© 1968 United Artists Corporation*

isn't a picture for children." Kelly also inquired about children at drive-ins and art houses and about children who are left unattended to see the film of their choice. He wrote, "Any theater manager will tell you he's tried to turn away children from adult movies, only to have the parent come in or phone up and demand that the youngsters be admitted. 'We know what's fit for our children,' they shout" (Kelly "Movie 'Censorship,'" 16).

United Artists gave worldwide release to the film, which was given the alternative title *You're the Muzzle/I'm the Trigger* in Japan. According to *Variety*, *Salt and Pepper* made $1,750,000 in the United States and Canada at the box office and was the sixty-third highest grossing film in 1969, thanks in part to the film getting a second wind at drive-in theaters in the spring of 1969 ("Big Rental Films of 1969"; "Movies: Salt and Pepper"). Although the team of Lawford and Davis did not become the next Abbott and Costello, *Salt and Pepper* did make enough money at the box office to garner a sequel, *One More Time* (1970). *One More Time* was directed by Jerry Lewis and abandoned most of the spy elements from *Salt and Pepper*.

Director Richard Donner would go on to direct a number of successful films, perhaps most notably *The Omen* (1976), *Superman* (1978), *The Goonies* (1985), and *Lethal Weapon* (1987).

The Chairman (1969)

As the 1960s progressed and the war in Vietnam continued to escalate, pop culture seemed to take a more serious tone. The same went for spy films. The spy spoof craze of the mid-1960s wore thin and was not delivering the same box office numbers it once did. As with any fad, the public had moved on. The spy genre began to look toward realism as opposed to the escapism it offered several years earlier. Films of the era also began to look at and distrust government institutions like the CIA, due in part to the escalation in the Vietnam War, and those institutions' willingness and ability to harm their own citizens to advance an agenda.

The Chairman is an example of producers taking that more serious tone and distrust with spy flicks. Directed by J. Lee Thompson, produced by Mort Abrahams, and presented by 20th Century Fox, along with a screenplay written by Ben Maddow and based on a novel by Jay Richard Kennedy; *The Chairman* was released as *The Most Dangerous Man in the World* in the United Kingdom ("The Most Dangerous Man in the World" was used as the film's tagline in the states).

Although the plot is still outlandish, the genre saw less eccentric villains and fictitious organizations. *The Chairman* has a real-life villain: "The Chairman" refers to the president of the People's Republic of China, Chairman Mao Zedong. Scientist Dr. John Hathaway (Gregory Peck) is sent into Red China by the United States, England, and the Soviets (at the time, the Sino-Soviet border conflict between China and the USSR was taking place) to recover an enzyme that will grow crops in any climate. Little does Hathaway know, the transmitter implanted in his head that he was told would be used as a tracking and communication device is set to explode if he does not complete his mission in time. The countdown clock monitored by agents in London is reminiscent of the atomic device seen in *Goldfinger* (1964). The explosive device could also be detonated remotely, and it is debated on whether it should be used to kill Chairman Mao when Hathaway arranges a meeting with him.

The film gained attention due to Gregory Peck's star power. Peck was best known for his roles in award-winning and critically acclaimed films *Roman Holiday* (1953), *The Guns of Navarone* (1961), *Cape Fear* (1962), and most notably his portrayal of Atticus Finch in *To Kill a Mockingbird* (1962), a role that earned him an Academy Award for Best Actor. At the time *The Chairman* was being made, Gregory Peck served as president of the Academy of Motion

Picture Arts and Sciences and chairman of the Board of Trustees of the American Film Institute.

The trailer declared, "The Chairman controls the destiny of one billion people. The Chairman is the most feared man in the world with the possible exception of the one man who could stop him." Footage of Chairman Mao graced the screen over footage from the movie.

The film's script was called too unrealistic and the film's hero "too noble" by *Chicago Sun-Times* critic Roger Ebert (Ebert "The Chairman").

Howard Thompson of the *New York Times* called it "an ambitious new thriller" that "begins so brilliantly that nothing in the rest of the title could match it. As the title credits of this 20th Century Fox release unfold to some tingling music by Jerry Goldsmith, the screen fairly bursts with fragmented images depicting Communist China. It is an extraordinary start for a film that makes provocative entertainment for the first half, hits a snag, begins to fall apart and came in for a tame, wobbly landing." Of course Thompson makes the inevitable comparison to films in the James Bond franchise: "007 flavoring that makes the first part of the film so engrossing, with some cool, biting dialogue, crisp direction by J. Lee Thompson and the pictorial splendor of the settings and excellent color photography in Hong Kong, Taiwan and simulated Oriental locales." He added, "The picture starts wavering conventionally. The rest is pure, predictable Hairbreadth Harry,* right to the Soviet border. As for Mr. Peck's continual beep-beeping all the way back to London, in the thick of it, viewers can forget James Bond and start believing in Santa Claus" (Thompson "Peck in Thriller," 44).

The *Fort Worth Star-Telegram*'s Elston Brooks believed the film had an "interesting premise" but had a problem with the title: "One drawback, however, is the film's say-nothing title, *The Chairman,* which hardly tells the story, nor motivates one to get a babysitter for a night at the movies" (Brooks "Peck Braves," 16). Nadine M. Edwards of the *Valley Times* of North Hollywood, California, believed the film was "surprisingly disappointing" and that it was "a pedestrian paced, unemotional vehicle whose main attraction is an aspirin sized transmitter implanted in Gregory Peck's head. Edwards added, "Always a fine performer, Peck does his best, but he can't rise above the tepid screenplay" (Edwards "Unemotional," 18).

Ultimately, *The Chairman* lost money, only grossing $2.5 million at the box office, according to *Variety* ("Big Rental Films of 1969").

---

* A *Philadelphia Press* syndicated comic strip by C. W. Kahles that ran in the early 1900s and often featured improbable scenarios.

4

HER MAJESTY'S SECRET SERVICE

Englishmen are so odd. They are like a nest of Chinese boxes. It takes a very long time to get to the centre of them. When one gets there the result is unrewarding, but the process is instructive and entertaining.

—Ian Fleming, *Casino Royale*

Producers in the United Kingdom, home of James Bond, were looking to make, release, and export as many Bond facsimiles as possible.

Carry On Spying (1964)

A continuation of the British comedy *Carry On . . .* series, *Carry On Spying* was the ninth installment of what grew to be a thirty-one-part film series that went from 1958 to 1992. Other entries in the series included *Carry On Sergeant* (1958), *Carry On Teacher* (1959), and *Carry On Cruising* (1962). All thirty-one films were produced by Peter Rogers with director Gerald Thomas.

Released in black-and-white in July 1964, *Carry On Spying* was set to quickly capitalize on the James Bond craze before people forgot the name "James Bond." It was released around the same time as *A Hard Day's Night* (1964), the Beatles' starring vehicle. Much like *Carry On Spying*, *A Hard Day's Night* was *originally* intended to quickly cash in on Beatlemania, with the general consensus being people would forget the names John, Paul, George, and Ringo.

When a secret chemical formula is stolen by evil organization STENCH (the Society for the Total Extinction of Non-Conforming Humans), the British Secret Service chief (Eric Barker) tasked Agent Desmond Simpkins (Kenneth Williams) and his three trainees, Daphne Honeybutt (Barbara Windsor), Charlie Bind (Charles Hawtrey), and Harold Crump (Bernard Cribbins), with recovering the formula from STENCH agents such as Fat Man (Eric Pohlmann) and Milchmann (Victor Maddern).

The majority of the cast were staples of the *Carry On . . .* series. Kenneth Williams and Charles Hawtrey appeared in all previous (and most future) *Carry On* films, while Bernard Cribbins appeared in *Carry On Jack*, which was released the same year as *Carry On Spying*. Barbara Windsor made her first *Carry On* appearance in *Carry On Spying* but went on to appear in nine other films in the series.

Eric Barker and Victor Maddern would make sporadic appearances in the series. Barker started with *Carry On Sergeant* (1958) and even made an appearance years later in the last *Carry On* film, *Carry On Emmanuelle* (1978), a takeoff on the semipornographic French *Emmanuelle* series of films popular in the 1970s. *Carry On Emmanuelle* also happened to be Barker's last film role. Victor Maddern would have appearances in five films in the series, also ending with *Carry On Emmanuelle*.

Also like many other British films, *Carry On Spying* did have a cast member in common with James Bond, but not one that ever appeared on screen. Eric Pohlmann was the voice of Ernst Stavro Blofeld in Bond films *From Russia with Love* (1962) and *Thunderball* (1965).

Although most of the other *Carry On* films had limited runs or were not shown at all in theaters outside Great Britain, *Carry On Spying* was an example of a film being imported simply due to the James Bond/spy film craze (there was not an abundance of American schoolteachers clamoring to see *Carry On Teacher*). Newspaper ads for the film, in spy spoof fashion, gave the film the tagline "They're at it again—O.O.OH!" (*Carry On Spying* advertisement).

"Some films are good box-office because they are so bad. *Carry On Spying* is so bad it has a S.T.E.N.C.H.," said Douglas Goodlad of England's *Illustrated Chronicle*. He later clarified that the movie was a "good old fashioned slapstick free-for-all" and that "the gags rely heavily on predictability" (Goodlad "How Good Is Bad?," 4).

Meanwhile, Patrick Fleet of the *Evening Post* in Bristol, Avon, England, seemingly had a bigger problem with what he called Kenneth Williams's, Barbara Winsor's, and Bernard Cribbins's "back alley accents." Fleet wrote, "Is inverted snobbery a substitute for humour? Is it pretended that only the ill-bred could be such utter nitwits? The voices in a slim piece like this might as well sound pleasant. As it is, they grate, they whine and they sound as tatty as the film's ideas." Fleet added that Mr. Williams, "whose oleaginous voice can be one of the most gurgle-some things in the cinema," had "curdled into a caricature of a caricature" (Fleet "Back-Alley," 6).

Wanda Hale of the *Daily News* in New York was not amused by the film, writing, "If the *Carry On* producers can't do any better than *Carry On Spying*, they had better quit carrying on." She called the film "a burlesque on all spy thrillers and just plain silly" (Hale "Strange Bedfellows," 544).

Carry On Spying was listed as a "money maker" in the British Isles in 1964 by British film industry trade magazine *Kine Weekly*, along with other 1964 releases like *The Gorgon, The Curse of the Mummy's Tomb, Dr. Strangelove, West Side Story*, and another "Carry On" film, *Carry On Jack* (Altria "British Films," 9).

Hot Enough for June (1964; a.k.a. *Secret Agent 8¾*)

Based on the 1960 novel *The Night of Wenceslas* by Lionel Davidson, *Hot Enough for June,* filled with James Bondesque gadgets and running gags, was released right before the peak of the James Bond spy spoof craze.

In the film's opening scene, Britain's MI6 agent "007" has been declared deceased by the British Secret Intelligence Service, and an agent is needed to pick up an important document in Prague. Aspiring yet unemployed writer Nicholas Whistler (Dirk Bogarde) is recruited by Colonel Cunliffe (Robert Morley) and given what he believes to be a job at a London glass manufacturing company. Whistler soon finds out his job will take him behind the Iron Curtain and in the middle of international intrigue. Although Communist agents *know* he is a spy and sent from the West, it takes a little longer for Whistler to realize he is one. To make matters worse, Whistler falls for his chauffeur, Vlasta Simenova (Sylva Koscina), whose father, Simenova (Leo McKern), is head of the Czech secret police. (The film's title is taken from a spy sign/countersign— "Hot enough for June"/"You should have been here in September"—used in order to make contact with a fellow agent.)

The film's star, English actor and World War II hero Dirk Bogarde, was best known in the United States for imported British films *So Long as the Fair** (1950), *Doctor in the House* (1954), and *The Mind Benders* (1963). Previous to *Hot Enough for June*, Italian actress Sylva Koscina was known mostly for her

---

* Released under the much more ominous title *The Black Curse* in the United States.

role as the bride of Hercules (Steve Reeves), Princess Iole, in Italian sword-and-sandal epics *Hercules* (1958) and *Hercules Unchained* (1960).

Bushy eyebrowed British character actor Robert Morley, an Academy Award nominee for Best Supporting Actor for his role as King Louis XVI in *Marie Antoinette* (1938), typically played British gentleman roles in films and onstage throughout his illustrious career, which spanned six decades. Morley even played two other monarchs before his role in *Hot Enough for June*: King George III in *Beau Brummell* (1954) and Louis XI of France in *The Adventures of Quentin Durward* (1955). American audiences at the time may have been unfamiliar with Morley, but he eventually would play his British gentleman character in *Oh! Heavenly Dog* (1980), with Chevy Chase and Jane Seymour, *The Great Muppet Caper* (1981), and made-for-TV movie *Alice in Wonderland* (1985).

Hot Enough for June marked the eighth movie that director Ralph Thomas and Dirk Bogarde would make together, which included dramas *Campbell's Kingdom* (1957), *A Tale of Two Cities* (1958), and *The Wind Cannot Read* (1958) and comedies in what was known as the Doctor series: *Doctor in the House* (1954), *Doctor at Sea* (1955), *Doctor at Large* (1957), and *Doctor in Distress* (1963). The script was written by Lukas Heller. Heller previously wrote *What Ever Happened to Baby Jane?* (1962) and would go on to write *The Dirty Dozen* (1967) with Nunnally Johnson.

Hot Enough for June was financed by British production company, the Rank Organisation. The Rank Organisation also funded the first two Harry Palmer espionage films, *The Ipcress File* (1965) and *The Quiller Memorandum* (1967), and Bulldog Drummond thrillers *Deadlier Than the Male* (1967) and *Some Girls Do* (1969).

Reports of the film's production were covered by Hollywood gossip columnist Sheilah Graham, who wrote, "Dirk Bogarde gets the prettiest young actress in Europe, Sylva Koscina, for his *Hot Enough for June* picture." She added, "Dirk at around 40 is a bachelor. He had a crush on Judy Garland that evaporated during their picture, *I Could Go on Singing*." Although Graham's column linked Bogarde to leading ladies, it presumably was an attempt to deflect the ongoing rumors and innuendo about Bogarde's sexuality (Graham "Hollywood," 5).

Released in the UK in London at the Odeon Theater on March 5, 1964, the film was given mixed reviews from London critics, who all made the obvious comparison to James Bond ("Amusements Guide"). Patrick Gibbs of the *Daily Telegraph* believed it was "sad to find a subject so full of comic possibilities as contemporary espionage being sent down the drain." He added, "Not even the saucy promise of the title is redeemed since June turns out disappointingly to be the name of a month, not a girl. And a James Bond joke for the first scene, inviting comparisons as it does, is soon shown to be tactless (Gibbs "Old Cloak," 13).

The *Daily Herald*'s Margaret Hinxman wrote, "The trouble with guying James Bond is that he is his own best caricature." She added, "But while a reference to 007 can send ripples of delighted expectation round a cinema, you can't blame film-makers for trying. . . . Its idea of fun is broad and foolproof. It simply commandeers the standard tricks of the spy film, then inflates them to outrageous proportions or shrinks them to absurdity (Hinxman "Having Fun," 6). Meanwhile, Richard Roud of the *Guardian* bluntly stated it was a "rather boring film which fails miserably in an attempt to cash in on the James Bond vogue" (Roud "New Films," 11).

Hot Enough for June was released by Continental Film Distributors in America in 1965 but was retitled *Secret Agent 8¾* when it debuted west of the Atlantic Ocean in Detroit, Michigan, on August 21, 1965. Several minutes were slashed from the film's runtime in the American version ("Now Showing"). Continental Film Distributors is the same company that distributed legendary midnight horror movie *Night of the Living Dead* (1968), Dr. Who adventures *Dr. Who and the Daleks* (1965) and *Daleks' Invasion Earth 2150 A.D.* (1966), and Godzilla films *Ghidorah, the Three-Headed Monster* (1964) and *Ebirah, Horror of the Deep* (1966) in the United States.

Kine Weekly, a British film industry trade magazine, listed the film as a moneymaker in the UK in 1964. There is no record of how the film fared in theaters stateside (Altria "British Films").

Bogarde would go on to costar as the villainous Gabriel in avant spy-fi spoof *Modesty Blaise* (1966) and 1970s spy thriller *Permission to Kill* (1975). Koscina would play in Euro-spy films *That Man in Istanbul* (1965) and *Agent X-77 Orders to Kill* (1966), and Rank Organisation's Bulldog Drummond flick *Deadlier Than the Male* (1967).

The Spy Who Came In from the Cold (1965)

At the time when James Bond and spy films were just about to hit their peak as a pop culture craze and spy films were about to reach extravagant levels of action, Salem Films Limited produced and Paramount released a spy film based on a novel of the same name by John le Carré with a more serious and realistic tone: *The Spy Who Came In from the Cold*. Coming in "from the cold" refers to when a spy is taken out of the field and assigned to a desk job.

A year before the film's release, *Washington Post* columnist Peter Potomac (a.k.a. Roy H. Hoops) wrote an article in 1964 comparing Beatlemania to Bondmania. Potomac ended the article stating, "And if you want to read a *real* spy book, I recommend *The Spy Who Came In from the Cold*. It makes James Bond look like he still uses the greasy kid stuff." That was a reference to a 1962 Vitalis hair product television commercial featuring Green Bay Packers quarterback Bart Starr saying to a rookie player, "Say, you still using that greasy kid stuff?" "Greasy Kid Stuff" was even turned into a brand of its own by a pair of enterprising college students and became a novelty song by Janie Grant, both in 1962 (Potomac "The James Bond Mania," 18).

Shot at Ireland's Ardmore Studios and England's Shepperton complex, the film was directed by Martin Ritt. Ritt was an award-winning director, best known for his films *The Long, Hot Summer* (1958), *The Black Orchid* (1958), and *Hemingway's Adventures of a Young Man* (1962) ("Spy Who Came In").

Richard Burton, star of stage and screen, was cast in the lead. The casting of Burton gave the film some gravitas. The Shakespearean actor was nominated for Best Actor at the 1954 Academy Awards for *The Robe* (1953) and in 1965 for *Becket* (1964).

But being a spy film from the 1960s, *The Spy Who Came In from the Cold* had its connections to James Bond. The film featured James Bond alum Bernard Lee. At the time of *The Spy Who Came In from the Cold*'s release, Lee starred in three James Bond movies as the MI6 chief known as M and would play the character eleven times. As an almost antithesis to the colorful, over-the-top world of James Bond, *The Spy Who Came In from the Cold* was shot in black-and-white at a time when increasingly, the standard for film was color.

Despite being an English production, *The Spy Who Came In from the Cold* had what was described as a gala premiere on December 16, 1965, at the DeMille Theater located on Seventh Avenue on Times Square in Midtown Manhattan (Cameron "Burton"). Perhaps the best description of the film came from *New York Times* critic Bosley Crowther in his review:

> This fellow in this chiaroscuric[*] film . . . is a genuine secret agent who doesn't quite make it in from the cold. He's the fellow who, for his last assignment before retiring from British Intelligence, undertakes to pass himself as a defector and thus get into East Germany, where he is expected to foil the espionage apparatus by incriminating a German agent named Mundt. But, of course, when he gets into Germany he finds himself in a fantastic trap that has been set by—but hold! That would be telling. There are still some who haven't read the book. (Crowther "Le Carre's Best Seller," 24)

---

* Use of strong contrasts between light and dark.

In his review, Crowther, clearly getting tired of spy films, wrote, "After all the spy and mystery movies of a romantic and implausible nature that we have seen, it is great to see one as realistic, and believable, too, as *The Spy Who Came In from the Cold.*" He also stated, "Whether its tale of subtle intrigue, double and triple-cross, among international espionage agents and Communist secret police is one that actually happened is of minor consequence. The film makes you believe it could have happened. And that's the remarkable thing." And he added that the film is "so sharply staged and directed that it looks like a documentary film. It looks as though Mr. Ritt has slipped in with a handheld camera and started recording the movements of a British secret agent at the Berlin wall, and then followed him all the way on a long adventure of extraordinary complexity and peril, shooting all the while from hiding places, until he follows his man back to the wall for the final scene" (Crowther "Le Carre's Best Seller," 24). Crowther also recommended that filmgoers read the book before checking out the movie.

Marjory Adams of the *Boston Globe* felt that the film was perhaps a little too close to the book and would have liked to see Richard Burton "tear up a little furniture." She called the camerawork "remarkable—one of the finest melding of plot and photography of the past year. In fact the camerawork deserves as much credit as Burton." In her review, Adams even foresaw a possible award for Burton for his role (Adams "Best Selling," 25).

Adams turned out to be correct about the camerawork. At the 1966 Academy Awards, Richard Burton was nominated for Best Actor for the third time, and the film was nominated for Best Art Direction (Black-and-White). That same year, Burton won Best Actor and the film won for Best Art Direction and Best Cinematography at the British Academy Film Awards (BAFA).

The Spy Who Came In from the Cold was the thirty-second highest grossing film of the year in North America, reportedly earning $3,100,000 ("Big Rental Pictures of 1966").

The 2nd Best Secret Agent in the Whole Wide World (1965; a.k.a. *Licensed to Kill*)

When Britain's best secret agent (or as he was referred to in the film, "the boy who settled that gold conspiracy" in reference to James Bond's adventure in *Goldfinger* [1964]) is unavailable, the second-best secret agent, Charles Vine (Tom Adams), is called on to protect Swedish scientist Henrik Jacobsen (Karel Štěpánek), who has invented an antigravity machine for England.

Tom Adams was best known for his appearances in *The Great Escape* (1963) and later Disney's *Prince of Donegal* (1966). Czech actor Karel Štěpánek spent much of his career playing German heavies and previously played in the big-budget English World War II flick *Operation: Crossbow* (1965) that same year.

Originally released in Great Britain under the title *Licensed to Kill,* it was reported in October 1965 that Embassy Pictures acquired the movie for worldwide distribution and would release the film under the title *The 2nd Best Secret Agent in the Whole Wide World*. Embassy Pictures, owned by Joseph E. Levine, had success with a number of foreign films, such as *Godzilla! King of the Monsters* (1956), *Hercules* (1959), and *Hercules Unchained* (1960), for the American market ("Virna Signs").

Embassy even acquired the services of Rat Pack member Sammy Davis Jr. to record the theme song for the American version of the film. The theme was written and composed by Sammy Cahn and Jimmy Van Heusen and released as a single on Reprise records. The single included the B side "If You Want This Love of Mine" written by Baker Knight and performed by Sammy Davis Jr. (Wallace "Nicely, Nicely"). The trailer, filled with innuendo to both James

Illustrated poster for *The 2nd Best Secret Agent in the Whole Wide World* (1965).
© *1965 Embassy Pictures*

Bond and sex, stated, "Killing comes easy! Danger comes often! Women come first!"

Embassy Pictures held an essay contest to promote *The 2nd Best Secret Agent in the Whole Wide World*. Limited to one hundred words or less, entrants were asked to write about "the most unforgettable second best secret agent I have known." Winners were given complimentary tickets to the film (Sparks "From This Viewpoint," 31).

Although released as *Licensed to Kill* in England, the world premiere of the film under its new title was held on November 26, 1965, in Florida: at the Plaza Theatre in Hollywood Shopping Plaza, five Miami theaters, and the Gateway Theatre in Fort Lauderdale. To promote the premiere, Tom Adams, described by Florida newsman Clarence Leino as a "27-year-old, six-foot, 170-pound British actor with brown hair and eyes and a debonair charm who photographs in a manner that is devastating to females of all countries—which is okay with Embassy Pictures," posed with a plastic model pistol with a silencer next to his plate while he had lunch at Pier 66 in Fort Lauderdale. Reporters and photographers interviewed him and snapped pictures. When interviewed, Adams gave his opinion on American girls and American food: "One thing about American women I do not like are the iron-works they wear to enhance their natural contours." But later he admitted that he "likes all girls—even the ones I haven't met yet," adding that he had the lofty goal of meeting every attractive girl in the world (Leino "The Second Best Secret Agent," 32).

The film later opened in Texas, then in New York, and finally had a much wider, national release on December 22, 1965. Advertisements for the picture exclaimed,

> Charles Vine is not the first . . . he's not the last . . . but he's THE SECOND BEST SECRET AGENT IN THE WHOLE WIDE WORLD, and that's why he has to spy harder, love more dangerously and fight more deadlier than the higher priced agent. Although known around spy circles as the "second best" secret agent. Charles Vine proves himself a first-class man killer and lady-killer in Joseph E. Levine's spy-spoof in color and wide-screen. He is, however, No. 1 at something: "THE SECOND BEST SECRET AGENT IN THE WHOLE WIDE WORLD" opens December 22nd . . . three days ahead of the high priced agent.

The "high priced agent" obviously referred to James Bond and his newest adventure, *Thunderball*, which was released at that time (*The 2nd Best Secret Agent in the Whole Wide World* advertisement).

Tom Adams was asked about his thoughts about being compared to the James Bond character and if he, like Sean Connery, feared being typecast. "I don't think much of it," responded Adams. "After all, where would he be with-out the Bond pictures? Not that he hasn't proven he could do other things but I get fed up with his attitude about being type-cast. I compare it to throwing away a mink coat when the pockets get filled up with trash" ("Adams Kids," 75).

Elston Brooks of the *Fort Worth Star-Telegram* noted that Tom Adams certainly used his license to kill, shooting seventeen people to death in the film, and rounded the total body count in the film to thirty. He added, "There are no survivors in this latest attempt by the movie industry to ride a once-good horse to death," in reference to the latest spy craze (Brooks "Sometimes Trying Harder," 10).

Buffalo News correspondent Ardis Smith believed that "the second best agent was surely no threat to replace 007" (Smith "Second Best Agent," 57). Henry T. Murdock of the *Philadelphia Inquirer* wrote that "as the title indicates *The Second Best Secret Agent in the Whole Wide World* has no intention of tak-ing itself seriously and completely lives up to that lack of intention" (Murdock "Movie Spoofs Spy," 10).

The Syracuse, New York, *Post-Standard* called the film "definitely 2nd Rate," writing that "Tom Adams, as Charles Vine, the pinch-hitter for what's his name, battles an assortment of counter-spies but his greatest enemy is a scrip which aims at spoof but falls into vulgar burlesque" ("2nd Best," 16). *Variety* wrote, "Almost every film-producing country in the world has jumped aboard the spy-wagon since 007 turned out to be the magic number that turned on the box office. Some imitations were made in such haste, however, that even Sean Connery wouldn't recognize them as carbons" (*Variety Film Reviews*, 271). The Catholic Church's Legion of Decency classified *The 2nd Best Secret Agent in the Whole Wide World* as A-3, meaning the film should be seen by adults only ("Legion of Decency").

The 2nd Best Secret Agent in the Whole Wide World did surprisingly well at the box office and grossed $900,000 in North America, according to *Variety* ("Big Rental Pictures of 1966"). The film generated two sequels: *Where the Bullets Fly* (1966) and *Somebody's Stolen Our Russian Spy* (1967).

Modesty Blaise (1966)

While many spy films of the era feature female characters, they are often rel-egated to a supporting role, a sex object for the male protagonist, or even an occassional villain. However, *Modesty Blaise*, based on a comic strip by Peter O'Donnell, featured Monica Vitti in the title role of a criminal mastermind–turned–secret agent for the British Secret Service in exchange for immunity.

At the time, Monica Vitti was relatively unknown to English-speaking audiences; mostly working in Italy, she starred in a number of comedies and dramas.

In the film, Blaise is tasked with protecting diamonds being sent to the Middle East in exchange for oil from Blaise's ruthless platinum-haired archnemesis Gabriel (Dirk Bogarde). Also featured is Terence Stamp as Blaise's sidekick, Willie Garvin. One year earlier, he received the Best Actor Award at the Cannes Film Festival for *The Collector* (1965). Three years earlier than that, Stamp was nominated for an Academy Award for Best Supporting Actor and received a Golden Globe Award for Most Promising Male Newcomer for his role in *Billy Budd* (1962). Also featured are character actors Harry Andrews and Michael Creig as two stereotypical uptight British secret agents, Sir Gerald Tarrant and Paul Hagen.

Associated Press writer Norman Goldstein was quick to note that *Modesty Blaise* was part of a new batch of imported films that were based on European comic strips, such as *Danger: Diabolik* (1968) and *Barbarella* (1968). Unlike previous works based on comic strips, the three movies he mentioned were adult features but reflected "the needs of a troubled society seeking the far-out, the pure escapism of the comic strip hero world in which we all don the mental cape of fantasy" (Goldstein "Comics Great," 23).

The film had a 1960s ultramod with futuristic pop art look and feel and was filled with sex, action, and comedy. The trailer also had the same stylings of *Modesty Blaise*'s European comic-strip counterpart *Barbarella*.

The movie was well reviewed at the Cannes Film Festival in 1966, but not every critic at the festival enjoyed the film. Bosley Crowther of the *New York Times* wrote, "What in blazes *Modesty Blaise* is supposed to be getting at, with all the op art and the comic-strip nonsense Joseph Losey has thrown into it, is something that puzzled this reviewer on first seeing it at the festival in Cannes. And it still puzzles me after seeing it again." Crowther added, "There's more fun in one good sequence of a Bond picture than there is in the whole of *Modesty Blaise*. . . . Maybe, if the whole thing were on a par with some of its flashier and wittier moments, or were up to its pictorial design, which is dazzling, it might be applauded as a first-rate satiric job. But it isn't. Nor is it consistent. It jumps between quick and clever gags and stretches of sheer sophomoric clowning" ("James Bond Spoof fff"; Crowther "Gaudy," 27).

Monica Vitti mainly worked in Italy following *Modesty Blaise*'s release and did not appear in many other English-language films. But a year after *Modesty Blaise* was released, it was rumored that James Bond producers were considering Terence Stamp to take over the role of James Bond after Sean Connery stepped away from the role after making *You Only Live Twice* (1967). However, that never came to fruition. Stamp notably would play General Zod in *Superman* (1978) and *Superman II* (1980) and would be a noted character actor, perhaps best known for his villainous roles, the rest of his career.

According to *Variety, Modesty Blaise* was the forty-first highest grossing film of 1966, earning $2.2 million ("Big Rental Pictures of 1966").

The Quiller Memorandum (1966)

Based on the best-selling novel *The Berlin Memorandum* by Adam Hall, *The Quiller Memorandum* features George Segal as Quiller, an American spy assigned to expose the headquarters of a neo-Nazi faction. Alec Guinness plays Quiller's boss, Pol, in a small but memorable role.

After discovering the headquarters with the help of schoolteacher Inge Lindt (Senta Berger), both are captured, but Quiller is released and must return with the location of American agents or they will murder Inge (whom Quiller has slept with). Now Quiller must run from the Nazis, led by Oktober (Max von Sydow), and expose the location of the headquarters to the British Secret Intelligence Service.

The Quiller Memorandum had its London premiere at the Odeon Leicester Square on November 10, 1966. It was released internationally soon afterward, making its screen debut in the United States a little more than a month later, on December 15, 1966. The film was later released in Japan under the title *Farewell Berlin Lights* ("Alec Guinness"; Cameron "Car Racing").

Reporters were quick to point out that the film was "disturbingly topical" due to an election of an ex-Nazi as chancellor of West Germany in 1967 and the rise of an ultra-right wing party in Germany, which some considered to be neo-Nazis (Stargazer's; Fox "Quiller"). George Segal was satisfied with his role in the film, stating, "As much as I cringe when I watch myself on the screen, my reaction when I saw *The Quiller Memorandum* was 'I like that guy'" (Crosby "Long Road," 8).

Despite Segal's assurance, reviews were mixed. Reviews throughout Great Britain called the film "a colorful and craftsman like thriller," "a refreshingly different kind of spy story," "elegant, well-made entertainment," and "the best of both kinds of spy films." Russell Claughton even remarked that the film had "no flaws." Theaters in London reported that *The Quiller Memorandum* was "doing the biggest business since *Goldfinger*" ("Unique Spy," 29; Claughton "Quiller," 2).

Lew Cedrone of the *Evening Sun* in Baltimore was concerned about the film's realism. "The film is done rather straight, but Segal goes about his work

Poster for *The Quiller Memorandum* (1966). © *20th Century Fox Film Corp.*

as though he is Humphrey Bogart in Berlin, every girl Lauren Bacall." Cedrone added, "[Segal] is very foolish when it comes to spying, going about it as though it were a game, as though he knows nothing really bad is going to happen to him because he's read the script" (Cedrone "Different Kind," 10).

Variety wrote the film was a "smoothly produced and directed topical spy drama devoid of gimmickry [in reference to the ever expanding and extravagant James Bond gadgets and gimmicks] and with compelling performances." In addition, the film had "good marquee value for all situations" (*Variety Film Reviews*, 415). Wayne Wilson of the *Valley News* in Van Nuys, California, told readers to "make a note to see *The Quiller Memorandum*" (Wilson "Capsule," 32).

Motion picture editor, Harry Haun, for the *Tennessean* in Nashville, Tennessee, wrote that *The Quiller Memorandum,* was a "spybrid" of "both Beat and Bond." Haun also wrote that though the film "leans strongly toward the beat breeds of spies, it [Segal's beat attitude] at least doesn't get in the way of his work. He skitters through a series of close calls in the Cold War era without once reaching for a quick-kill gimmick or even a functional .44. His weapon is his wit, which eventually wins the fray . . . since he's not dealing with the usual dumbkopf movie-villains" (Haun "Spybrid," 7).

The Quiller Memorandum was filmed in Deluxe Color and shot in Panavision on location in Berlin, Germany, and included a number of scenes in and around famous Berlin landmarks. John Barry, who arranged and performed the "James Bond Theme" for *Dr. No* (1962), composed *The Quiller Memorandum*'s soundtrack, which featured the song "Wednesday's Child." The song was performed by Matt Monro, who also recorded the theme to the second James Bond movie, *From Russia with Love* (1963).

The Quiller Memorandum was the fifty-ninth highest grossing film of 1967 in North America, earning approximately $1,500,000 at the box office ("Big Picture Rental Films of 1967").

Where the Bullets Fly (1966)

In September 1966, it was announced that Joseph E. Levine of Embassy Pictures was releasing a sequel to 1965 Bond spoof *The 2nd Best Secret Agent in the Whole Wide World* (1965), titled *Where the Bullets Fly*. The film marks the return of Tom Adams as England's number-two secret agent Charles Vine. The announcement noted that the company planned a Thanksgiving release and that in the new film, "Vine attempts to protect 'Spurium,' a new substance for atomic radiation shields, from foul play." Angel (Michael Ripper), the chief villain and head of "International Export Limited," subjects Vine to hypnotic gas, bullet-shooting umbrellas, and an electronic torture room, among other diabolical devices ("New Spy Thriller").

The plot does go deeper, however. The "Spurium," which enables the Royal Air Force to fly nuclear aircrafts, is stolen by Angel. To make matters worse, Angel's organization kidnaps Agent Tom Vine, keeps him in what R. H Gardner of the *Baltimore Sun* called an "LSD dungeon," and replaces him with an evil agent named Seraph, played by Tim Barrett (Gardner "'Second Best Agent' Sequel," 23).

Michael Ripper notably appeared in Hammer horror films *The Revenge of Frankenstein* (1958), *The Mummy* (1959), *The Curse of the Mummy's Tomb* (1964), and *The Plague of the Zombies* (1966). Best known in England for his work on television, Tim Barrett appeared in the miniseries *Quatermass and the Pit* (1959) and the spy series *The Avengers* (1961–1967).

Royal Air Force pilot Lt. Felicity "Fiz" Moonlight, the film's true hero and love interest of Vine is played by a real-life princess, Dawn Addams. At the time Addams was married to Don Vittorio Emanuele Massimo, Prince of Roccasecca. The royal couple divorced in 1971. Addams was a regular on the big screen in films like Charlie Chaplin's *A King in New York* (1957) and more notably on television, appearing in espionage favorites on *The Saint* (1962–1969) and on the second run of *Danger Man* (1964–1968).

The film would be directed by John Gilling, who was not a stranger to action/adventure films. Gilling directed films such as *Fury at Smugglers' Bay* (1961) and *Panic* (1963). He also directed a string of Hammer horror films: *The Shadow of the Cat* (1961), *The Plague of the Zombies* (1966), and *The Reptile* (1966). Gilling stated, "We're not just out to have fun. We're also showing that espionage is a business, just like any other." He added, "In *Where the Bullets Fly*, you not only will see the hero face exotic obstacles like hypnotic gas and electronic torture but also will see comic scenes of gadgets trying to cope with making out their expense accounts and espionage directors with personal problems. The Foreign Service or the CIA, like any other big organization, must deal with these mundane problems. This gives us great latitude for some pointed humor" ("Like Us All," 6).

It was also announced that the movie's theme "Where the Bullets Fly" was recorded by Susan Maughan. Maughan was best known for recording the Marcie Blane song "Bobby's Girl," which reached number three on the UK Singles charts in December 1962. The *Runcorn Weekly News* in Runcorn, Cheshire, England, reviewed the theme and said it "owes a lot to *Goldfinger*, same tempo, same backing, just new words" ("Hollies Chart," 5).

Where the Bullets Fly was released in both England, where it often played with *The Night of the Grizzly* (1966) as its double feature, and the United States in November 1966. Mostly ignored by major critics, *Where the Bullets Fly* was poorly received when it was reviewed. The aforementioned R. H. Gardner of the *Baltimore Sun* said the film was not as funny as its predecessor *The 2nd Best Secret Agent in the Whole Wide World* ("a lot of spy-spoofs have gone under the bridge since [*2nd Best*]—it is still entertaining"). And the *Lincolnshire Echo* in Lincolnshire, England, wrote, "The glut of spy spoof films has tended to make one more critical about them." In addition, the film was a "dismal, padded-out story which limpingly unfolds. Nearly everything that occurs has happened before, and much better" (Gardner "*Second Best Agent* Sequel," 23; "Tricky Film," 4). Like *The 2nd Best Secret Agent in the Whole Wide World*, the Catholic Church's Legion of Decency classified *Where the Bullets Fly* as A-3, recommending the film should be seen by adults only ("Moral Evaluations").

Where the Bullets Fly was followed up the next year by *Somebody's Stolen Our Russian Spy*, again starring Tom Adams as Charles Vine. In the film, Vine rescues a Soviet spy from the Albanian Secret Service, which planned on blaming the Soviet's kidnapping on the British. The film was not released until 1976, when it finally played in a small number of theaters in England after sitting on the shelf for eight years.

Where the Spies Are (1966)

Originally titled *Passport to Oblivion* and based on a novel written by James Leasor, *Where the Spies Are* began production under the direction of Val Guest in 1964 in Beirut, Lebanon. It was called a "light-hearted adventure in the Middle-East" with "beautiful women and sinister men" (Scheuer "Story of Taj Mahal," 54).

Where the Spies Are starred David Niven as a World War II–era intelligence agent turned medical doctor Jason Love. Love was recruited to return to his former occupation and was tasked with finding the whereabouts of a missing agent. French star Françoise Dorléac portrayed a fashion model and Love's love interest, Vikki. The film quickly takes the pair around the globe, uncovering international intrigue and avoiding death via enemy spies in a number of exotic locations.

Newspaper ads for the film leaned into the James Bond fad writing, "From Russia, Beirut, London, Rom and Byblos with LOVE!" and "That's secret agent Jason Love who takes you where the spies are!" (*Where the Spies Are* advertisement).

Variety wrote that "Metro [Goldwyn-Mayer] is latest to board the spy melodrama bandwagon" in order to exploit profitability of spy films but noted that *Where the Spies Are* was not a low-budget production. *Variety* touted the film's "excellent production values" and "outstanding" photography in Panavision and Metrocolor (*Variety Film Reviews*, 280).

Released in January 1966, the film had a nationwide release in the United States but was eclipsed by *Thunderball*, which was released in the states around the same time. Many critics also preferred Bond. Phyllis Funke of the *Courier-Journal* in Louisville, Kentucky, wrote that the film "offers deeply entangled and sometimes fast moving adventure" and that it "may not have the dash and splash of many of its recent predecessors, but, in its own quite self-reliant way, it plays a good game of hide-and-seek." Anne Miller Tinsley of the *Fort Worth Star-Telegram* in Fort Worth, Texas, wrote that "there is some interesting photography, and the plot is suspenseful in a few places. But the picture is disjointed and transparent" and that Niven's talent and Dorléac's looks were "wasted on such a flimsy movie." Tinsley added that the film is "another of those you-know-what movies-copy catting you-know-who" (Funke "Where the Spies Are," 33; Tinsley "No Escape," 20).

One of the only positive reviews came from the notoriously difficult to impress *New York Times* critic Howard Thompson: "As head-on entertainment, the new picture is a peach. Don't believe those teasing Bond-style ads." In addition, "with excellent dialogue, the scenes click along with deceptive casualness. . . . The general tone ranges from wry to grim, with some touches of genuine amusement and one splash of sex, with Françoise Dorléac that seems as reasonable as the rest. Furthermore, even as the action gathers crescendo, Mr. [Val] Guest keeps a restraining hand on the throttle" (Thompson "An Original Spy?," 29).

Three years prior to the film's release, David Niven was considered for the role of James Bond in the first James Bond film, *Dr. No.* Niven, who looked close to Ian Fleming's description of Bond in his novel *From Russia with Love* (slim build . . . blue-grey eyes; a "cruel" mouth; short, black hair, a comma of which rests on his forehead), was rumored to be Fleming's personal choice for the character. In 1967, a year after *Where the Spies Are* was released, Niven would play the "original" James Bond in Columbia Pictures' parody film *Casino Royale.*

The spy genre kept director Val Guest busy throughout the mid-1960s. Although Guest was perhaps best known for making a number of horror films for Hammer Films, such as *The Quatermass Xperiment* (1955), *Quatermass II* (1957), and *The Abominable Snowman* (1957), Guest directed spy flicks

Ian Fleming's choice to play James Bond, David Niven, in *Where the Spies Are* (1966). © *1966 Metro-Goldwyn-Mayer, Inc.*

Where the Spies Are (1966), segments of *Casino Royale* (1967), and *Assignment K* (1968).

Before the film's release, in 1965, the *Los Angeles Times* reported MGM planned on producing more adventures featuring Dr. Jason Love. The studio even optioned the contracts of Val Guest and David Niven for a total of five films, presumably hoping the films would become the next James Bond franchise. *Where the Spies Are* was the only Dr. Jason Love film produced (Martin "Movie Call Sheet").

Danger Route (1967)

Released as a double feature with *Attack on the Iron Coast* (1967), a World War II action film starring Lloyd Bridges, *Danger Route* was based on a novel titled *The Eliminator*, by Andrew York. Before resigning his post, top British secret agent Jonas Wilde (Richard Johnson) is given one more mission by his commander Tony Canning (Harry Andrews): to assassinate a defector being held by the Americans. Of course, Wilde encounters a number of enemy agents and femme fatales throughout the film.

The film's star, Richard Johnson, who was rumored to be *Dr. No* (1962) director Terence Young's first choice to play the role of James Bond, previously starred in the World War II spy picture *Operation Crossbow* (1965), the Bulldog Drummond adventure *Deadlier Than the Male* (1967), and, later, its sequel, *Some Girls Do* (1969).

Produced by Amicus Productions, *Danger Route* was clearly made to exploit the popularity of the James Bond films. The theme was even composed by Lionel Bart, who provided the theme to the second James Bond film, *From Russia with Love* (1963). Director Seth Holt was not a stranger to the spy genre, previously directing episodes of the first incarnation of British television's *Danger Man* (1960–1962) and an episode of *Espionage* (1963–1964). He was the original director of *Danger: Diabolik* (1968), a film that was later taken over by Mario Bava.

New York Times columnist Howard Thompson believed that *Danger Route* "trails a host of predecessors with spies, counterspies and more spies, but it packs considerable punch and tension along the way." He added, "*Danger Route* ... is one of those espionage packages where nobody, including the hero, is quite what he seems. This includes the baby-faced Carol Lynley, cast as a sleek worldling. In any case, Mr. Johnson, treacherously assigned to polish off the wrong victim, shoots and karate-chops his way from London to the countryside and the Channel Islands, stalked by some suave killers and protectors.

. . . What hoists *Danger Route* to the level of pretty good pulp melodrama is the incisive dialogue, especially the clipped direction of Seth Holt, who gathers it all up at about mid-point, and hurls it at the camera. Fair enough. At least it's fast, for all the plot absurdities" (Thompson "British Double Bill," 54). The *Monthly Film Bulletin* believed the film was confusing, a "tired, and tiring muddle of a film with characters interestingly introduced and then abruptly dropped only to turn up later as though nothing has happened in the meantime" ("Danger Route," 8).

Danger Route was a failure at the box office, and a year after the film's release, director Seth Holt said that the film was "dreadful," stating that he "scarcely saw it finished. I had a very difficult schedule. I was waiting between one and another and I needed the bread" (Gough-Yates "Seth Holt," 17).

Deadlier Than the Male (1967)

In 1920, H. C. McNeile released the book *Bull-Dog Drummond*, the first in a long-running series of books featuring the title character Hugh "Bulldog" Drummond. Originally, Drummond was a decorated British World War I veteran who was looking for action and adventure in his life. Drummond would routinely take down the likes of enemy saboteurs, counterfeiters, and terrorists. Two years later, films featuring Drummond began to be produced, starting with the silent film *Bulldog Drummond* (1922). In total, prior to *Deadlier Than the Male*, the character was featured in twenty-two feature-length films, and *Deadlier Than the Male* was the first Bulldog Drummond film produced in sixteen years. But there were talks of reviving the franchise as early as 1962 because of the box office success of *Dr. No* earlier that year ("Comeback for Hero").

Drummond (Richard Johnson), now presented as a Korean War veteran–turned–private insurance investigator, is tasked to track down two deadly female assassins for hire, Irma Eckman (Elke Sommer) and Penelope (Sylva Koscina), along with their boss, Carl Petersen (Nigel Green). Capitalizing on the James Bond and spy craze, Drummond was presented as a James Bond type—a well-dressed, sophisticated, womanizing gentleman action hero.

Richard Johnson was reportedly *Dr. No* (1962) director Terence Young's first choice to play James Bond and played in the big-budget WWII spy film *Operation Crossbow* (1965). The same year *Deadlier Than the Male* was released, Johnson would later go on to play another Bondesque character in *Danger Route* (1967). Sylva Koscina was in spy adventures *Hot Enough for June* (1964), *That Man in Istanbul* (1965), and *Agent X-77 Orders to Kill* (1966). Elke Sommer would go on to play in *The Wrecking Crew* (1968), which starred Dean Martin as secret agent Matt Helm. Character actor Nigel Green also had experience in the spy field, previously playing in *The Ipcress File* (1965), and would also go on to appear in *The Wrecking Crew* (1968).

Upon announcement of the film's production and that Drummond would be portrayed as a character more akin to James Bond, Australian newspaper *The Age* asked, "Is Bondmania finally on the wane?" And it opined that Drummond fans' excitement would presumably be "tempered by the thought of what the modern 'treatment' will do to the old hero's image" ("Out?," 2).

The film was released by the Rank Organisation. The Rank Organisation also brought audiences 1960s spy flicks *Hot Enough for June* (1964) and the first two Harry Palmer films *The Ipcress File* (1965) and *The Quiller Memorandum* (1967). Producer Betty E. Box was one of the few female producers in the genre, having produced *Hot Enough for June* and later *Deadlier Than the Male*'s sequel *Some Girls Do* (1969) for the Rank Organisation. The reportedly $1.7 million production began in London on May 23, 1966, previewed in both the UK and the United States in February 1967, and was released in both countries on February 12, 1967 (Weiler "Comedians"; Martin "The Visitors' Film Roles").

Critics did not like the new Bond oriented Drummond. *Variety* wrote, "There is no doubt that *Deadlier Than the Male* is loaded with colorful and exciting production values . . . production will strike some as okay dual bill escapism, and others as overly raw, offensive and single entendre. Sadism, sex and attempted sophistication mark this latest Bulldog Drummond pic, with Richard Johnson starred. Elke Sommer heads a long list of lookers. Femme audiences may be repelled by the abundant sadism, and [box office] prospects appear most promising for Universal release in male-oriented." *Variety* continued to talk about the film's violence: "There are about nine explicitly gory episodes . . . these are made deliberately obvious and are protracted to excess. Also, there are three major explosions which take human life. Adding up, it works out to one death-dealing event every eight minutes or so." Although the publication called Ralph Thomas's direction "routine," the "lush eye appeal in sets, locations, wardrobe and femmes" was praised (*Variety Film Reviews*, 444).

Bill Strobel of the *Oakland Tribune* wrote that Bulldog Drummond was "back and looking very much like James Bond if Bond were appearing in a comic strip written by [*Playboy* magazine owner and editor] Hugh Hefner." He continued, "I shudder to think what the filmmakers could do for instance to Sherlock Holmes. I can almost see the old boy now prancing around Baker Street pad in a mod suit, chasing chicks while Doc Watson orders another bottle of booze from sexy Mrs. Hudson downstairs" (Strobel "Drummond Back," 9).

Motion picture editor of the *Nashville Tennessean* Harry Haun believed that the new Drummond film "could well have been shaped by the James Bond cookie-cutter" and that the film "toying with contemporary sex 'n' sadism is a ghastly end for such a civilized sleuth" (Haun "All Bite," 20).

Deadlier Than the Male was followed up by the sequel *Some Girls Do* (1969).

Assignment K (1968)

Philip Scott (Stephen Boyd) runs an English toy company that in reality is a front for a British Secret Intelligence Service, the same organization James Bond works for, a branch headed by its chief, a man simply known as Harris (Michael Redgrave). When Scott's cover is blown while at a ski resort in Kitzbühel, Austria, and his girlfriend Toni (Camilla Sparv) is kidnapped by a man named "Smith" (Leo McKern) and his evil spy crew, Scott must rescue his girlfriend while making sure that Smith's crew does not get ahold of valuable microfilm and state secrets.

Based on the pulp novel *Department K* by Hartley Howard, the British-produced spy thriller *Assignment K* was directed by Val Guest. Guest previously

Assignment K (1968) lobby card featuring Stephen Boyd and Camilla Sparv. © 1968 Columbia Pictures Corp.

directed Hammer Films science fiction/horror films *The Quatermass Xperiment* (1955), *Quatermass II* (1957), and *The Abominable Snowman* (1957). He was not a stranger to the spy genre, having directed the David Niven spy spoof *Where the Spies Are* (1965) and segments of MGM's James Bond film *Casino Royale* (1967).

Assignment K marked Stephen Boyd's first espionage film in twelve years. Boyd previously played a pro-Nazi Irish spy in *The Man Who Never Was* (1956) and was best known for his roles in *Ben-Hur* (1959) and *Fantastic Voyage* (1966). Two years earlier, Camilla Sparv played in Dean Martin spy spoof *Murderers' Row* (1966). Leo McKern appeared in the British spy comedy *Hot Enough for June* (1964) and episodes of the spy-fi television show *The Prisoner* (1967–1968). Michael Redgrave was knighted in 1959 by Queen Elizabeth II and was best known for *The Browning Version* (1951), *The Night My Number Came Up* (1955), and *Time without Pity* (1957).

The film also featured a number of skiing scenes filmed in Kitzbühel, Austria, a trope that would not be seen in Bond films until a year later, in *On Her Majesty's Secret Service* (1969). Although new and exciting in the early 1960s, by 1968 the secret agent film genre was losing steam and originality. Critics clearly felt this way as well.

Los Angeles Times entertainment editor Charles Champlin showed his frustration with the genre in his review of *Assignment K*: "It's secret agent time again, the murky battles of Them vs. Us, the clandestine meetings, the messages in cigarette butts and coffee cans, the microfilm in a match-box left on a train the double-crossing and the femme fatale." He added, "The dialog is intermittently sophisticated, very intermittently, and the total effect is old chapeau, very old chapeau"* (Champlin "K Opens," 91).

Vincent Canby of the *New York Times* wrote that *Assignment K* was "earnest and totally confusing" (Canby "Fright Seeds," 18). David Adams of England's *Kensington Post* believed *Assignment K* was "hardly worth commenting on . . . another example of a movie with a hopeless script trying to cover the default up by having the characters say the words with beautiful sights in the background" (Adams "Snow and Satire," 17). However, the *Fort Lauderdale News* felt that *Assignment K*, which was almost always the second film on a double feature, deserved better even if it was not "a Landmark spy adventure film" but felt that the film was "pleasant and often suspenseful entertainment" ("*Assignment K* Suspenseful," 37). Newspaper ads and the trailer attempted to explain what the "K" in *Assignment K* stood for, exclaiming: "K is for: Kissing, Killing, Kitzbühel, Karate, and a big new Kind of Excitement!" (*Assignment K* advertisement).

---

* Old hat (uninteresting, predictable, old-fashioned).

Assignment K had a very limited run in theaters in the United States and ran in Southern California drive-ins as the second feature to the avant-garde melodrama *The Swimmer* (1968), starring Burt Lancaster. Nationally the film often played along with the James Coburn and James Mason comedy *Duffy* (1968) or the horror film *Torture Garden* (1967), starring Burgess Meredith and Jack Palance.

Some Girls Do (1969)

In May 1968 it was announced that Richard Johnson would return to the role of Bulldog Drummond in *Some Girls Do*, the sequel to *Deadlier Than the Male* (1967), and that producer Betty E. Box and director Ralph Thomas would be returning as well. Production on the film, written by David Osborn, began that month at Pinewood Studios—at the same time and at the same location as the filming of the sixth James Bond adventure *On Her Majesty's Secret Service* (1969) ("James Bond's Sixth").

Not long afterward, Dahliah Lavi and Beba Loncar joined the cast. Israeli-born Lavi previously appeared in the Matt Helm film *The Silencers* (1966) and as one of the many James Bonds (that is, a female 007, going by the nickname The Detainer) in *Casino Royale* (1967). Yugoslavian-born Loncar, who mostly appeared in films throughout the European continent, was not a stranger to the spy genre. Loncar previously appeared in Euro-spy films *Lucky, the Inscrutable* (1967) and *The Fuller Report* (1968). Also cast was British character actor James Villiers, known for his role in the horror film *The Damned* (1963), who would go on to play in the Bond film *For Your Eyes Only* (1981) starring Roger Moore ("Smith, Carr").

Some Girls Do had a similar plot to *Deadlier Than the Male*—but with one twist. When Britain's new supersonic plane, the SST-1, is involved in what is believed to be an accident, Bulldog Drummond is called to investigate. While on assignment, several attempts are made on Drummond's life, and he is captured by the evil Carl Peterson (James Villiers) and his two female assassins—however, this time the two female assassins (Dahliah Lavi and Beba Loncar) are really sexy humanoid robots.

In this film, Bulldog Drummond manages to lean in even further to the obvious comparisons to James Bond by driving Bond's signature Aston Martin DB5.

While many previews and reviews of the film focused on the sex appeal of Dahliah Lavi and Beba Loncar, Loncar hoped audiences looked at more than her beauty. "I think people think of me as more of an actress than a sex symbol," said Loncar. "I'm not sure if it's a good thing. Sex symbols earn more money than I do" ("Killer Legs," 98; "Beguiling," 8; "Dubbing Removes," 23).

The movie premiered in the United Kingdom in January 1969 but had a wider release in the country two months later. The film had screenings in the United States in late 1968, but it did not have a wide US release until 1971. Although just three short years had passed, by the time *Some Girls Do* was widely released in the United States, the movie seemed like a relic of the past.

The New York *Daily News* wrote that the plot of *Some Girls Do* was "so antiquated by now it practically creaks," and *The Record* in Hackensack, New Jersey, said, "Just when we thought, wished, hoped we'd seen the last of James Bond imitations, along comes *Some Girls Do*." ("Spy Film Is Just," 89; "Much Derring-Do," 37).

The *New York Times* noted, "There's a gaggle of gorgeous lovelies who could be enlivening *Playboy* centerfolds in *Some Girls Do*." And it called the film a "British pseudo-comic adventure" that was a "distant cousin of James Bond" ("*Some Girls Do* Arrives," 55).

Some Girls Do was the last Bulldog Drummond film produced.

5

EURO-SPY ESPIONAGE

The great trains are going out all over Europe, one by one, but still, three times a week, the Orient Express thunders superbly over the 1,400 miles of glittering steel track between Istanbul and Paris.

—Ian Fleming, *From Russia with Love*

Throughout the European continent, especially in Italy, West Germany, and France, filmmakers looked to capitalize on the spy craze and occasionally the Bond name.

That Man from Rio (1964)

A French-Italian international coproduction, *That Man from Rio* was directed by Nouvelle Vague* (French New Wave) director Philippe De Broca and was shot on location in France, the jungles of the Amazon, and (as the title suggests) Rio De Janeiro, Brazil ("Presenting 'That Man'").

Adrien Dufourquet (Jean-Paul Belmondo), an airline pilot on leave in Paris, quickly gets caught up in international intrigue when his fiancée Agnès (Françoise Dorléac) is abducted along with a museum curator, Professor Catalan (Adolfo Celi), and an Amazonian statue by indigenous South Americans. Adrien finds himself in a chase around the globe to rescue his fiancée, find Professor Catalan, and reclaim the stolen statue.

---

* A French art movement that began in the 1950s and rejected conventional aesthetics and conventions in art and film.

Many of the film's stars had links to other spy films of the era. Previously starring in the 1960 French crime drama written and directed by leading Nouvelle Vague director Jean-Luc Godard, *Breathless* (1960), Jean-Paul Belmondo would star in French films *Pierrot le Fou* (1965), *Borsalino* (1970), and *The Professional* (1981). A year after *That Man from Rio*'s release, Belmondo began a relationship with Ursula Andrews, Bond girl from *Dr. No* (1962).

Françoise Dorléac later starred in spy genre films *Where the Spies Are* (1966), directed by Val Guest, and the final Harry Palmer adventure *Billion Dollar Brain* (1968). Adolfo Celi would go on to play SPECTRE agent Emilio Largo in the Bond film *Thunderball* (1965) and also in fellow Euro-spy film *OK Connery* (1967), which starred Sean Connery's younger brother, Neil Connery, and also went under the title of both *Operation Kid Brother* and *Operation Double 007*.

That Man from Rio was released in France on February 5, 1964, but did not premiere in the United States until June 8, 1964, at the Paris Theaters in New York. The "gala American premiere," as it was described by New York's *Daily News*, was sponsored by La Maison Française* of New York University ("*Man from Rio* Premiere," 69).

Soon the French language film with English subtitles began popping up in theaters throughout the United States. Although critics knocked many of the spy films of the era, especially ones that did not star Sean Connery, they had a positive take on *That Man from Rio*.

An advertisement for the film ran in the *Los Angeles Times* on January 20, 1965, touting the film's critical acclaim:

"Best foreign film of the year!" *New York Film Critics*

"A riotous affair!" *Herald-Examiner* (New York, New York)

"IRRESISTIBLE . . . a kind of James Bond thriller New Wave fashion." *Los Angeles Times*

"Wacky and crazy . . . a lot of fun!" Louella O Parsons, *Chicago's American*

"A wild and wonderful time! Continually hilarious! 1,000 thrills 1,000." *Time Magazine*.

(*That Man from Rio* advertisement)

On the other side of the country, an advertisement in New York's *Daily News* provided a number of additional reviews:

---

* A cultural exchange between the French-speaking world and the United States, based out of NYU.

Full-size American poster for *That Man from Rio* (1964). © *1964 Lopert Films, Inc.*

"A Lulu! Bubbles . . . exaltation of the absurd! It's more reckless than James Bond's adventures! Every complication, involving imminent peril pulled in such rapid continuity and so expansively played, with such élan against such brilliant backgrounds . . . they take your breath away. Belmondo is dandy as a fast, fearless modern day Harold Lloyd. There's just fun for fun's sake!" Bosley Crowther, *New York Times.*

"Knocks your eyes out! A stylish, amusing, hilarious takeoff on adventure intrigue films! *That Man from Rio* leads us on a merry chase." Judith Crist, *New York Herald Tribune.*

"Belmondo sparkles in comic adventure! The astonishing Jean-Paul Belmondo projects comedy on the screen with a vengeance! The pictures moves swiftly and amusingly across the screen!" Kate Cameron, *New York Daily News.*

(*That Man from Rio* advertisement: The Paris Theater)

William Mootz, drama critic for the *Courier-Journal in* Louisville, Kentucky, called *That Man from Rio* "irreverent and delightful" (Mootz "*Man from Rio* Proves," 42). Harold V. Cohen of the *Pittsburgh Post-Gazette* called the film a combination of James Bond adventures mixed with silent film comedy, calling it tongue-in-cheek "spoof and satire" (Cohen "Danger and Delirium," 26). Les Wedman of the *Vancouver Sun* had a similar assessment but added that Adrien Dufourquet's "indestructibility is never in doubt but he proves it the hard way, and in doing so dances on the graves of departed tough guys and swashbucklers like Humphrey Bogart, Douglas Fairbanks, Errol Flynn or any Hollywood star who has ever saved a damsel in distress" (Wedman "That Man from Rio Review," 18).

Hollywood gossip columnist Sheilah Graham called it "wild, wild, wild, packed with action and derring-do. And that's what movies were made for" (Graham "Charlie Chaplin's," 13). Seemingly, everyone wanted to get a look at *That Man from Rio.* New York nightlife columnist Earl Wilson reported seeing *The Bridge on the River Kwai* (1957) star Sir Alec Guinness waiting in line "just like non-royalty to see the movie *That Man from Rio*" (Wilson "Gleason's Score," 11).

French composer Georges Delerue's soundtrack for the movie, which syndicated gossip columnist Walter Winchell described as "sexciting" in 1964, was not released on vinyl in the 1960s. It was not commercially available until 2009, when it was released on compact disc on the Kritzerland label.

That Man from Rio holds more gravitas than the typical film of the genre and more than James Bond could ever hope for. *That Man from Rio* was nominated for Best Original Screenplay at the 1965 Academy Awards. The *New York Times* reported in 2015 that celebrated French essayist Roland Barthes "cited the movie repeatedly in a 1964 interview on semiology and cinema" and that director Steven Spielberg used the film as inspiration for *Raiders of the Lost Ark* (1981) and went to see *That Man from Rio* nine times when it was released (Hoberman "Jet-Setting").

Operation: Lovebirds (1965; a.k.a. Slå først Frede! and Strike First Freddy!)

Although films produced in Denmark are rarely released extensively throughout the United States, *Operation: Lovebirds* is yet another example of a film being brought to the United States as a result of James Bond and the 1960s spy craze.

Gag novelty toy salesman, Frede Hansen (Morten Grunwald) is mistaken by both an unnamed democratic counterintelligence agency and by enemy agents and soon becomes a reluctant participant in espionage to save the world from Dr. Pax (Martin Hansen) and his evil unnamed organization. Frede becomes Secret Agent Frede Hansen and is given a number of spy gadgets, like a backward firing gun, a shoe with a knife in the heel, and an exploding cigarette case. Now Secret Agent Frede Hansen is guided by Agent Smith (Ove Sprogøe), a by-the-book secret agent. Frede fumbles his way through his mission to save the world from Dr. Pax's Operation: Lovebirds, a plot to incite a world war with the help of pigeons. In the process, Frede falls for an enemy catsuit-wearing agent named Sonya (Essy Persson). Throughout the movie, Frede Hansen even wears a white tuxedo dinner jacket, black bowtie, and red corsage, as James Bond wore in *Goldfinger* (1964).

A year prior, Essy Persson starred in the Danish sexploitation film *I, a Woman* (1965), which also was imported to fulfill the growing demand for adult content in films that American studios were still apprehensive to release. So American news outlets began to cover her career and reported on the progress of *Operation: Lovebirds*. Despite the international attention, Persson only starred in two other films with international appeal: the erotic yet artistic French film *Therese and Isabelle* (1968) and British horror film *Cry of the Banshee* (1970), starring Vincent Price ("Spy Spoof Coming").

Premiering in Denmark with the title *Slå først Frede!* (*Strike First Freddy*) in 1965, *Operation: Lovebirds* was acquired by American distribution company Emerson Film Enterprises in 1967. Emerson Film Enterprises released notorious shlock exploitation titles *Manos: The Hands of Fate* (1966), *The Doctor and the Playgirl* (1963), and *Wife Swappers* (1965). Emerson would later put out films *Psyched by the 4D Witch* (1973), *Mondo Hollywood: Hollywood Laid Bare!* (1967), and *The Sexterminators* (1970), among others (Martin "Operation: Lovebirds").

Morten Grunwald as Agent Frede Hansen, wearing his James Bond–style tux, with Essy Persson as Sonja in *Operation Lovebirds* (1965). *Author's collection*

Emerson Film Enterprises did not release the film overseas until January 1968, when it began to play throughout Canada. The film later debuted in the United States on June 21, 1968, in Hartford, Connecticut, at the Arts Cinema ("Movie Directory"; "Get More Out of Life").

Operation: Lovebirds did not play in major markets such as New York, Los Angeles, or Chicago, so it did not receive many write-ups in newspapers and was ignored by major outlets such as *Variety*. With some exceptions, theaters running the film did not spend advertising dollars to promote the feature.

Operation: Lovebirds was often shown in Canada with Japanese import *Agent 101* (1966), though the latter was never shown in the United States. The advertisement for the Canadian double feature promised "Double Action That Out-Bonds James Bond!" and "The riotous fun of *Thunderball*, the *Flint* pictures, *Casino Royale*" (*Operation: Lovebirds* Double Feature advertisement).

The film's follow-up, *Relax Freddie* (1966), was originally titled *The Whistler* and reportedly alternatively titled *Solitaire*. There is no record of the sequel being dubbed or playing in *any* English-speaking country (Gaghan "Lack").

Secret Agent Fireball (1965)

December 1965 was a great time for spy film devotees. Not only did the fourth James Bond film *Thunderball* hit theaters but the action-packed American International Pictures double feature by American International Pictures (AIP) released a pair of Italian-Euro superspy films, *Spy in Your Eye* and *Secret Agent Fireball*, as a double feature.

In *Secret Agent Fireball* (also released under the titles *The Spies Kill in Beirut* and *Message from 077*) Secret Agent 077 Bob Fleming (Richard Harrison) travels on assignment to Hamburg, Germany, and Beirut, Lebanon, to investigate the killing of several Soviet scientists who had defected to the West. It turns out the Soviets are on the hunt for microfilm in the scientists' possession that contains information about the Soviet hydrogen bomb project. As it turns out, Western nations also would like to get their hands on the microfilm. The Soviets torture and kill for the microfilm.

Secret Agent Bob Fleming, who shares the same last name as James Bond creator Ian Fleming and holds a similar number (077) to Bond has a license to kill and an eye for the ladies.

Secret Agent Fireball starred American Richard Harrison, who found his fortune overseas in Italy mostly making spaghetti Westerns such as *$100,000 for Ringo* (1965), *Vengeance* (1968), and *Between God, the Devil and a Winchester* (1968). Dominique Boschero played Fleming's love interest, Liz Grune. Boschero previously worked with Harrison on *Between God, the Devil and a Winchester* and also starred in the Italian spy/superhero film *Argoman the Fantastic Superman* (1968). Wanda Guida and Luciano Pigozzi played Russian spies Elena and Yuri. Guida would later appear in Euro-spy flicks *Lightning Bolt* (1966; a.k.a. *Operazione Goldman*) and *Killers Are Challenged* (1966; a.k.a *Bob Fleming: Mission Casablanca*). Pigozzi starred in a treasure trove of Italian horror, giallo, spaghetti Westerns, and spy films such as *Baron Blood* (1972), *The Whip and the Body* (1963), *And God Said to Cain* (1970), and in an unrelated film using the 077 monicker, *Agent 077: From the Orient with Fury* (1965).

The trailer exclaimed, "London, Paris, Hamburg, Beirut. The world's capitals of intrigue. Where the cheapest thing is life. Here attractive women lure wanted men into death traps then find themselves victims of counterespionage." It added, "He goes where the action is hottest!" *Variety* called the film an "okay entry into the present espionage upsurge, but lacks the finish of most of its predecessors" believing that the film's audience will be "moderately entertained" (*Variety Film Reviews*, 301).

Advertisements for the *Spy in Your Eye* and *Secret Agent Fireball* double feature called the films "2 of the GREATEST Spy Thrillers Ever Made! Both in Action Color! More Gals, More Guns, More Gimmicks than 007 ever thought of!!!" and an "action-packed adventure thriller in color that is double-billed with *Spy in Your Eye*" (Anchor Drive-In advertisement; "Movie Premiers," 15).

Richard Harrison returned to the role of 077 Bob Fleming in *The Killers Are Challenged* (1966; a.k.a. *Bob Fleming: Mission Casablanca*), which played on television in the United States throughout the late 1960s and 1970s but never in theaters.

Spy in Your Eye (1965; a.k.a. Berlin, Appointment for Spies)

When *Goldfinger* (1965) was released, James Bond barely scratched the surface on gadgets that he would accrue throughout the years. At that point his fully loaded Aston Martin was the most outlandish item given to him by the Q branch at MI6. Movies like *Spy in Your Eye* forced James Bond's producers to push the envelope in future Bond films. The trailer promised, "He hasn't a double-O number but he lives a doubly dangerous life with sexier gals, groovier gimmicks, and more out and out guts than anything or anyone you've ever seen."

When a Nobel Prize–winning scientist is killed attempting to defect from Communist East Germany to the West with his daughter, Paula Krauss (Pier Angeli), and with a formula for a death ray in tow, his daughter is captured by the Soviets. American secret agent Bert Morris (Brett Halsey) must paratroop behind enemy lines to rescue Paula before she is tortured and potentially gives up her father's secret death ray formula. In the meantime, Chinese agents are on the ground to kidnap Paula and acquire information on the death ray for themselves. To make matters worse, unbeknown to the Americans, eye patch–wearing colonel Lancaster (Dana Andrews) is given a prosthetic eye that in reality is a camera, giving the Soviets an insider's view of all of the American's plans.

Brett Halsey in action in *Spy in Your Eye* (1965). *Author's collection*

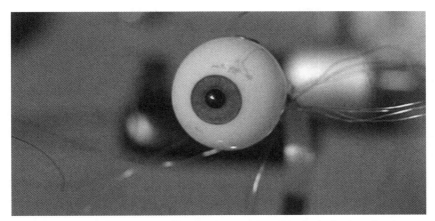

The electronic eye in super-spy film *Spy in Your Eye* (1965). *Author's collection*

While the film was still in production, an article by the Associated Press ran in newspapers throughout the county talking about the film's star, Pier Angeli, and her return to Italy from Hollywood in order to make the film. At that time, Angeli was married to Italian composer Armando Trovajoli and in the past had been romantically linked to Kirk Douglas, Vic Damone, and James Dean ("Pier Making Italian").

Released in Europe under the title *Berlin, Appointment for Spies*, American International Pictures released the film in the United States as *Spy in Your Eye*, along with Italian-French production *Secret Agent Fireball* (1965). Both films played together at drive-ins and grindhouse theaters throughout the country from December 1965 through most of 1966.

Although the film was being shown regularly, it was mostly ignored by critics and media outlets, the exceptions being stills and blurbs to promote local showings. The *Los Angeles Times* staff writer Margaret Harford wrote an article in January 1966 about the spy craze happening in American cinema. Harford noted that the spy craze had "too many gimmicks" but added both *Spy in Your Eye* and *Secret Agent Fireball* "are swift action spoofs of the Bond films that should do fairly well, though I doubt that they will win any prizes" and *Variety* called the film a "confusing espionage meller [melodrama] hard to follow" (Harford "Spies," 7; *Variety Film Reviews*, 301).

That Man in Istanbul (1965)

A US CIA agent, known simply as Kelly (Sylva Koscina), is called in after the government paid a $51 million in ransom for a top atomic scientist, Professor

Pendergast (Umberto Raho), who was kidnapped in Istanbul but replaced by a body double in the exchange. Nightclub owner Tony Mecenas (Horst Buchholz) becomes involved in the hunt for the atomic scientist after Kelly applied to be a stripper at Mecenas's nightclub as a cover. Of course, Kelly and Mecenas become *romantically* involved, battle the criminal underworld in Istanbul, and encounter a Red Chinese spy ring.

The film was produced in Europe and had an international cast. American audiences would have been unfamiliar with most of the cast with the exception of stars Horst Buchholz and Sylva Koscina. Buchholz played Chico in the popular Western *The Magnificent Seven* (1960) and Communist Otto Ludwig Piffl in Billy Wilder's *One, Two, Three* (1961). Koscina played Hercules's wife in imported Italian sword-and-sandal films *Hercules* (1958) and *Hercules Unchained* (1960) and would later be featured in the Bulldog Drummond spy adventure *Deadlier Than the Male* (1967).

Columbia Pictures had high hopes for the film at the US box office, since the film had "record-breaking engagements" after *That Man in Istanbul* was released to theaters in Europe in August 1965. The film's star Horst Buchholz even told newspaper gossip columnist Hedda Hopper that he believed that the picture would be a hit ("Columbia Plans," 33; Hopper "Edgar Bergen").

That Man in Istanbul was released in the United States in January 1966, at a time when seemingly one or more new spy flicks were coming out every week and critics around the country were already sick of the spy genre.

Philip K. Scheuer, motion picture editor for the *Los Angeles Times*, tore into the film. Scheuer compared it to one of 1966's most popular but camp television shows, writing, "The foolishment in all these Bond imitations (as in the Bond capers themselves) is just a matter of degree. In this latest one it is sometimes hard to tell whether the camp is intentional or not; the dialogue however, is almost as awful as that in *Batman*—and certainly as stilted." Scheuer even had problems with the music: "The music score is just corny enough to be noticed. But then so is everything else about *That Man in Istanbul*" (Scheuer "Spy Foolishment," 79).

Nadine M. Edwards of the *Los Angeles Evening Citizen News* wrote, "*That Man in Istanbul* seems familiar," insinuating that the film was just another Bond knockoff: "Beautiful girls, death-dealing Tommy guns, knife wielding underwater duels, loaded steam baths . . . another action-packed film dealing with spies, counterspies and unadulterated lies" (Edwards "That Man in Istanbul Seems Familiar," 9).

Eliot Fremont-Smith echoed Edwards's sentiment, in the *New York Times*:

Poster for *That Man in Istanbul* (1966). © 1966 Columbia Pictures Corp.

Here we go again. An exotic locale. A rugged, very cool hero. Gorgeous girls in bikinis. A kidnapped atomic scientist. Gangsters, Chinese Communists, secret agents. Underwater fights, helicopter drops, screeching tires, even a melee in a ladies' steam bath. Sound familiar? It all is in *That Man in Istanbul*. That man is not James Bond, but Our Man Tony Mecenas (Horst Buchholz) who is—what else—a playboy, the owner of a gambling casino, a sort of pubescent Turhan Bey and apparently the greatest lover since "The Sheik." Just in case we might forget it, he takes off his shirt every 15 minutes. And if the message still isn't clear, at least every 20 minutes a different girl appears on the screen, smiles knowingly and whispers: "Ciao, Tony." (Fremont-Smith "Lady L," 51)

Fremont-Smith added, "Through it all, Tony maintains a sense of humor that would undoubtedly make James Bond cringe. . . . For the audience there are some lovely views of Istanbul, a few first-rate action scenes and, of course, those girls in bikinis whispering 'Ciao, Tony'" (Ibid.).

Readers could almost hear Sy Oshinsky of the *Motion Picture Daily* yawning when he wrote, "Add another jet-propelled adventure yarn to the ever growing list of motion pictures dealing with international intrigue." The same could be said about Dick Banks of the *Charlotte Observer*, when he declared that *That Man in Istanbul* was "another OK spy show" and that the film is "a spy picture made apparently by people who are wild about spy pictures." Dick Shippy of the *Akron Beacon Journal* simply believed, "We don't need bad imitations." Shippy added that making the movie was a "bad idea all the way around" and "we certainly do not need one as clumsily done as *That Man in Istanbul* which is determinedly unfunny with its spoof and as diligently asinine with the straight heroics, unless this is a grotesque put-on" (Oshinsky "New Films in Review"; Banks "That Man," 15; Shippy "We Don't Need," 14).

Occasionally, *That Man in Istanbul* did receive a positive review. An uncredited review that was published in smaller publications throughout the country called the film "a thoroughly enjoyable addition to the present screen flood of secret agent adventures" as well as "wild, ingenious and suspenseful comedy." It concluded, "*That Man in Istanbul* is a happy combination of fun and action" ("Secret Agent Is Theme," 24).

Even before *That Man in Istanbul* was released to theaters in the United States, in November 1965, syndicated gossip columnist Earl Wilson reported that Buchholz would return as Tony Mecenas in a sequel, *That Man in Rangoon*. There was even talk that it would be the start of an entire series of films. However, the film was never produced, nor were any other films in the planned series (Wilson "Barbra's," 35).

Two Mafiosi against Goldginger (1965)

Perhaps the most direct spoof of James Bond came from Italian director Giorgio Simonelli in the film *Two Mafiosi against Goldginger*. While many spoofs of the era alluded to James Bond, or had a James Bond–inspired character, *Two Mafiosi against Goldginger* actually has a James Bond character. Although not authorized by James Bond's copyright holders, Danjaq LLC and United Artists Corporation, the film's producer Edmondo Amati took advantage of Italy's copyright laws and cast George Hilton, a Uruguayan actor best known for his roles in spaghetti Westerns and giallo films, as 007 James Bond.

However, the character of James Bond does not last very long and is killed by his nemesis Goldginger (an obvious takeoff on Goldfinger). Goldginger plans world domination by replacing government agents around the world with humanoid robots while based in his ginger-flavored soda factory. Before Bond was killed, his secrets were picked up by two Italian photographers Franco Franchi and Ciccio Ingrassia (Franco & Ciccio), who now are the only ones who can save the world from Goldginger.

The film steals a number of themes from *Goldfinger*, including lasers used to splice Franco & Ciccio, a woman covered in gold paint, and even an Odd-job duplicate named Molok, played by South American professional wrestler Dakar.

Franco & Ciccio had a long and illustrious career; they starred in 112 Italian films from 1960 to 1984, even working with famous and influential directors Lucio Fulci and Sergio Corbucci prior to *Two Mafiosi against Goldginger*'s release. Aside from appearing on film, the duo appeared in a number of mediums, including television and radio theater, and they even released a number of musical albums throughout their thirty-eight-year career. The film's director, Giorgio Simonelli, specialized in Italian comedy films and directed Franco & Ciccio in *Two Mafiamen in the Far West* (1964) and *Two Sergeants of General Custer* (1965).

Released and dubbed into English by American International Pictures (AIP) Television, *The Amazing Dr. G* became a television staple throughout the United States in 1969 and the early 1970s, often playing late night and/or in the wee hours of the morning alongside black and white sit-com reruns, B-grade monster flicks, old Westerns, and pro wrestling. However, *The Amazing Dr. G* did get some screen time in several movie theaters throughout the country in 1969.

Two Mafiosi against Goldginger was not seen west of Milan in its original form and language until 1970, when it played at the Orpheum Theater in Sault

St. Marie, Ontario, Canada, with spaghetti Western *Arizona Colt* (1966) in an adults-only Italian-language double feature (Follow Me advertisement).

Dr. Goldfoot and the Girl Bombs (1966), released as *Le spie vengono dal semifreddo* (*The Spies Who Came In from the Cool*) in Italy, was directed by Italian director Mario Bava and served as an indirect sequel to both *Two Mafiosi against Goldginger* and the AIP film *Dr. Goldfoot and the Bikini Machine*. *Dr. Goldfoot and the Girl Bombs/Le spie vengono dal semifreddo* featured both Franco & Ciccio's characters from *Two Mafiosi against Goldginger* and Vincent Price's titular character from *Dr. Goldfoot and the Bikini Machine*, along with his gold-bikini-wearing army of sexy humanoid robot girls.

Later, the film also became known as *Two Crazy Secret Agents* or simply *Goldginger*.

Bang! Bang! You're Dead! (1966; a.k.a. Our Man in Marrakesh)

Fresh off a string of successful films alongside Doris Day, future *Odd Couple* (1970–1975) star Tony Randall starred in the English-produced spy spoof *Bang! Bang! You're Dead!* (1966). In the states, the film was originally scheduled to be titled simply *Bang, You're Dead* (perhaps not to confuse the film with the alternative title to the 1965 spy film *Spy in Your Eye*, which was billed as *Bang, You're Dead* in some markets), but it was released in England under the title *Our Man in Marrakesh* (McHarry "Play for Bette").

Bang! Bang! You're Dead! is another spy film revolving around the "reluctant spy." While on a bus to Casablanca, Andrew Jessel (Tony Randall) is believed to be holding two million dollars and intending to bribe delegates at the United Nations. Soon a melee ensues, with counterintelligence agents from different organizations chasing Jessel and trying to capture him and, more importantly, the money. While on the run, he comes into contact with the attractive Kyra Stanovy (Senta Berger), who may also have the money in her possession and may be a foreign agent.

The film, shot on location in Morocco, was produced by Harry Alan Towers. Towers may be best known as the producer of several Euro films directed by Jesús Franco that starred Christopher Lee: *The Brides of Fu Manchu* (1966), *The Vengeance of Fu Manchu* (1967), *The Blood of Fu Manchu* (1968), *The Castle of Fu Manchu* (1969), *Eugenie . . . The Story of Her Journey into Perversion* (1970), and *The Bloody Judge* (1970). *Circus of Fear* (1966) and the first of the Fu Manchu films, *The Face of Fu Manchu* (1965), both starred Christopher Lee and were produced by Towers but not directed by Franco. Although *Bang! Bang! You're Dead!* was an English production, the film was written and directed by a pair of Australasians: written by Peter Yeldham and directed by Don Sharp. Sharp directed a pair of horror films for Hammer Films—*The Kiss of the Vampire* (1963) and *Rasputin, the Mad Monk* (1966)—and the Harry Alan Towers–produced *The Face of Fu Manchu*, while Yeldham worked mostly with Harry Alan Towers throughout his career, previously writing his films *Code 7, Victim 5* (1964), *Twenty-Four Hours to Kill* (1965), and *Ten Little Indians* (1965).

Tony Randall's costar was spy film veteran Senta Berger. Berger played on a 1964 episode of the television show *The Man from U.N.C.L.E.* (1964–1968) titled "The Double Affair," which was turned into a feature-length film, *The Spy with My Face* (1966), and she costarred in the film *The Quiller Memorandum* (1965). Berger brought plenty of sex appeal to *Bang! Bang! You're Dead!* and was often featured wearing a short, low-cut dress throughout the film. The trailer even remarked, "Tony [Randall] really enjoyed making *Bang! Bang! You're Dead!* . . . and Senta Berger is one gal that is a pleasure to work with. If you call this work," while showing many of the scenes in the film involving Berger kissing Randall or wearing revealing outfits.

Also appearing is British character actor and comedian Terry-Thomas as El Caid, an intelligence agent living in the Middle East, not unlike Lawrence of Arabia. Thomas may be best recognized by an extremely large and noticeable gap between his two front teeth. The same year *Bang! Bang! You're Dead!* was released, Terry-Thomas also appeared in another spy spoof, *Kiss the Girls and Make Them Die* (1966).

Bish Thompson of the *Evansville Press* in Evansville, Indiana, noted the film was "another spy spoof, loaded with chases through streets of Marrakesh and across the desert; international intrigue at its zaniest." Hollywood gossip columnist Sidney Skolsky wrote that Tony Randall is a "comical take-off of a Bond-Flint-Helm man." *Abilene Reporter-News* amusements editor Patrick Bennett called the film a "cloak and dagger romp" (Thompson "Khartoum," 12; Skolsky "Gossipel Truth," 6; Bennett "Big Features," 26).

The *New York Times* critic Bosley Crowther felt *Bang! Bang! You're Dead!* would possibly kill the spy spoof all together, stating, "Spies and spy spoofs may be the hot film items these days, but *Bang, Bang, You're Dead!* . . . should help to cool off both genres." Crowther added, "The scenery, in color, is exotic and easy on the eyes. Senta Berger and Margaret Lee, in bikini or dress, also help make the convoluted plot redundant" (Crowther "Venetian Affair," 36).

Bang! Bang! You're Dead! often played as the second half of a double feature with the Italian-produced *Dr. Goldfoot and the Girl Bombs* (1966) or alongside *The Pawnbroker* (1964).

Kiss the Girls and Make Them Die (1966)

Kiss the Girls and Make Them Die, an US-Italian coproduction, was released in the United States by Columbia Pictures and produced by Italian producer Dino De Laurentiis. De Laurentiis was coming off the production of *The Bible: In the Beginning . . .* (1966) for his production company Dino de Laurentiis Cinematografica.

Directed by Henry Levin, who during the same year directed the Dean Martin spy spoof *Murderers' Row* (1966), *Kiss the Girls and Make them Die* is set in Rio De Janeiro and stars future *Mannix* (1967–1975) star Mike Connors as CIA agent Kelly and Dorothy Provine as beautiful British MI6 agent Susan Fleming. Kelly and Fleming attempt to stop a Chinese-funded, Brazilian industrialist and scientist known as Mr. Ardonian (Raf Vallone) from sterilizing the entire globe and repopulating the earth in his image, using women he's kidnapped and has on ice in suspended animation.

After production wrapped on *Kiss the Girls and Make Them Die*, Raf Vallone described his character as a "jolly mad scientist who wants to create a happier, more peaceful mankind" but who gets led down the wrong path. Vallone

The theatrical poster for *Kiss the Girls and Make Them Die* (1966) presented the film as an over-the-top, big-budget Bond spoof. *© 1966 Columbia Pictures Corp.*

believed the film had a message: "In our current world science and technology have gradually come to condition everything in our lives, our brains, our emotions." He added, "This has given an extraordinary power to scientists. And this extraordinary power has gone to the head of the hero of my movie. This is the theme of the film" (Mennella "What Next?," 113).

Mike Connors was coming off playing in a low-budget Italian comedy with Jayne Mansfield, *The Panic Button*, that was released in America in 1964. Connors clearly wanted to forget *The Panic Button*. "I congratulate you on missing me doing a scene in *Panic Button* for the film was bad," Connors told Pittsburgh reporter Kaspar Monahan while in town to plug *Kiss the Girls and Make Them Die*. However, Connors clearly had higher hopes for *Kiss the Girls and Make Them Die*. "Let's say I'm a lot better in my latest film," said Connors (Monahan "Noted Actors' Daughters," 39). The *Banner Press*, a David City, Nebraska, newspaper, described it as "a science fiction melodrama in James Bond style combining violence and tension with polished villainy and flippant espionage" ("At the 4th," 2).

Howard Thompson wrote that *Kiss the Girls and Make Them Die* was "such a coy label for a strictly one-horse James Bonded adventure crammed with gadgetry and pretty girls," adding that the script was "meandering" and a waste of the color Brazilian scenery (Thompson "Kiss the Girls," 134). The *Los Angeles Times* staff writer Kevin Thomas had a different take on the film: what the film lacked in originality it made up for in action. He wrote, "From the spectacular beginning, which has Connors being rescued by helicopter atop Rio's famed landmark, the Statue of Christ on Corcovado Peak, director Henry Levin maintains a rapid pace." Thomas added that Levin focuses on the characters and action rather than the movie's "overly familiar plot" (Thomas "Pair of," 66).

Similarly, Dale Munroe of the *Valley Times*, a North Hollywood newspaper, believed that the film "may do for Rio De Janeiro what *Dr. No* did for Jamaica. The Dino De Laurentiis production combines secret agents, villains, action, sex, gimmicks and the kind of colorful location photography that highlighted the first James Bond thriller." However Munroe felt the movie "suffers from too many gimmicks and spy-film clichés, but does manage to be an entertaining film despite itself. The plot is weak, but the action is hard-fisted and in abundance" (Munroe "Gimmicks," 8)

The United Press International (UPI) offered a reason, aside from the action, to go see the film. The news outlet described one of the film's stars, Beverly Adams, in an article that both announced her 1967 engagement to famed hair stylist Vidal Sassoon and plugged *Kiss the Girls and Make Them Die*, as "a beautiful dark-haired, green-eyed girl best known for taking a bubble bath with Dean

Martin in *The Silencers*." The article added that Adams, who also appeared in *Murderers' Row* (1966) and *Torture Garden* (1967), "says she's only 21, has all the physical equipment going for her. In addition to her enchanting face, she has a figure that is at once arresting without being obtrusive" ("Promising Starlet," 8).

Kiss the Girls and Make Them Die, also released under the title *Operazione Paradiso* and *If All the Women in the World*, much like many spy spoofs of the era, had very James Bond–inspired posters that promised "Swinging adventure!," "Wow women & pow action!," and "Sizzling kisses."

Producer Dino De Laurentiis would go on to produce big-budget spectacles, namely, *King Kong* (1976), *Flash Gordon* (1980), and *Dune* (1984), along with a number of critically acclaimed films, namely *Serpico* (1973), *Death Wish* (1974), and *Blue Velvet* (1986).

Lightning Bolt (1966; a.k.a. Operazione Goldman)

While many spy flicks revolve around agents in the CIA, MI6, or any number of fictitious clandestine organizations, *Lightning Bolt* revolves around agents of the "S Division" of the US Federal Security Investigation Commission (FSIC). Harry Sennitt (Anthony Eisley), who is given an unlimited expense account backed by the US government and nicknamed "Goldman," is sent along with FSIC leader, Captain Patricia Flanagan (Diana Lorys), nicknamed "Agent 36-22-36" for obvious reasons, to investigate the sabotage of American rockets to the moon lifting off from Cape Kennedy, much like in *Dr. No* (1962). However, Sennitt and Flanagan soon uncover a much more sinister plot, beyond the destruction of US rockets. They uncover a secret underwater base run by mad scientist Rehte (Folco Lulli) who intends to conquer the world with a laser cannon he plans to build on the moon. To make matters worse, Rehte runs the underwater base with the help of a number of masked ninja scientists. He also houses a number of cryogenically frozen prisoners, whom he keeps alive for his enjoyment and to blackmail their family members.

Anthony Eisley, the film's only American cast member (the rest are Italian or Spanish), was known to American audiences as the star of the ABC detective show *Hawaiian Eye* (1959–1963), and he appeared on episodes of *Dragnet* (1967–1970), *Perry Mason* (1957–1966), *The Outer Limits* (1963–1965), *Combat!* (1962–1967), *The F.B.I.* (1965–1974), and *The Wild Wild West* (1965–1969). Spanish actress Diana Lorys previously appeared in a number of European films, most notably the horror exploitation film *The Awful Dr. Orloff* (1962), which also was a financially successful film in the United States.

Captain Patricia Flanagan, a.k.a. "Agent 36-22-36" (Diana Lorys), enjoys a shower on her top-secret mission to stop a madman with a laser beam in *Lightning Bolt* **(1966).** *Author's collection*

The film's villain, Folco Lulli, was a well-known Italian character actor who appeared in over one hundred films in his career, very few of which played outside the European continent.

The film was directed by Antonio Margheriti, who previously directed Italian genre films *Space-Men* (1960), *Castle of Blood* (1964), and *Hercules, Prisoner of Evil* (1964), among other similarly themed films. In the American version, Margheriti went under the anglicized alias Anthony M. Dawson. *Lightning Bolt* was released in the United States by the Woolner Brothers, who notably also released *Swamp Women* (1956), *Attack of the 50 Foot Woman* (1958), *Hercules in the Haunted World* (1961), *The Las Vegas Hillbillies* (1966), and *Hillbillies in a Haunted House* (1967).

Leaning into the James Bond fad, the film was given the tagline "Strikes Like a Ball of Thunder," and Harry Sennitt was full of Bondesque quips, such as when he was poolside at an all-secret-agent resort and said to one of the many beautiful agents, "I'll step aside, baby, I'm sure you don't want to be shadowed."

Released to theaters in the United States in 1967, *Lightning Bolt* often played as a double feature with German-Italian coproduction *Red Dragon* (1967) and occasionally with World War II–period spy film *Triple Cross* (1966) or James Bond adventure *You Only Live Twice* (1967). The film played in more than three thousand theaters across the United States and Canada (in French-speaking Quebec, the film was released under the European title *Operazione Goldman*) and was also sold to television (Gewertz "Alexandrian").

Even before *Lightning Bolt* made its debut in the United States, Betty Martin of the *Los Angeles Times* reported in July 1966 that Anthony Eisley would return to his role as Harry Sennitt in a film titled *Fury in Tahiti*. However, *Fury in Tahiti* was never produced (Martin "Delon to Return").

Ring around the World (1966)

Insurance investigator Fred Lester (Richard Harrison) is tasked to look into the death of a colleague. Lester uncovers a number of large life insurance policies on the deceased investigator's life and finds that, strangely, banks and businesses were listed as his beneficiaries. With the help of his fellow insurance investigator's daughter (Hélène Chanel), the seemingly mundane case takes Lester around the globe, where he fights in gun battles and even jumps out of a plane to uncover a nefarious criminal ring and a killer (Giacomo Rossi Stuart) who uses a gun that uses chemical bullets.

Richard Harrison was coming off starring roles in Euro-spy films *Secret Agent Fireball* (1965) and *Bob Fleming . . . Mission Casablanca* (1966), and spaghetti Westerns *$100,000 for Ringo* (1965) and *El Rojo* (1966). Before *Ring around the World,* French actress Hélène Chanel played in a trio of spy films that did not play in the United States: *Operation Counterspy* (1965), *Ischia operazione amore* (1966), and *Agente segreto 777* (1966). But Chanel may have been best known stateside for her role in imported Italian sword-and-sandal films such as *Samson and the Seven Miracles of the World* (1961), *The Witch's Curse* (1962), and *Hercules of the Desert* (1964). Giacomo Rossi Stuart was also a veteran of the Italian sword-and-sandal genre, appearing in *Seven Slaves against the World* (1964) and *The Revenge of Spartacus* (1964). The Italian actor also appeared in a number of horror films like *Kill, Baby, Kill* (1966) and—the role American audiences may have best known him for—the American-Italian coproduction *The Last Man on Earth* (1964), starring Vincent Price.

Earlier in 1966, the film's director Luigi Scattini directed the comedy *War Italian Style* (1966), which starred American silent-film star Buster Keaton and Italian comedy team Franco & Ciccio. Franco & Ciccio previously starred in spy spoofs *Two Mafiosi against Goldginger* (1964) and *Dr. Goldfoot and the Girl Bombs* (1966).

Writer Ernesto Gastaldi, who occasionally wrote under the anglicized name Julian Berry and was known for writing sword-and-sandal, giallo, and gothic horror films, also wrote the screenplay for another Italian spy film starring Richard Harrison: *Secret Agent Fireball* (1966).

The Italian film's swinging 1960s score was provided by Piero Umiliani. Umiliani's compositions could be heard on a number of Italian exploitation, mondo, spaghetti Westerns, Euro-spy, and giallo films, and even on American television screens, when the Muppets made his song "Mah Nà Mah Nà" an earworm in 1969 on *Sesame Street* (1969–Present).

The film had a very limited showing in the United States, only appearing as the second feature with *Gambit* (1966) in Green Bay, Wisconsin, with *Who's Minding the Mint?* (1967) in Hackensack, New Jersey, and with *Birds Do It* (1966) in Wilmington, Delaware.

Secret Agent Super Dragon (1966; a.k.a. *New York chiama Superdrago*)

Often playing as the second feature in American theaters, *Super Agent Super Dragon* first appeared in American theaters on June 12, 1966, in El Paso, Texas. The first showing of the film was seen on double bills with *One Way Wahine* (1965) a comedy starring Joy Harmon ("Movies for Everyone").

Super Agent Super Dragon, an Italian production by Films Borderie S.A. (C.I.C.C.) Constantin Film, was filmed in Technicolor and was shot in Italy, France, and West Germany. The film was the first foreign film released in 1966 by United Screen Arts, along with, most notably, *Atomic War Bride* (1960) and *SS Strike at Dawn* (1958), in a package of nineteen films ("Miss Parker").

When an evil crime syndicate plots to take over the world using a new drug called "Syacron 2," enter CIA agent Super Dragon (Ray Danton), who is seemingly impervious to assault from enemies due to his practice of both yoga and karate. Like James Bond, Super Dragon carried a number of gadgets such as a bullet-firing sweater, pocket-sized tape recorder, and a transponder watch as he came out of retirement to save humankind. The gadgets are invented by a career criminal turned sidekick, Babyface (Jess Hahn), who was released from a stretch at Sing Sing and lent to Super Dragon by the American government to help with the assignment. Of course, Super Dragon makes time to also be with beautiful women Charity Farrel (Marisa Mell) and Cynthia Fulton (Margaret Lee).

All four stars had previous experience in the spy genre. Prior to *Super Agent Super Dragon*, Ray Danton played in Euro-spy film *Code Name: Jaguar* (1965) and notably appeared on American television shows *Bourbon Street Beat* (1959–1960), *Hawaiian Eye* (1959–1963), and *The Roaring 20's* (1960–1962). Jess Hahn appeared in the French spy spoof *The Great Spy Chase* (1964) and the Woody Allen–written sex comedy *What's New Pussycat?* (1965). A year earlier, Marisa Mell was considered for a role in James Bond film *Thunderball* (1965) but ultimately was not cast; she later appeared in Mario Bava's *Danger: Diabolik* (1968). And Margaret Lee previously played in a trio of Euro-spy films: *Our Agent Tiger* (1965), *Agent 077: From the Orient with Fury* (1965) and *Kiss the Girls and Make Them Die* (1966).

The stylish and jazzy trailer, full of sex, violence, and spy gadgets, exclaimed, "Introducing the screen's newest, hottest, fastest, undercover operator. You name it he can handle it, killers, foreign agents, master criminals, blondes, brunettes, redheads; the screen's most luscious, curvaceous beautiful assassins." The trailer went on to call Ray Danton as Super Dragon "the cool cool spy" and Marisa Mell "smoldering." It added, "Super Agent Super Dragon, the man that makes the other secret agents look like softies. You've never seen a secret agent with as many weapons as Super Dragon. Ask his enemies. Ask his women. He's like no other man you've ever met or imagined before!"

Newspaper ads mirrored the trailer: "Blondes, Brunettes, Redheads, Murderers, Smugglers or Criminals His Fire Could Take Them All!" (*Secret Agent Super Dragon* advertisement 2). But reporters all but ignored *Super Agent Super Dragon* in the United States, with some exceptions. The *Anniston Star* from Anniston, Alabama, called the film "lavishly mounted on a major scale as a top-budgeted production," and called Ray Danton "ruggedly handsome" and Marisa Mell "arrestingly voluptuous." The *Sunday News and Tribune* in Jefferson City, Missouri, called the film an "action-packed espionage thriller," while Reggie Capes of the *Columbus Ledger* in Columbus, Georgia, called the film "another James Bondish action film" ("Ritz to Offer," 31; "Spies, Tarzan," 29; Capes "Holdovers," 18).

O.K. Connery (1967; a.k.a. *Operation Kid Brother* or *Operation Double 007*)

Nepotism was alive and well for Neil Connery. In January 1966 the Associated Press (AP) announced that twenty-eight-year-old Neil Connery, the younger brother of 007 himself, Sean Connery, signed a contract with Italian movie producer Dario Samatello. Samatello previously produced a number of Italian films, most notably the spaghetti Western *Seven Guns for the MacGregors* (1966). At the time, Neil Connery was earning approximately $9 a day as both a house-painter and photographer. Although he had no previous acting experience, he jumped at the chance to follow in his brother's footsteps. The film he signed on to make was reported to be a "James-Bond type" secret agent film, *O.K. Connery*, a title that clearly exploits the star's relations ("007 the Second," 38).

A number of James Bond alumni were cast: Daniela Bianchi (*From Russia with Love*), Adolfo Celi (*Thunderball*), Anthony Dawson (*Dr. No*), and Yasuko Yama (Yama had a minor role in *You Only Live Twice* and was romantically linked to actor James Mason). Samatello even managed to cast current James Bond stars Bernard Lee, who played MI6 chief M, and Lois Maxwell, MI6

Neil Connery, younger brother of Sean Connery, was too much in *Operation Kid Brother* **(1967).** © *1967 United Artists Corporation*

secretary Miss Moneypenny. Both were still actively playing their roles in Eon Productions' James Bond franchise.

Lois Maxwell, whose character had limited screen time in all the previous James Bond films, in particular was excited for the film. Maxwell was able to step out from behind a desk and play a secret agent like Bond in the film. "I get to shoot 18 people with a machine gun," exclaimed Maxwell (Petzold "An Adventurous," 18).

The cast also included a pair of spaghetti Western regulars: Agata Flori, wife of producer Dario Sabatello, who played in *Seven Guns for the MacGregors* (1965) and *Up the MacGregors!* (1967), and Italian racecar driver and cousin of famed Italian actress Gina Lollobrigida, Guido Lollobrigida. Guido Lollobrigida had notable roles in *$100,000 for Ringo* (1965), *Django Shoots First* (1966), and *Mexican Slayride* (1967).

Neil Connery played the bearded, world-renowned plastic surgeon, Dr. Neil Connery, the younger brother of an unnamed top British Secret Service secret agent. When Dr. Connery's secret agent brother is killed in action, he is brought in to save the world from the evil organization THANATOS. THANATOS planned on using a magnetic wave generator that would cause all metal-based machinery to stop working. Fortunately, Dr. Connery happens to be a master of disguise, an expert in martial arts and hypnotism, and like his brother, an infamous playboy.

Although a film made to exploit the spy craze and the Connery name, *O.K. Connery* reportedly had a budget of $1.6 million, and Samatello shot the film on location in Turin and San Remo, Italy; Monte Carlo and Tetuan, Monaco; and Malaga and Barcelona, Spain (Hall "It's 006").

Dario Sabatello brought on Alberto De Martino to direct. De Martino was known at the time for directing and writing a number of Italian horror, spaghetti Western, Euro-spy, and sword-and-sandal (peplum) films such as *Medusa against the Son of Hercules* (1963), *The Blancheville Monster* (1963), *$100,000 for Ringo* (1965), *Django Shoots First* (1966), and *The Spy with Ten Faces* (1966).

Producer Dario Sabatello also employed prominent composers Bruno Nicolai and Ennio Morricone. Nicolai was best known for composing music for a number Euro-spy films and spaghetti Westerns and worked on other Alberto De Martino projects *The Spy with Ten Faces* (1966), *$100,000 for Ringo* (1965), and *Django Shoots First* (1966). Morricone, a highly influential and fabled composer, at the time was best known for composing the score for *The Good, the Bad and the Ugly* (1966). Morricone composed epic scores for more than four hundred film and television productions throughout this lifetime, working until his death in 2020.

Neil Connery made it clear to the press that he was not simply imitating the character his brother made famous. "Let's get one thing straight. I'm not James Bond and I'm not my brother." He added, "And my brother is a professional actor and a very good one. I'm just a learner. . . . We're completely different, both on screen and off. Sean's a man of action, high strung and impulsive. I'm calmer and more reflective" (Hollander "Watch Out, 007!," 138). Before the film was released, Neil Connery told *San Francisco Examiner*'s William Hall, "I'm taking the job as seriously as I can, but it isn't easy. I'd like to succeed as an actor, even take lessons. But if I'm a flop I'll be quite happy to go back to my old work" (Hall "Neil Connery," 223).

Dario Samatello said that Neil Connery was a "satisfactory lover" in his screen test and got even better as filming progressed. "He's doing wonders for a guy making his first picture," said Samatello. "I'm convinced that in three years he'll be even better than his brother." Daniela Bianchi, who costarred with Sean Connery in *From Russia with Love*, said, "I had a fine time with Sean but Neil is even more fun in some ways. Maybe it's me. I could hardly speak any English when I worked with Sean and once the scene we concluded we had nothing to say to each other. Now I can talk and joke with Neil so we get along very well even when the cameras are spotted" (Hollander "Watch Out, 007!," 138).

Although the film was announced in early 1966, in January 1967, *Hollywood Scene* columnist Dorothy Manners wrote that Sean Connery was not happy about the film. She stated that the more Sean heard about *O.K. Connery*, "a nervy title to start with, the madder he gets" (Manners "Connery Not Amused," 40).

Neil later refuted Dorothy Manner's claim, stating "People have said that Sean doesn't like what I'm doing, but that's not true." He added, "I've seen all Sean's work, and there's no danger of our being rivals or anything like that" (Hall "It's 006," 5). Sean Connery never directly addressed his feelings toward the film.

James Bond coproducer Harry Saltzman of Eon Productions brushed off the film and was quoted as saying, "Looks like an attempt by the Italian to make a fast buck," with reference to Dario Samatello. Meanwhile Samatello stated that he heard "Sean [Connery] and his producers [Harry Saltzman and Albert Broccoli]) will try to stop us legally. Not a chance. There's no law against a brother playing a spy role on screen—even if he's the brother of Sean Connery" (Manners "Connery Not Amused," 40).

No legal action was ever taken by Eon Productions or Sean Connery. However, the film was released as *Operation Kid Brother* in the states to avoid possible legal disputes. The film had another name change in 1993. *Operation Kid Brother* was renamed *Operation Double 007* when it was shown on the original run on the cult satirical series *Mystery Science Theater 3000* (1988–1999). The film was released to European theaters on April 20, 1967, and began to play theaters in the United States on October 27, 1967.

The trailer featured the tagline "Neil Connery Is Too Much," a soundalike "James Bond Theme," a number of beautiful girls, and most of the film's action sequences. Bosley Crowther of the *New York Times* wrote, "Anyone prepared to pay $2.50 just to see what Sean Connery's brother looks like probably deserves *Operation Kid Brother*, a wobbly carbon copy of the James Bond thrillers." Crowther stated that it was obvious the film was Neil Connery's acting debut and that "there's a determined but one-horse trickling of Bond-type gadgets, murderous and otherwise. The scenery and the girls, especially Daniela Bianchi (*From Russia with Love*), are nifty. For good measure and out of the same film, there's even an iron-jawed lesbian killer briefly pawing a fair captive. Call it *Operation Turkey*" (Crowther "Mr. Kennedy," 58).

Tony Mastroianni of the *Cleveland Press* panned the film and saw it as a cheap Bond knockoff. "Dreary and dismal is the espionage movie *Operation Kid Brother* which derives its name and even some of its plot from the fact that it stars Neil Connery, younger brother of Sean (James Bond) Connery. His name in the movie also is Neil Connery, lest audience members forget, and there are frequent references to the fact that he has an older brother who is a spy. . . . What is missing are the flair and skill with which the Bond films are made. The script is labored, the direction slow and the acting is barely adequate," wrote Mastroianni. "I don't know if the movie will cause any sibling rivalry among the Connerys. Among audiences, however, it is likely to cause a distinct sibling depression" (Mastroianni "*Kid Brother* Is Poor Relation," 42).

A review published in the *Knoxville News-Sentinel* stated, "At best, the film, its director, Alberto de Martino, and the large cast deserve an 'E' for effort. . . . The junior Connery is a wooden actor, and he and the whole cast suffer for very poor dubbing and post-synchronization." But the writer concedes, "All the continental gals should help male movie-goers enjoy the fast-paced and outlandish antics all the more" ("New Films in London," 64).

Not all reviews were terrible. The *Miami Herald* described the film in an announcement that *Operation Kid Brother* would be providing local theaters with "edge-of-the-seat thrills, punctuated by shots, fights, karate, plastic surgery and even a strange kind of Tibetan hypnosis" ("New Hero," 207). Henry T. Murdock of the *Philadelphia Inquirer* called the film "a wild spoof which can hijack a lot of laughs from its audience" (Murdock "*Kid Brother* Spoofs," 11).

But Marjory Adams of the *Boston Globe* believed Neil Connery didn't have the right "ZING." She wrote that he "hasn't the dash, the personality, the attractiveness, the talents of brother Sean. . . . *Operation Kid Brother* is a mishmash of spying and beautiful girls; boudoirs and subterranean caves, knife wielding women and arrow shooting males. It could never be taken seriously by the most gullible moron" (Adams "Neil Connery Lack," 17).

One *Boston Globe* advertisement for the New England–based theater chain, Sack Theaters erroneously claimed that *Operation Kid Brother* was "the latest of the James Bond Films" (Sack Theaters advertisement).

After production wrapped, Neil Connery reportedly returned to his family and to his career as a housepainter and photographer in Scotland. Neil Connery only made one other big screen appearance, two years later appearing in the British science fiction film *The Body Stealers* (1969) (Graham "Sean Connery's," 10).

6

SOUTH OF THE BORDER SECRET AGENTS

"Where am I?" he asked and was surprised that his voice sounded firm and clear.

—Ian Fleming, *Casino Royale*

The Mexican film industry was running on all cylinders in the 1960s, producing romance, comedies, horror, Western, and action/adventure films (and sometimes all five in one film) at a staggering pace. Studios south of the border were also eager to put out their own versions of the 007 character.

Operación 67 (1966; a.k.a. Operation 67)

El Santo: El Enmascarado de Plata (The Saint: The Man in the Silver Mask)—Mexican silver-masked luchador (professional wrestler), comic book star, and folk hero—made his mark in the world of film being portrayed as Mexico's resident monster slayer. El Santo, like all masked Mexican luchadores, did not have a secret identity; the mask *was* his identity, and he was not seen without his mask on or offscreen or in or out of the wrestling ring. In his films El Santo took on vampires, werewolves, zombies, mad scientists, witches, Martians . . . just to name a few.

But in 1966, El Santo changed direction, took a break from monster hunting, and starred in the James Bond–inspired spy thriller *Operación 67*. El Santo starred alongside the tall, dark, and handsome Jorge Rivero. The duo play secret agents who attempt to stop a counterfeit money ring that intends to bring down Latin American governments.

Operación 67 takes a lot from the James Bond playbook and includes lots of bikini-clad girls, swinging music, action, car chases, over-the-top spy gadgets, an airplane attack, flamethrowers, a bazooka, and numerous fight sequences. Like most other El Santo films, it contains several wrestling matches featuring El Santo (one with Jorge Rivero as his tag-team partner).

Although the film played all over Latin America, *Operación 67* played in the United States exclusively in Spanish-language theaters, namely, at drive-ins in California, Michigan, Arizona, and Texas.

El Santo continued to rack up wrestling championships, continued to star in his own comic book that was published from the 1950s through the 1970s, and appeared in over fifty films on the big screen but never came back to the spy genre. Occasionally El Santo portrayed a crime fighter, but only in *Operación 67* is El Santo explicitly a secret agent. Following *Operación 67*, El Santo returned to mostly fighting classic horror monsters throughout the rest of his film career, which ended two years before his death in 1984.

El Santo and Jorge Rivero taking a break from being secret agents and professional wrestlers with two unnamed beach beauties in *Operación 67* (1966). *Author's collection*

A folk hero throughout Mexico, El Santo can even be seen in religious iconography throughout the country. *Author's collection*

A statue commemorating El Santo stands in Tulancingo de Bravo, Mexico, and his mask was passed down to his son, El Hijo del Santo, and later to his grandson, Santo Jr., both celebrated and decorated luchadores in Mexico.

S.O.S. Conspiración Bikini (1967; a.k.a. S.O.S. Bikini Conspiracy)

Mexican production *S.O.S. Conspiración Bikini* stars Julio Alemán as secret agent Alex Dinamo and his partner Adriana (Sonia Furió). The pair do battle with an international terrorist organization, Secret Organizational Service (S.O.S.), an evil group that exclusively recruits beautiful bikini-clad women via a modeling-agency front run by Madame Bristol (Sonia Infante).

Writer-director René Cardona Jr., who has ninety-nine films to his directing credit, talked about his new film before the film's release: "Terrorism in Latin America is the basis of this first adventure. Alex Dinamo faces a terrorist organization only known as S.O.S. The initials stand for nothing." But Cardona added another reason why someone would want to go see his film: "But of course, apart from deeds of daring, Alex Dinamo is surrounded by a lot of female beauties—Latin beauties. . . . And, of course, they are all dressed in minute bikinis" (Zubryn "Latin America's," 128).

Alex Dinamo (Julio Alemán) in action in *S.O.S. Conspiración Bikini* **(1967).** *Author's collection*

Cardona saw the film as a possible watershed moment for Mexican cinema to gain international attention: "Mexico's industry must break out of the rut of singing charros who are fumbling gunfighters and indifferent horsemen. The time has come for Mexico to internationalize and while I admit action pictures are good bets at the box office, there has been far too little action in our films in the past and far too much talk—and singing—and sobbing!" (Ibid.).

While many other spy movies attempted to shy away from James Bond, Cardona did not deny his inspiration. "Alex Dinamo is a Latin American James Bond. Why deny it? But Alex is a rugged individualist, and uses Latin ingenuity in coping with his problems and situations. Something James Bond never does" (Ibid.).

Although Cardona hoped the film would do better north of the Mexican border, the only showing of *S.O.S. Conspiración Bikini* in the United States was at a Spanish-language drive-in theater in Tucson, Arizona, in November 1968 ("Show Schedule").

Alex Dinamo would return in *Peligro . . . Mujeres en Acción* (1969; a.k.a. *Danger Girls*), a film that also had a limited run in the United States.

Agente 00 Sexy (1968)

Agente 00 Sexy is another attempt to capitalize on the 007 name, but any correlation to James Bond is purely coincidental.

After Ernesto Romero's (Fernando Lujan) dreams of being a singing star are crushed (because he is an awful singer), he is whisked away by a gang who believe Ernesto is their leader, Louie. As it turns out, Ernesto is an exact double for Louie (Fernando Lujan plays Louie as well). Ernesto even becomes acquainted with Louie's blond American girlfriend, Angora (Amadee Chabot).

Ernesto is soon rescued by the police and is convinced to go undercover to take on Louie's gang. To help with his mission, he is given James Bond–type gizmos and gadgets, a watch with a mini tape recorder inside, and a cigarette lighter equipped with a camera.

Most reviews and synopses of the film point out that Amadee Chabot's voice, although she spoke Spanish in other films without a problem, was dubbed. The dubbing gave Chabot a "gringo" accent. She spoke loudly in broken Spanish and occasionally in English, presumably to play up her dumb blond American character.

Because Angora is not a secret agent, it is unclear who exactly is supposed to be "Agente 00 Sexy."

Amadee Chabot in her infamous Catwoman outfit in *Agente 00 Sexy* (1968). *Internet Archive*

Like many Mexican flicks at the time, *Agente 00 Sexy* featured comedy, action, rock and roll, musical numbers, dancing, and beautiful women. The film also attempted to exploit another 1960s fad, *Batman* (1966–1968). Although *Agente 00 Sexy* features Amadee Chabot in a number of revealing outfits and bathing suits, most famously the film and the film's poster feature her dressed as Batman villain Catwoman (in a much more revealing outfit than what was seen on the *Batman* television show).

Amadee Chabot was a former Miss California and was featured in a number of films and TV shows in the states, most notably appearing in two 1964 episodes of *The Beverly Hillbillies* (1962–1971), *Muscle Beach Party* (1964), and even two uncredited roles in Dean Martin's spy spoofs *The Silencers* (1966) and *Murderers' Row* (1966). But in 1968 Chabot made her way south of the border to find fame with a Spanish-speaking audience. Within the first year, she starred alongside Mexican professional wrestler, comic book hero, and movie star El Santo in *Treasures of Montezuma* (1968) and in *Agente 00 Sexy*. Chabot would go on to play in Latin America's answer to James Bond: *Peligro . . . Mujeres en Acción* (1969, a.k.a. *Danger Girls*).

In the United States, *Agent 00 Sexy* played only at Spanish-language theaters in California, Texas, and Florida.

Peligro . . . Mujeres en Acción (1969; a.k.a. *Danger Girls*)

In a sequel to *S.O.S. Conspiración Bikini* (1967), secret agent Alex Dinamo (Julio Alemán) once again takes on the evil S.O.S. organization composed of beautiful, bikini-wearing girls who are hell-bent on taking over the world by sabotaging oil fields in Ecuador and inserting a biological weapon in Latin America's drinking water after smuggling an international terrorist out of prison.

American actress Elizabeth Campbell, who migrated south of the border to find success in movies, played S.O.S. mastermind Salva. Campbell may be best known for her roles in Mexican exploitation flicks *Las Luchadoras contra el Médico Asesino* (1963; a.k.a. *Doctor of Doom*), *Las Luchadoras contra la Momia* (1964; a.k.a. *The Wrestling Women vs. the Aztec Mummy*, *El Planeta de las Mujeres Invasoras* (1966; a.k.a. *Planet of the Female Invaders*), and *Operación 67* (1966; a.k.a. *Operation 67*).

Alma Delia Fuentes played Dynamo's love interest, Maura. Like Elizabeth Campbell, Fuentes is best known for her roles in Mexican exploitation cinema, appearing in films such as *Dr. Satán* (1966; a.k.a. *Dr. Satan*), *La Isla de los Dinosaurios* (1967; a.k.a. *The Island of Dinosaurs*) and *Blue Demon: Destructor de Espías* (1968; a.k.a. *Blue Demon: Destructor of Spies*).

Filmed in Miami, Puerto Rico, and Ecuador the film features more sex, explosions, shootouts, karate fights, and action on the land, in the water, and in the skies than its predecessor. *Peligro . . . Mujeres en Acción* also features a jazzy stylish soundtrack, beautiful scenery, and colorful characters. The film's trailer promised "A storm of intrigue! Of terror! Of murder! Of cruelty!" and that the film was "the most spectacular film ever made in Latin America."

Although René Cardona Jr. envisioned Alex Dinamo as Latin America's James Bond and hoped to have an ongoing series, *Peligro . . . Mujeres en Acción* is the last of the Alex Dinamo films. However, Alex Dinamo was turned into a popular Latin American comic book. *Peligro . . . Mujeres en Acción* only played in the United States at three locations: the Apache Drive-in, Tucson, Arizona; Los Angeles area's Floral Drive-in, Monterey Park, California; and the historic Art Deco movie palace BAL Theater in San Leandro, California.

7

DOUBLE AGENT
TELEVISION

*Bond sat down on his rumpled bed and lost himself in drink
and gloomy reflections.*

—Ian Fleming, *Casino Royale*

The three major American television networks (NBC, ABC, and CBS) all had their share of espionage to fill their prime-time lineups, and shows from Great Britain could not be imported fast enough to keep up with the demand.

Danger Man (1960–1962 and 1964–1968; a.k.a. *Secret Agent*)

Inspired by Ian Fleming's James Bond novels but two years before James Bond hit the big screen, *Danger Man* aired on ITV in Great Britain and starred Patrick McGoohan as NATO agent John Drake. Drake, like James Bond, defends order and democracy across the globe.

Despite the show being canceled in 1962, the 1960s spy craze, with James Bond at the forefront, was about to hit its peak, and that caused renewed interest in the show and a comeback in 1964. The original series of episodes were a brisk thirty minutes, but when brought back in 1964, the show was extended to an hour, giving viewers the equivalent of a mini–James Bond–type adventure every week. The show also featured a fair amount of blood and violence for 1960s prime-time viewing.

Danger Man first made an appearance in the United States in 1961 when the show was imported by CBS as a replacement for the newly canceled Western

Promotional still for *Secret Agent* (1960–1962 and 1964–1968). *ITC Entertainment Corporation*

Wanted: Dead or Alive (1958–1961). CBS brought back the show in 1964 and renamed it *Secret Agent*. *Secret Agent* ran in the United States until the spring of 1966. The show also aired on a number of independent local channels throughout the United States.

Along with a different title, CBS gave the show a different theme song; Johnny Rivers's "Secret Agent Man." The song proved to be so popular it reached number three in 1966 on the *Billboard* Hot 100 charts. "Secret Agent Man" proved to be as synonymous with the 1960's spy craze as "The James

Bond Theme." In England the original series theme was "The Danger Man Theme," composed by Edwin Astley, and later "High Wire," composed by Edwin Astley as well.

The Avengers (1961–1969)

Predating *Dr. No* (1962), perhaps the most iconic British spy program was *The Avengers*. The show originally featured two male leads, John Steed (Patrick Macnee) and David Keel (Ian Hendry). The next season replaced Keel with black knee-high boots–wearing Cathy Gale (Honor Blackman). The presence of Cathy Gale added much needed sex appeal to the show. However, Blackman left the show at the end of the 1963–1964 season to play the role of Pussy Galore in the third James Bond movie *Goldfinger* (1964).

Blackman was replaced by superspy Emma Peel (Diana Rigg), who proved to be even more popular with audiences than her predecessor. Peel's signature one-piece bodysuits were designed by Alun Hughes and were known in England as "Emma Peelers."

"What man wouldn't be overcome by an Amazon in sex-kitten's clothing?" asked Roslyn Owen of *TV Week*. "Take Emma's white lace over flesh-fabric cat suit—what could be sexier? Only, perhaps, her blue lamé bra and matching hipster trousers, which she wears for scenes in an old Scottish castle. Of course, she does wear clothes of a more 'butch' type. Like her black stretch jersey fighting suits for daytime. Or even a black leather fighting suit with a side-buckled waist and gun-pouch. But even the black-leather number is softened by a white crepe blouse. And it fits like a second skin" (Owen "Dressed to Kill," 22).

The show received attention from American media outlets like the *New York Times* in 1964, but *The Avengers* was not brought to the United States until it aired on ABC Monday March 28, 1966, at 10:00 p.m. as a summer replacement for *Ben Casey* ("What the Networks").

New episodes once again aired in January 1967, when the show made the jump to color, the newly minted television standard. Excitement and interest for the British import were high, and Diana Rigg and Patrick Macnee even appeared on the January 21, 1967, cover of *TV Guide*.

But Diana Rigg left *The Avengers* in 1967; she, too, went on to play in a James Bond film as Bond's love interest (and future Mrs. James Bond) Countess Tracy di Vicenzo, in *On Her Majesty's Secret Service* (1969), starring George Lazenby as James Bond.

In the sixth and final season of *The Avengers*, Linda Thorson took over as secret agent Tara King (1968–1969).

Emma Peel (Diana Rigg) in her "Emma Peelers" alongside her partner John Steed (Patrick Macnee). *Author's collection*

The Saint (1962–1969)

Future James Bond, Roger Moore starred as Simon Templar, a former criminal who now travels the world to protect the helpless and is known as "The Saint."

Before debuting in the United States, British show *The Saint* aired in Great Britain on ITV and amassed a cult following in the United States when it aired on local stations late at night and on UHF stations throughout the country.

Although the show did not air in prime time on NBC stateside until May 21, 1967, the show aired in syndication throughout the United States starting in 1963. Roger Moore acknowledged that up until the show aired on NBC in prime time, *The Saint* did not have much competition in the United States. Moore stated, "We've been doing remarkably well against nothing . . . we're seen on Sunday night opposite an assortment of old, old movies all playing for the 50th time." He added, "NBC checked the ratings and found we had a higher share than many of their other programs. But next season we go in against regularly scheduled programs and we may fall flat on our faces" (Jordan "Politicos, Election Special," 52; Pack "NBC Signs," 22).

Despite taking the role of James Bond and playing the famous MI6 agent in seven films, at the time Roger Moore said that "Bond is an immoral, amoral character. He's a man who is glamorized because he can kill, and this is rather

The future James Bond, Roger Moore, in *The Saint* (1962–1969). *Author's collection*

sick" as opposed to Simon Templar who never killed anyone in his six seasons on the air (Van Gelder "Roger Moore," 10D).

The Saint also had some real-life Cold War intrigue. The show was reportedly a favorite in Eastern European Communist Bloc nations such as Czechoslovakia, Romania, Hungary, Bulgaria, and Poland. The Saint was so popular in Poland that it was reported that Communist Party branches never scheduled meetings when The Saint was on the television schedule ("Red Viewers").

Espionage (1963–1964)

Airing in America on Wednesday nights at 9:00 p.m. on NBC, Espionage was a British anthology series with stories of spy adventures around the globe and in different historical periods. Episodes involved World War II, the Irish Rebellion, Israeli agents in Spain, and the CIA manipulating an African government, to cite a few examples.

Although the show did not have any recurring characters or actors, it did feature a number of noticeable personalities, including Dennis Hopper, Steven Hill, Donald Pleasence, Jim Backus, and Patricia Neal. Donald Kirkley of the Baltimore Sun called the show "one of the best spy stories that I have seen in any medium." He added, "In its category, I think it is a masterpiece" (Kirkley "Look and Listen," 28).

The hour-long show suffered in the ratings, airing Wednesday night opposite popular shows Ben Casey (1961–1966) on ABC and The Beverly Hillbillies (1962–1971) and The Dick Van Dyke Show on CBS. Cincinnati Enquirer TV-radio editor James Devane wrote that he "heard NBC intended to continue Espionage even if it goes unnoticed by a major portion of the population of the United States. Since I'm not among those who find the week unbearable without seeing either gruff Ben or the Clampett clan, this is fine with me, for the spy series generally is upper class entertainment" (Devane "TV's 'Espionage,'" 17).

Devane was wrong. Despite being well-produced, the show only lasted one season.

Get Smart (1965–1970)

A satirical take on James Bond spy adventures, Get Smart chronicled one of television's most iconic characters: Agent 86 Maxwell Smart (Don Adams), a bumbling secret agent for the US top secret counterintelligence organization CONTROL. Smart was joined at CONTROL by partner, love interest, and future wife Agent 99 (Barbara Feldon); Chief (Edward Platt); humanoid,

Don Adams and Barbara Feldon use Maxwell Smart's signature shoe phone in promotional stills for *Get Smart* **(1965–1970).** *Author's collection*

good-natured, and emotional robot Hymie (Dick Gautier); and the Chief's forgetful assistant Larabee (Robert Karvelas). Every week, the agents of CONTROL took on the evil agents of KAOS, Ludwig Von Siegfried (Bernie Kopell) and his sidekick Shtarker (King Moody).

Get Smart had a number of takes on James Bondesque spy gadgets—perhaps most notably Maxwell Smart's then futuristic shoe phone and CONTROL's top-secret, giant apparatus for keeping conversations a secret that rarely worked, the Cone of Silence. *Get Smart* even parodied a number of movies, books, and television shows, including Bond films *Dr. No* (1962) and *Goldfinger* (1964), and spy shows *I Spy* (1965–1968) and *Mission: Impossible* (1966–1973).

Critics almost universally praised *Get Smart* for its sharp writing by Buck Henry and Mel Brooks:

> "The ha-ha, and even ho-ho, quota is refreshingly high."—Harry Harris, *Philadelphia Inquirer*.

> "The wackiest farce."—Martin Hogan Jr., *Cincinnati Enquirer*.

> "He almost succeeds in being the straight man to himself."—Jack Anderson, *Miami Herald*.

"Pure fun from start to finish."—Aleen MacMinn, *Los Angeles Times.*

"Maybe the best of the 30-minute comedies."—Allen Rich, *Hollywood Citizen-News.*

"Great Comic Possibilities."—Rick DuBrow, United Press International.

("Critics' View, Part 2," 69)

Like James Bond, *Get Smart* was seen on every conceivable piece of merchandise. United Artists Records released a *Get Smart* record album. On the album, Don Adams in character as Maxwell Smart recalls his adventures. Barbara Feldon got in on the act and recorded a 7", 45 rpm single titled "Max," and B side, which has become a *Get Smart* fan favorite, "99." Dell Comics published a series of *Get Smart* comic books, and Tempo books released nine *Get Smart* novels written by William Johnson. Toy stores also sold board games, trading cards, lunch boxes, jigsaw puzzles, coloring books, and toy spy kits adorned with the *Get Smart* moniker.

Get Smart's popularity rode the wave of the 1960s spy craze. The first season of *Get Smart*, in 1965–1966 during the height of the craze, was the twelfth most watched show on television; in the second season, 1966–1967, the show fell to the twenty-second highest rated. By the 1967–1968 season, when the craze was in a steep decline, ratings fell off and never recovered. However, when the show was canceled by NBC in 1969, the show was picked up by CBS for the 1969–1970 season (Brooks and Marsh 1979).

Amos Burke: Secret Agent (1965–1966)

For two seasons, *Burke's Law* (1963–1965) chronicled the story of Amos Burke (Gene Barry), a millionaire Los Angeles police captain who was chauffeured around to solve crimes in his Rolls-Royce. But in 1965, the show changed with the spy trend and was transformed into *Amos Burke: Secret Agent.* Burke took on the role of secret agent for a secret government organization. His Rolls-Royce was even given a bulletproof-glass windshield. Instead of being confined to Los Angeles, Burke now traveled the world, taking on evil organizations and counterintelligence organizations. Switching formats did not work for *Amos Burke: Secret Agent*, which routinely found itself at the bottom of the ratings heap. The show was canceled after only seventeen episodes ("Bottom 15").

The Baron (1965-1966)

Originally airing on ITV in Great Britain, ABC imported the show to the US prime-time schedule as a winter replacement for the drama *The Long, Hot Summer* in 1966. *The Baron* featured John Mannering (Steve Forrest) as a British Intelligence agent who travels the world to solve crime under the guise of being an antiques dealer from Texas. Steve Forrest was coming off a successful string of featured roles on shows such as *The Twilight Zone* (1959-1964), *The Virginian* (1962-1971), and *Twelve O'Clock High* (1964-1967).

Debuting in the states around the same time as the wildly popular *Batman* (1966-1968), ABC spent much of its time and effort in the winter of 1966 on promoting the Caped Crusader and not *The Baron,* which did not make the next season's schedule.

The Man from U.N.C.L.E. (1964-1968)/The Girl from U.N.C.L.E. (1966-1967)

"James Bond on television" is how *The Man from U.N.C.L.E.* (1964-1968) star Robert Vaughn, described his show. U.N.C.L.E. (United Network Command for Law and Enforcement) was an international organization that even included Cold War foes the United States and the Soviet Union. U.N.C.L.E. agent's Napoleon Solo (Robert Vaughn), Illya Kuryakin (David McCallum), and U.N.C.L.E. chief, Mr. Alexander Waverly (Leo G. Carroll), took on the evil THRUSH organization when an innocent person got caught up in international affairs.

The comparison was not unwarranted. James Bond creator Ian Fleming was involved with the creation of the show, originally titled *Mr. Solo* and later *Solo* from October 1962 until he signed his rights away for one British pound sterling in June 1963. Fleming signed away the rights due to pressure from James Bond's film producers Albert Broccoli and Harry Saltzman, who did not want Fleming to be involved with both *The Man from U.N.C.L.E.* television show and the James Bond film franchise. According to letters between Fleming and *The Man from U.N.C.L.E.* producer Norman Felton, Fleming came up with the character Napoleon Solo and a number of the show's key elements. Because Fleming signed away his rights, MGM Studio head Robert M. Weitman released the following statement: "There have been, from time to time, references in the press to the effect that Ian Fleming is the creator of, or associated with this MGM-TV series. The series is based upon an original idea of Norman Felton's and was developed into a pilot script by Sam Rolfe. Neither

Mr. Fleming nor the James Bond books are involved in the production of this television series" (Koenig Letters).

In its first season, *The Man from U.N.C.L.E.* had a difficult time finding a foothold in the ratings, but by the second season, when the show made the jump to color, *The Man from U.N.C.L.E.* was the thirteenth highest rated show (Brooks and Marsh 1979). *The Man from U.N.C.L.E.* never saw the same kind of rating success as it did in its second season, dropping to forty-sixth in 1966–1967 (Spencer "TV's Vast").

The drop in ratings perhaps is due in part to changes in the show's production and vision. The show introduced a new producer each season, and each season the new producer brought their own ideas and concepts to the show, thus making *The Man from U.N.C.L.E* a very different show than originally conceived. In an interview with the Academy of Television Arts & Sciences, Robert Vaughn put it best when he stated, "It went from being a straight James Bond kind of show . . . by the third season it had become almost a farce because we were shooting cupcakes out of guns on the sides of cars. It was no longer James Bond. It was something very silly and it went off the air the fourth year for that very reason" ("Robert Vaughn").

The National Association for Better Broadcasting (NABB) published a report on television shows it believed to be unacceptable for children and wrote that *The Man from U.N.C.L.E*'s "vividly depicted horror make it unsuitable for children" (Leonard "What's Out," 78).

The Man from U.N.C.L.E., like James Bond, was not short of merchandising opportunities. Despite the NABB's recommendation, children were clearly fans of the show, and store shelves were lined with official U.N.C.L.E. identification badges, character action figures, car model kits, invisible ink pens, toy gun sets, puzzles, lunch boxes, board games, and a number of novelizations.

The Man from U.N.C.L.E LP was released in 1965, and *More Music from The Man from U.N.C.L.E.* was released in 1966; they included the show's theme and soundtrack arranged and conducted by Hugo Montenegro. Montenegro would also produce the music for two Matt Helm spy spoofs, *The Ambushers* (1967) and *The Wrecking Crew* (1968).

Between 1964 and 1968, eight movies that were lengthened and reedited versions of *The Man from U.N.C.L.E.* were released in the United States and in international markets like Australia and Great Britain and presented as feature-length films: *To Trap a Spy* (1964), *The Spy with My Face* (1965), *One Spy Too Many* (1966), *One of Our Spies Is Missing* (1966), *The Spy in the Green Hat* (1966), *The Karate Killers* (1967), *The Helicopter Spies* (1968), and *How to Steal the World* (1968). Called a "bridge picture" in the film industry, *Variety*

This *Man from U.N.C.L.E.* (1964–1968) card game has very little to do with the show. Players must collect the highest number of cards (numbered 1–6) that equal multiples of 10. *Author's collection*

called the films a "confusing spy meller [melodrama] expanding a *Man from U.N.C.L.E* segment" ("Hybrid"; *Variety Film Reviews*, 306).

Called "*The Man from U.N.C.L.E.* in high heels" by Paul Molloy of the *Chicago Sun-Times,* spin-off *The Girl from U.N.C.L.E.* (1966–1967) debuted in the fall of 1966 and featured Stefanie Powers as rookie U.N.C.L.E. agent April Dancer. *The Girl from U.N.C.L.E.* had the same general plot and feel of *The Man from U.N.C.L.E* and was given similar merchandising and promotional opportunities, including an age-inappropriate *Girl from U.N.C.L.E.* garter gun holster. Stefanie Powers famously appeared on the cover of *TV Guide* wearing an all silver jumpsuit ("Critics' Views," 67).

The Girl from U.N.C.L.E. even had her own soundtrack LP composed by Dave Grusin. Grusin also composed the score for *The Wild Wild West* (1965–1968) and would go on to notably score films such as *The Graduate* (1967) and *Heaven Can Wait* (1978).

Also much like *The Man from U.N.C.L.E.*, NABB called out the show's violence and wrote that the show was "an illustration of network television's irresponsibility to children. Explicit terror. Torture for fun. This is a worse show even than *Man from U.N.C.L.E.*" NABB added, "Ordinary violent death is too mild a form of entertainment for this show. It has to be accomplished with pits of boiling oil, with carnivorous fish, electricity or chemical solvents to reduce the body to dust. It has to be produced by people who delight in creating nightmares," stating that its "cynical treatment and macabre humor make this violent suspense program unsuitable for young children" (Horn "Rating Shows," 10; Leonard "What's Out," 78).

Although gruesome deaths and Powers's skintight jumpsuits may be an attraction to some viewers, poor reviews did not help the show. "Honestly, in one season how many spoofs can you take? If a spoof is going to be effective, it must surely have to begin with something serious to spoof off from," said a review in *TV Guide*. *The Girl from U.N.C.L.E.* is "about as believable as women's wrestling. And it has as much wit as a roller derby." "The acting in *The Girl from U.N.C.L.E.* is enough to make you cry aunt" (Amory "Review," 21).

Despite the promotional effort, *The Girl from U.N.C.L.E* was the second least watched show of the 1966–1967 season and was ultimately canceled by NBC at season's (Spenser "TV's Vast").

I Spy (1965–1968)

Robert Culp and Bill Cosby starred as US Intelligence agents Alexander "Scotty" Scott (Bill Cosby) and Kelly Robinson (Robert Culp) in *I Spy* (1965–1968). The agents traveled undercover as a pair of tennis bums.

In 1965, when Cosby was cast in NBC's *I Spy*, it became one of the first weekly network television shows to feature an African American star in what was called at the time an "integrated cast." NBC feared that some local affiliate stations would not air a show with an integrated cast. Although 180 network affiliates throughout the United States carried *I Spy*, 5, mostly southern, stations refused (Adams "*I Spy* with Negro").

Cosby later thanked NBC "for having guts" to air *I Spy* (Adams "Bill Cosby of 'I Spy,'" 68). Robert Culp stated, "The fact that they—a white man and a Negro—work together as friends also carries an underlying message of the brotherhood of man, though there is never any preaching about it" (Thomas "Robert Culp Happy," 32).

I Spy debuted in color on Wednesday, September 15, 1965, at 10:00 p.m. on NBC and received positive reviews:

"This could be the one to watch."—Bob Hull, *Los Angeles Examiner*.

"The best spy series we've ever encountered."—Jack O'Brian, *New York Journal-American*.

"There are tones of Bond . . . a cross between *Espionage* and *Hong Kong*."—Louis Cedrone Jr., *Baltimore Evening Sun*.

Robert Culp and Bill Cosby posing as tennis bums on *I Spy* (1965–1968). *Allstar Picture Library Ltd./Alamy Stock Photo*

"Creditable cloak-and-dagger series"—Bill Irwin, *Chicago American*.

"A show in search of an attitude and also the style to go with it."—Jack Gould, *New York Times*.

"A fast moving, slick production."—Cynthia Lowry, Associated Press.

("How Critics See," 39)

Although clearly inspired by James Bond, Culp described James Bond as an "amoral figure who treats his enemies and women with equal cruelty," and he felt that even the villains in *I Spy* were more lighthearted and fun (Thomas "Robert Culp Happy," 32). But *I Spy*'s fate lived and died with James Bond and the spy craze. When interest waned, so did ratings and the NBC network's faith in the show's future. *I Spy* was canceled after the 1967–1968 season.

The Secret Squirrel Show (1965-1967)

Screen Gems produced a James Bond spoof for kids, *The Secret Squirrel Show* cartoon. *The Secret Squirrel Show* aired alongside cartoon superhero Atom Ant on NBC from 1965–1967 and was seen in a block of daytime cartoons. Mel Blanc voiced Secret Agent 000 who fought crime with a Peter Lorre–sounding and fez-wearing sidekick Morocco Mole (Paul Frees) and his chief, Double Q (also voiced by Frees). Like James Bond, Secret Squirrel used a number of gadgets (including a limousine that folds up into an attaché case when a button is pushed) and his ingenuity to fight the evil organization Hi-Spy and bad guys such as Yellow Pinkie and international submarine snatcher Captain Ahab.

Mel Blanc was best known for voicing numerous characters in television and film on *The Looney Tunes*, *Tom and Jerry*, *The Flintstones*, and *The Jetsons*.

Secret Squirrel and Morocco Mole on assignment. *RGR Collection/Alamy Stock Photo*

Frees most notably provided voices on *The Adventures of Rocky and Bullwinkle* (1959–1964) but worked with every major Hollywood studio. Both voice actors worked on the feature-length Flintstones-Bond parody cartoon, *The Man Called Flintstone* (1966)

Bangor, Maine's *Bangor Daily News* columnist Ed Matheson wrote in 1965 that *The Secret Squirrel Show* "is a takeoff on all the other 'secret agent' shows that have made their appearance on television the past few months" (Matheson "Talk of the Town," 10).

The Wild Wild West (1965–1969)

The Wild Wild West (1965–1969) creator Michael Garrison and the show's star Robert Conrad both described the CBS spy Western as "James Bond on horseback." Set in the Old West following the American Civil War, James T. West (Robert Conrad) and master of disguise Artemus Gordon (Ross Martin) were secret agents who traveled via secret railcar to prevent Confederate and other nefarious groups. Like Bond, West had a number of futuristic gadgets (for the 1800s) to assist his mission. Robert Conrad stated, "You might call me Agent 001 because I'm 95 years ahead of Bond, who as everybody knows, is 007. I have my own special train. If Bond could have his sports car armed why shouldn't I have a train with all the weaponry known at the time?" (Musel "New Fall TV," 22).

Character actor Robert Conrad was coming off a starring role on ABC's *Hawaiian Eye* (1959–1963), and before *The Wild Wild West* hit the airwaves, Ross Martin was best known for starring on *Treasury Men in Action* (1950–1955), which aired on ABC and then NBC. *The Wild Wild West* rode the wave of popularity of the new spy craze and the continued popularity of Westerns. In its first season, the show was the twenty-third highest rated show of the season (Brooks and Marsh 1979).

Although the show never received particularly high ratings, it remained a favorite of the network. But following the assassinations of Martin Luther King Jr. and Robert Kennedy in 1968, activist groups focused their attention on television violence and made *The Wild Wild West* public enemy number one. The groups urged CBS to cancel the show. Initially, producers and stars of the show pushed back against the criticism. *The Wild Wild West* producer Bruce Lansbury said, "We are a different kind of show—unrealistic, preposterous, escapist—a comic strip," while Robert Conrad asked, "The question is, did or did not John Wilkes Booth's mother let him watch television?" (Crosby "Tube Moves Boobs," 14; Kleiner "Hollywood Making Reappraisal," 30).

Ross Martin and Robert Conrad in *The Wild Wild West* (1965–1969), circa 1965.
PictureLux/The Hollywood Archive/Alamy Stock Photo

Groups kept up their crusade, often focusing solely on *The Wild Wild West*. The *Christian Science Monitor* wrote that the show was one of the most violent shows on television and the National Association for Better Broadcasting (NABB) listed *The Wild Wild West* as one of the most detrimental shows on TV for children. Senator John O. Pastore (D-RI) began holding Congressional hearings, which condemned the show's sex and violence. The Congressional group National Commission on Violence believed that *The Wild Wild West* "encourages violent forms of behavior and fosters moral and social values about violence in daily life which are unacceptable in a civilized society" ("TV Violence Continues," 8; Pearson "Reappraising TV Violence," 6; Inman "New Violence," 25; Mohbat "TV Scored," 3).

The network caved to pressure, and the last episode of *The Wild Wild West* aired on April 11, 1969. The *Associated Press* wrote of the reasoning behind the cancellation of *The Wild Wild West*: "Despite high ratings, because of criticism. It was seen by the network as a gesture of good intentions" ("TV Linked," 3).

Activist groups tried to keep reruns of *The Wild Wild West* off the television airwaves as well. The Foundation to Improve Television filed suit in US District Court seeking an injunction to keep the show off television before 9:00 p.m., believing that children were "being force fed a steady diet of murder and mayhem, [and] television viewers . . . have the right to be free from the daily diet of violence and horror served by the broadcast industry." The group said *The Wild Wild West* was chosen because "it is a good example of the kind of program the foundation is trying to stop." It added that "children have a constitutional right under the 5th amendment to be free from mental harm caused by viewing television programs that portray fictional violence and horror" and that the First Amendment does not "license anyone to poison our nation's youth by educating them in violence." The suit failed (Hall "Group Files," 15).

The Double Life of Henry Phyfe (1966)

Comedian Red Buttons starred as Henry Phyfe, an accountant pressed into service by the CIA to impersonate a now dead foreign agent in order to infiltrate and disrupt an enemy organization in the very short-lived *Double Life of Henry Phyfe*. Each week, Phyfe would be given an assignment and skills to learn, all while keeping his new secret agent status from his family and coworkers and holding on to his day job.

The show marked Red Buttons's return to television after an almost eleven-year hiatus following the cancellation of his CBS variety show *The Red Buttons Show* (1952–1955). The show was immediately hit with bad reviews, notably that of the *New York Times'* Jack Gould: "Bad luck continues to dog Red Buttons in television. The comedian made his debut last night in a series called *Double Life of Henry Phyfe* and the part isn't worth his time" (Gould "Red Buttons," 79).

Producers insisted the show was not a takeoff on *Get Smart* or James Bond: "This is not a spoof. This is the story of a reluctant spy. We are doing it for fun, fun, fun" (Newton "Don't Lose," 17). But the fun did not last long. The show, which was continuously at the bottom of the ratings barrel, only lasted seventeen episodes on ABC ("Batman Still Flying").

The Man Who Never Was (1966–1967)

The Man Who Never Was starred Robert Lansing as Peter Murphy, an American spy in Europe. In a case of mistaken identity, millionaire Mark Wainwright (also played by Robert Lansing), who bears an uncanny resemblance to Peter Murphy, is killed by assassins sent to kill Murphy. Murphy then assumes

Wainwright's identity, even taking Wainwright's wife, who knew the difference but did not seem to mind, in order to continue his work while still under the guise of having been killed.

Robert Lansing previously starred on ABC's World War II Air Force drama *12 O'Clock High* (1964–1967), but after the first season, producers wanted the show to feature a more youthful looking star. Nonetheless, ABC still wanted Lansing on its prime-time schedule.

The Man Who Never Was received less-than-positive reviews for many critics around the country:

> "A study in puzzlement."—Joseph E. Sullivan, *Boston Herald*.

> "Pretty preposterous."—Bernie Harrison, *Washington Evening Star*.

> "Poorly executed and scripted."—Don Page, *Los Angeles Times*.

> "It makes the plots on *Batman* seem high drama."—Lawrence Laurent, *Washington Post*.

However some saw it as a positive direction for the spy craze:

> "A cool and cleverly done espionage series."—Rex Polier, *Philadelphia Bulletin*.

> "Has an impressive list of attributes which should make it appealing to spy buffs."—Clay Gowran, *Chicago Tribune*.

> "If you can swallow the first episode, it may turn out exciting."—Dean Gysel, *Chicago Daily News*.

> ("Critics Reviews," 37)

The Man Who Never Was had a true Cold War–era feel, thanks to being shot almost exclusively in Berlin (although shooting was later moved to European cities Munich, Germany; Nice, France; and Athens, Greece) and to taking advantage of abandoned World War II–era subway lines and even the Berlin Wall ("Man Who Never")

The show lasted seventeen episodes. Several episodes of *The Man Who Never Was* were pieced together to make two made-for-television movies, *The Spy with the Perfect Cover* and *Danger Has Two Faces*, in 1967.

Although being shot in Europe was part of the appeal of *The Man Who Never Was*, Lansing believed that Hollywood trade unions pressured ABC and sponsors not to promote the show because it was being filmed overseas and not using American union labor in its production ("Man Who Never Wins").

Mission: Impossible (1966–1973)

Mission: Impossible, and its iconic theme by Lalo Schifrin, lasted seven seasons with 171 color episodes. The show was described by *TV Guide* in the "1966–1967 Fall Preview" before the show debuted as "exactly what it sounds like: An elite team of undercover agents hop from one hotspot to another, performing incredible feats. One week they're south of the Border swiping two nuclear warheads from an impenetrable vault. Another week they're behind the iron curtain breaking into and out of a maximum-security prison" ("Fall Preview 1966–1967," n.p.).

In the first season, Dan Briggs (Steven Hill), leader of the Impossible Mission Force (IMF), each week received a seemingly impossible mission and chose a team of undercover agents to assist in the mission. Most often, the team consisted of model and actress Cinnamon Carter (Barbara Bain); electronics, mechanical, and forgery expert Barney Collier (Greg Morris); strongman Willy Armitage (Peter Lupus); and master of disguise and impersonation Rollin Hand (Martin Landau).

Each episode followed a basic format. The IMF leader would receive a tape with a mission and this reminder: "As always, should you or any of your IM Force be caught or killed, the Secretary will disavow any knowledge of your actions. . . . This tape will self-destruct." The IMF leader would then go through the dossiers of agents that he chooses for the mission. Once assembled, the team would plan out and execute the mission.

Mission: Impossible received mostly positive reviews:

"Level of suspense throughout the hour rarely achieved in television."—Don Page, *Los Angeles Times.*

"Very likely [will] catch on."—Jack Gould, *New York Times.*

"A taut tale."—Bob Hull, *Los Angeles Herald Examiner.*

"May be the best-of-breed of the new network series batch."—Bob Williams, *New York Post.*

("How Critics Assess," 74)

But the show was too much for some critics:

"Strained credulity will be beyond the breaking point."—Lawrence Laurent, *Washington Post.*

"It was virtually an impossible mission for the viewers to sort out the good guys from the bad guys and still keep track of the plot."—Bill Irvin, *Chicago's American*.

("How Critics Assess," 74)

In the second season, Peter Graves replaced Steven Hill, taking on the role of IMF leader Jim Phelps. At the time, Graves was best known for his appearance

Promo photo of Peter Graves for *Mission: Impossible* (1966–1972). *Author's collection*

on numerous television shows and work in horror films *Killers from Space* (1954) and *It Conquered the World* (1956). Graves would later be best known for his hosting and narration gig on the documentary series *Biography* on the cable network A&E, from 1987 to 1999, or his role in the disaster film parody *Airplane!* (1980).

Mission: Impossible hit its stride in the third season and was the eleventh highest rated show that year. That would be the highest rating the show would receive in the seven years it was on the air.

The 1968–1969 season was Martin Landau's last. Landau was replaced in the 1969-1970 season by Leonard Nimoy, in one of his first post-*Star Trek* roles, as IMF agent Paris, in forty-nine episodes in two seasons. Nimoy remained with the show until its cancellation at the end of the 1972-1973 season ("CBS Ups"; "Burnett Gains").

Unlike many spy shows or films of the era, *Mission: Impossible* bucked the spy trend and was rarely compared to James Bond's adventures. Perhaps this led to the show's longevity. When the show hit its ratings stride, the spy craze was on the downswing, and *Mission: Impossible* lasted much longer on the air than any of its television spy contemporaries.

Man in a Suitcase (1967–1968)

Following the second cancellation of *Danger Man*, United Kingdom channel ITV green lit another spy series, *Man in a Suitcase*. *Man in a Suitcase* first aired in the United States on ABC in the summer of 1968 and was the story of a former American intelligence agent simply known as McGill (Richard Bradford) who now is a private detective/spy living a nomadic lifestyle in England.

Man in a Suitcase was the breakout role for Richard Bradford, who would later go on to appear in the big-screen version of *The Untouchables* (1987) with Kevin Costner, Robert De Niro, and Sean Connery.

The theme was provided by Ron Grainer. Grainer was best known for composing the iconic original electronic theme to *Dr. Who* (1963–1989) and would compose the theme to *The Prisoner* (1967–1968) that same year.

The Prisoner (1967–1968)

Psychedelic science fiction spy thriller, *The Prisoner* starring and created by *Danger Man*'s Patrick McGoohan aired on ITV in Great Britain and was brought to the United States in 1968. However, it only aired on NBC in the summer months.

The Prisoner was unlike any show at the time or since and told the story of a newly resigned British secret agent who was knocked out via gas and awoke trapped on a mysterious island known as "the Village." While on the island, the former agent was only known as Number Six. Throughout his time in "the Village" he is drugged, brainwashed, and driven to madness along with other prisoners who are mostly former spies as well. None of the prisoners on the island knows why they are there or who are good agents or bad agents. They are monitored by a voice that demands "information" from them. Anyone on the island who attempts to escape is tracked, captured, and occasionally killed by a white, translucent balloon known as the Rover.

Although *The Prisoner* never mentions Patrick McGoohan's *Danger Man* character or any of his adventures, many viewers saw the show as the spiritual successor to *Danger Man/Secret Agent Man*.

The Prisoner was canceled after one season. Reports from England indicated that *The Prisoner* was canceled in part due to the cost. It reportedly cost £50,000 an episode to produce, at a time when the average television show cost £35,000 to produce. In addition, viewers complained that they could not "follow or understand" the show ("Prisoner to Be Freed," 11).

Prisoner Number Six (Patrick McGoohan) is forced to play a literal game of human chess on *The Prisoner* (1967–1968). *Author's collection*

Although *The Prisoner* only lasted seventeen episodes, interest in the show persisted following the show's cancellation despite audiences never finding the true identity of McGoohan's character, Number Six.

The Champions (1968–1969)

British-produced *The Champions* was an ABC summer replacement for *Rowan & Martin's Laugh-In* 1968. The show, in the vein of American spy shows *Mission: Impossible* and *The Man From U.N.C.L.E.*, is about an international law enforcement agency but with a twist: four agents acquired telepathic super-powers in the mountains of Tibet, unbeknown to the agency's higher ups. *The Champions* starred Stuart Damon, Alexandra Bastedo, William Gaunt, and Anthony Nicholls.

The show was created by Dennis Spooner and Monty Berman. Spooner wrote a number of episodes of *The Champions* and episodes of spy shows *The Avengers* (1961–1969), *The Baron* (1965–1966), and *Man in a Suitcase*

Stuart Damon, Alexandra Bastedo, and William Gaunt in an episode of *The Champions* (1968–1969) in 1968. *Allstar Picture Library Limited./Alamy Stock Photo*

(1967–1968). Berman also served as a producer of *The Champions* and produced spy series *The Saint* (1962–1965) and *The Baron* (1966–1967).

The show was not a ratings success and was only broadcast throughout the summer months in 1968 in the United States.

EPILOGUE

The 1960s spy craze lasted seven years, ostensibly from 1962 to 1969, peaking in 1966. Although James Bond films continue to be made, James Bond films of the 1970s and beyond lost the charm, originality, and freshness we saw in 007 in the 1960s.

Throughout their history, Bond films often became even more outlandish but remained popular. The films also began to steal concepts from other popular films of their day. For example, Bond used a Smith and Wesson 44 Magnum in *Live and Let Die* (1973), similar to the one used by Harry Callahan (Clint Eastwood) in *Dirty Harry* (1971), and a laser gunfight was featured in *Moonraker* (1979), to capitalize on the popularity of *Star Wars* (1977). As for other spy flicks, studios and the American public moved on to the latest fads.

As the United States entered the 1970s, audiences demanded grittier and more realistic crime films like *The French Connection* (1971), *Serpico* (1973), and *The Conversation* (1974), brought about in part by the growing distrust in government institutions due to the escalation of the Vietnam War. In addition, major movie studios abandoned the Hays Motion Picture Code in favor of the MPAA rating system. Although weakened by the 1950s, the Hays Motion Picture Code loomed large over Hollywood film productions from 1934 to 1968 and set guidelines for films made by major studios in the United States that forbade pointed profanity, nudity, drugs, and "sexual perversion," among other things, as a form of self-censorship to avoid government interference with productions. Hollywood was also forced to evolve due to the increased availability of independent and foreign films without major studio distribution that were made without the Hays Motion Picture Code in mind. In 1970 the Hays

Code seemed like a distant memory, with even the largest studios producing and distributing films, such as *M*A*S*H*, *Joe*, and *Beyond the Valley of the Dolls*, that just several short years earlier would have been out of the question.

On television, the spy craze was declared "all but dead" by syndicated columnist Rick DuBrow by 1967 and was being replaced by situation comedies, Westerns, police procedurals, variety shows, and panel shows. All spy shows except for CBS's *Mission: Impossible* (1966–1973) were canceled by 1970 (DuBrow "Spy Series Slump," 36).

Spy novelty songs, secret agent toys, and even imported Euro-spy films were no longer on America's collective pop-culture radar.

The public learned more about secret agents through documents that were declassified after the Cold War. Although not much was known about the work of secret agents in the 1960s, the International Spy Museum, founded in 2002 in Washington, DC, displays a number of declassified tools of the trade that allowed spies to covertly monitor, infiltrate, sabotage, and kill. Many of the items used, once thought of as science fiction, are not too far from what was seen on film.

By the late 1990s and early 2000s, spy films were ripe for parody. James Bond, Matt Helm, Derek Flint, Harry Palmer, and themes of the entire 1960s spy genre were parodied in films *Spy Hard* (1996), *Johnny English* (2003), and most famously in the Austin Powers trilogy: *Austin Powers International Man of Mystery* (1997), *Austin Powers: The Spy Who Shagged Me* (1999), and *Austin Powers in Goldmember* (2002). Although the Austin Powers films took concepts from mostly James Bond and a number of other 1960s spy flicks, Powers notably used Matt Helm's signature rotating round bed, used Derek Flint's signature telephone ringtone, and wore Harry Palmer's signature eyeglasses and spoke in Palmer's Cockney accent. Harry Palmer himself, Michael Caine, even appeared as Powers's estranged father, Nigel Powers, in *Austin Powers in Goldmember*.

Although the American public moved on from outlandish spy adventures of the 1960s, those adventures left a legacy of stylish, sensational, often exciting, sometimes weird—and at times forgotten—spy films, television shows, toys, memorabilia, music, and soundtracks.

WORKS CITED

Ackerman, Forest J. "Fang Mail." *Monster World*, no. 5 (October 1965): 48.

"Actor Caine Kept Busy in England." *The Spokesman-Review* (Spokane, Washington), September 26, 1965, 59.

"Actress Visiting Here." *Miami Herald*, November 16, 1967, 73.

Adams, David. "Snow and Satire." *Kensington Post* (Kensington and Chelsea, England), February 16, 1968, 17.

Adams, Marjory. "Allen, Rossi Falter in 1st Film." *Boston Globe*, May 28, 1966, 10.

Adams, Marjory. "Best Selling Spy Novel Becomes Forceful Film." *Boston Globe*, December 23, 1965, 25.

Adams, Marjory. "Neil Connery Lacks Sean's Zing." *Boston Globe*, October 30, 1967, 17.

Adams, Val. "Bill Cosby of 'I Spy' Set." *New York Times*, May 23, 1966, 68.

Adams, Val. "*I Spy* with Negro Is Widely Booked," *New York Times*, September 10, 1965, 71.

"Adams Kids Agent Roles." *Fort Lauderdale News*, November 26, 1965, 75.

"Agent 007 Filming in the Alps." *Herald Statesman* (Yonkers, New York), October 24, 1968, 31.

"Agent 007 'Personifies Fascism.'" *Press and Sun Bulletin* (Binghamton, New York), December 20, 1965, 4.

"Alec, Gina Will Team in French Farce." *Los Angeles Times*, May 11, 1965, 63.

"Alec Guinness, Playing the Spy Game with Currant Buns." *Evening Standard* (London, England), November 10, 1966, 8.

"Alexander Signed for 'Candy Web.'" *Press and Sun-Bulletin* (Binghamton, New York), February 9, 1963, 24.

"Allen and Rossi Team Spoof Present Day Spies." *Winona Daily News* (Winona, Minnesota), July 24, 1966, 34.

"Allen, Rossi in Person and on Film." *Daily Register* (Red Bank, New Jersey), May 24, 1966, 24.

Altria, Bill. "British Films Romp Home—Fill First Five Places." *Kine Weekly*, December 17, 1964, 9.

Amory, Cleveland. "Review—The Girl from U.N.C.L.E.," *TV Guide*, December 17, 1966, 21.

Amos, Bill. "The Revenue Men Cometh." *Liverpool Echo*, March 18, 1967, 2.

"Amusements Guide." *Evening Standard* (London, England), March 5, 1964, 20.

Anastasi, Joel. "*From Russia with Love* Mixes Sex and Suspense." *Asbury Park Press*, April 9, 1964, 29.

Anchor Drive-In Theater advertisement. *Daily Press* (Newport News, Virginia), December 23, 1965, 18.

Anderson, Gail. "A Producer Tells How." *Miami News*, March 26, 1966, 10.

"Another Sinatra in Spotlight." *Memphis Press-Scimitar*, May 12, 1967, 54.

Archer, Eugene. "007 Is Still S.R.O. as a Rerun Here." *New York Times*, June 1, 1965.

"Arrives in London Airport." *Latrobe Bulletin*, May 3, 1967, 4.

Assignment K advertisement. *Oklahoma City Times*, August 24, 1968.

"*Assignment K* Suspenseful Spy Film." *Fort Lauderdale News*, August 29, 1968, 37.

"At the 4th Street Theatre." *Banner Press* (David City Nebraska), April 13, 1967, 2.

"Aussie as 007?" *Sydney Morning Herald* (Sydney, Australia), September 22, 1968, 25.

Bacon, James. "Belinsky Shuns Acting after Riding Accident." *Asbury Park Press*, January 25, 1963, 14.

Banks, Dick. "Icy-Nerved 007 Is Back—Swiftly." *Charlotte Observer*, December 22, 1965, 15.

Banks, Dick. "*That Man in Istanbul* Is Another OK Spy Show." *Charlotte Observer*, April 16, 1966, 15.

Barker, Felix. "Versatile." *Liverpool Echo*, June 16, 1967, 5.

Bart, Lionel. "On Britain's Bustling Film Scene; 'Maggie May' Heads toward Screen—Blue Chip Bonds—'She' Returns." *New York Times*, November 1, 1964, 13.

"Batman Still Flying." *Broadcasting*, January 31, 1966, 10.

"Beauties Receive Instructions on Finer Points of Game." *Herald-Sun* (Durham, North Carolina), July 28, 1966, 19.

Beck, Marilyn. "Dean Martin's Pout Postpones Matt Helm Epic." *Press and Sun-Bulletin* (Binghamton, New York), December 22, 1969, 19.

Beck, Marilyn. "Moore Ready for More Bond Action." *Pensacola News Journal* (Pensacola, Florida), June 29, 1979, 38.

"Bedsole in Movies." *News-Pilot* (San Pedro, California), June 5, 1965, 12.

"Beguiling an Old Bulldog." *Evening Chronicle* (Newcastle, England), January 24, 1969, 8.

Benjamin, Sid. "Listening Post." *Times-Tribune* (Scranton, Pennsylvania), January 11, 1969, 88.

Bennett, Collin. "Another Williams Heroine in Pain." *The Age* (Melbourne Australia), March 30, 1963, 19.

Bennett, Patrick. "Big Features Due in National Movie Month." *Abilene Reporter-News* (Abilene, Texas), October 2, 1966, 26.

Bentley, Jack. "From the Censor with Love." *Sunday Mirror* (London, England), October 13, 1963, 31.

"Best Sellers." *The Morning Call* (Allentown, Pennslyvania), January 10, 1965, 31.

Betts, Ernest. "Oh, No!" *The People* (London, England), October 7, 1962, 16.

"Big Rental Films of 1967." *Variety*, January 3, 1968, 25.

"Big Rental Films of 1968." *Variety*, January 8, 1969.

"Big Rental Films of 1969." *Variety*, January 7, 1970, 15.

"Big Rental Films of 1970." *Variety*, January 6, 1971.

"Big Rental Pictures of 1963." *Variety*, January 8, 1964.

"Big Rental Pictures of 1964." *Variety*, January 6, 1965.

"Big Rental Pictures of 1965." *Variety*, January 5, 1966.

"Big Rental Pictures of 1966." *Variety*, January 4, 1967.

"Bikini Plot Foiled." *St. Louis Post-Dispatch*, March 12, 1967, 279.

"Bill Lear." *Cincinnati Enquirer*, March 5, 1967, 84.

"*Billion Dollar Brain* Now Filming in England." *Calgary Herald* (Calgary, Alberta, Canada), February 2, 1967, 10.

"Bit Parts." *Arizona Republic*, April 13, 1966, 22.

Bjorkman, Carol. "The 'In' Mr. Flint." *San Francisco Examiner*, July 10, 1966, 124.

Black, Jeremy. *The Politics of James Bond: From Fleming's Novels to the Big Screen.* University of Nebraska Press, 2005.

Black, Robert. "The Case against James Bond." *Adam Film Quarterly*, April 1968, 18.

Bladen, Barbara. "Fred Flintstone vs. James Bond." *The Times* (San Mateo, California), August 8, 1966, 15.

"Bond Films Revive Serial." *Daily Reporter* (Dover, Ohio), November 10, 1966, 6.

"Bond Is Up to His Tricks Again." *Middlesex County Times and West Middlesex Gazette* (Ealing, London, England), April 9, 1965, 38.

"Bond Packs Box-Office Punch on Both Sides of the Atlantic." *Kingston Whig-Standard* (Kingston, Ontario, Canada), January 7, 1966, 16.

"Bond Rolls On." *Pittsburgh Press*, July 21 1967, 11.

"Bond to Marry." *Evansville Courier and Press* (Evansville, Indiana), February 2, 1969, 72.

"Bond Uses Gimmicks but Harry Uses Brains." *Stockton Evening and Sunday Record*, September 30, 1965, 31.

"Bond without Connery." *Fresno Bee*, January 13, 1966, 48.

"Bond's 'Friend' Picked." *Fort Lauderdale News*, February 19, 1965, 19.

"Bond's New Girl." *Standard-Speaker* (Hazleton, Pennsylvania), February 18, 1965, 17.

"Bond's Volcano Takes the Tube." *Windsor Star* (Windsor, Ontario, Canada), March 17, 1967, 23.

Borsch, Linda. "'You Must Be Joking!' Descriptive of 'Lily.'" *Courier-Journal* (Louisville, Kentucky), November 10, 1966, 34.

"The Bottom 15." *Broadcasting*, October 18, 1965, 93.

Bourke, George. "*Our Man Flint* Invades World of Secret Agents." *Miami Herald*, December 12, 1965, 211.

Bourke, George. "Producer Likes Our Film Climate." *Miami Herald*, March 25, 1966, 49.

Bourke, George. "*Thunderball* Unit Plans Beach Invasion Monday." *Miami Herald*, May 2, 1965, 63.

Bourke, George. "Work Begins Soon on *Thunderball*." *Miami Herald*, January 28, 1965, 68.

Boyle, Hal. "Bond Film Star: Heroine to World's Secretaries." *Dixon Evening Telegraph* (Dixon, Illinois), June 1, 1967, 8.

Boyle, Hal. "British Actress is a 'Tough' on Film." *Corpus Christi Times* (Corpus Christi, Texas), November 20, 1964, 40.

Bradford, Jack. "Hollywood Highlights." *Honolulu Star-Bulletin*, June 26, 1968, 58.

Bradford, Jack. "Natalie Wood's Warming Up for Her 'Hot Time' Film." *Honolulu Star-Bulletin*, May 22, 1967, 24.

Bradford, Jack. "Notes from Hollywood." *Pasadena Independent*, February 2, 1967, 16.

"*Brainstorm* Cast Named by Warners." *Los Angeles Times*, January 1, 1965, 64.

Brass, Kevin. "L.A. Comedy Group Makes Film Dubbing an Art Form." *Los Angeles Times*, July 22, 1988.

Brayson, Johnny. "When Did Post-Credits Scenes Start? The Trend's History Is Filled with Twists & Turns." *Bustle*, November 14, 2017. https://www.bustle.com/p/when-did-post-credits-scenes-start-the-trends-history-is-filled-with-twists-turns-3235313.

"Briefing." *The Observer* (London, England), August 16, 1964, 18.

"Britt Is on Her Way." *The Record* (Hackensack, New Jersey), March 4, 1967, 50.

Brooks, Elston. "Girls from 'Murderer's Row' Come On Like Gangbusters." *Fort Worth Star-Telegram*, December 14, 1966, 16.

Brooks, Elston. "Movie Critic Will Sleep Better with Valenti In." *Fort Worth Star-Telegram*, April 27, 1966, 10.

Brooks, Elston. "Peck Braves Duel Enemy in Meeting 'The Chairman.'" *Fort Worth Star-Telegram*, July 25, 1969, 16.

Brooks, Elston. "Sometimes Trying Harder Proves Why You're Second." *Fort Worth Star-Telegram*, January 21, 1966, 10.

Brooks, Tim, and Earle Marsh. *The Complete Directory to Prime Time Network TV Shows 1946–Present*. Ballantine Books, 1979.

Brown, Thomas M. "Michael Caine Returns Again in British Agent Role." *Fort Lauderdale News*, March 19, 1967, 62.

Browning, Norma Lee. "A New Monroe?" *Chicago Tribune*, January 28, 1971, 55.

"Burnett Gains in Rescheduling." *Broadcasting*, February 5, 1973, 44.

"Burton to Play Bond." *Daily Herald* (London, England), February 21, 1964, 1.

Bustin, John. "Show World." *Austin American-Statesman*, December 24, 1966, 13.

"Camera Angles." *Valley Times* (North Hollywood, California), May 22, 1968, 25.

Cameron, Kate. "Burton Comes in from the Cold." *Daily News* (New York, New York), December 5, 1965, 25.

Cameron, Kate. "Car Racing Thriller." *Daily News* (New York, New York), December 4, 1966, 71.

Cameron, Kate. "Gem Robbery Comedy Due in May." *Daily News* (New York, New York), March 27, 1966, 23.

Cameron, Kate. "A Thriller Film Trend Is On." *Daily News* (New York, New York), May 26, 1963, 28.

Canby, Vincent. "007 to Multiply." *New York Times*, October 5, 1966, 38.

Canby, Vincent. "Fright Seeds, 'Torture Garden' and *Assignment K* Bow." *New York Times*, July 20, 1968, 18.

Canby, Vincent. "The Glass Bottom Boat: Comedy at Radio City Stars Doris Day, a Chris Marker Film at the New Yorker." *New York Times*, June 10, 1966, 54.

Canby, Vincent. "Matt Helm Back in Town." *New York Times*, February 6, 1969, 32.

Canby, Vincent. "The Ten Worst Films of 1969." *New York Times*, January 4, 1970, 81

The Candy Web advertisement. *The Age* (Melbourne, Australia), March 22, 1963, 21.

"Candy Web Setting Move to Arrowhead." *Memphis Press-Scimitar*, December 12, 1962, 27.

Capes, Reggie. "Holdovers Holding On at Theaters." *Columbus Ledger* (Columbus, Georgia), August 7, 1966, 18.

Carlile, Tom. "Sean's Exit Won't Stop Bondwagon." *Fort Worth Star-Telegram*, July 3, 1967, 3.

Carroll, Kathleen. "*In Like Flint*—Gals, Action but Weak Plot." *Daily News* (New York, New York), March 16, 1967, 83.

Carry On Spying advertisement. *Evening Post* (Bristol, Avon, England), August 22, 1964, 6.

Carthew, Anthony. "All Honor Honor." *New York Times*, March 1, 1964.

"Cast Grows." *Los Angeles Times*, June 2, 1965, 27.

"CBS Ups Shares." *Broadcasting*, January 15, 1973, 48.

Cedrone, Lew. "Different Kind of Spy." *Evening Sun* (Baltimore, Maryland), February 9, 1967, 10.

Century City advertisement. *Los Angeles Evening Citizen News*, June 10, 1965, 14–16.

Champlin, Charles. "*K* Opens Citywide Showings." *Los Angeles Times*, September 19, 1968, 91.

Claughton, Russel. "Quiller: No Flaws." *Kensington News and West London Times*, January 6, 1967, 2.

"Cliff Richard Again Most Popular Star." *Daily Telegraph* (London, England), January 3, 1964, 20.

"Coburn, Jet Press Agent." *Pittsburgh Post-Gazette*, January 19, 1966, 9.

Cochnar, Bob, and Dave Burgin. "Toyota Vehicle Comes On Strong." *Odessa American*, May 20, 1967, 22.

Cohen, Harold V. "Brief Encounter." *Pittsburgh Post-Gazette*, July 8, 1968, 22.

Cohen, Harold V. "Danger and Delirium." *Pittsburgh Post-Gazette*, December 8, 1964, 26.

Cohen, Harold V. "In One Ear." *Pittsburgh Post-Gazette*, June 29, 1964, 10.

"Columbia Plans Thriller Spoof." *Morning Call* (Allentown, Pennsylvania), October 14, 1965, 33.

"Columbia to Film Hamilton Movie in Santa Fe Vicinity." *Santa Fe New Mexican*, May 5, 1965, 1.

"Comeback for Hero of Twenties. Wanted £5. Bulldog Drummond for Screen." *Herald Express* (Torquay, Devon, England), October 29, 1964, 10.

"Comfortably Chic." *Albuquerque Journal*, August 5, 1966, 32.

"Connery Insists He Wants Out of Bond Films." *Stockton Evening and Sunday Record* (Stockton, California), May 16, 1967, 25.

"Connery to Return as Bond in 'Diamonds are Forever.'" *Arizona Republic*, March 9, 1971, 53.

"Connery-Bond Wants a Million Next Time." *Bucks Examiner* (Chesham, Buckinghamshire, England), August 25, 1967, 8.

Connolly, Mike. "Hollywood." *Philadelphia Inquirer*, April 27, 1965, 35.

Connolly, Mike. "Mike Connolly on TV." *Sunday News* (Lancaster, Pennsylvania), April 3, 1966, 60.

Connolly, Mike. "Notes from Hollywood." *Pasadena Independent*, March 29, 1965, 19.

Connolly, Mike. "Taylor Joins Wayne." *Arizona Republic*, July 12, 1966, 29.

"Coral Ridge Books 'Only Live Twice.'" *Fort Lauderdale News and Sun-Sentinel*, March 25, 1967, 10.

"Creator of Secret Agent James Bond Dies." *Southern Illinoisan* (Carbondale, Illinois), August 12, 1964, 5.

"The Critics Reviews the Season's First Preview." *Broadcasting*, September 12, 1966, 37.

"The Critics' View, Part 2." *Broadcasting*, September 27, 1965, 69.

"Critics' Views of Hits, Misses." *Broadcasting*, September 19, 1966, 67.

Crosby, Joan. "A Long Road: Killer Cop to Cop Killer." *Central New Jersey Home News* (New Brunswick, New Jersey), February 18, 1967, 8.

Crosby, Joan. "Raising Caine to Stardom." *Guam Daily News*, September 22, 1965, 10.

Crosby, Joan. "Tube Moves Boobs." *Desert Sun* (Palm Springs, California), May 30, 1969, 14.

Crowther, Bosley. "Agent 007 Meets *Goldfinger*: James Bond's Exploits on Film Again." *New York Times*, December 22, 1964, 36.

Crowther, Bosley. "007's Underwater Adventures: Connery Plays Bond in *Thunderball*." *New York Times*, December 22, 1965, 23.

Crowther, Bosley. "*Dr. No*, Mystery Spoof: Film Is First Made of Ian Fleming Novels Sean Connery Stars as Agent James Bond." *New York Times*, May 30, 1963, 20.

Crowther, Bosley. "Flag Is Down at Warner for 'Grand Prix.'" *New York Times*, January 22, 1966, 39.

Crowther, Bosley. "*Funeral in Berlin* Begins Run: Michael Caine Returns as Harry Palmer Soft-Sell Secret Agent Betrayed by Script." *New York Times*, December 23, 1966, 17.

Crowther, Bosley. "Gaudy 'Modesty Blaise,' Girl Secret Agent: Monica Vitti Co-Stars with Dirk Bogarde, Imported Farrago Has Flashes of Humor." *New York Times*, August 11, 1966, 27.

Crowther, Bosley. "*In Like Flint* Opens at Capitol: Durable Hero Defeated by Deficient Script Usual Bevy of Beauties Doesn't Help Much." *New York Times*, March 16, 1967, 53.

Crowther, Bosley. "Inferior Burlesque of Bond: *Our Man Flint* on View at Forum and Baronet." *New York Times*, January 26, 1966, 23.

Crowther, Bosley. "James Bond Travels the Orient Express." *New York Times*, April 9, 1964, 25.

Crowther, Bosley. "Le Carre's Best Seller Adapted to Film." *New York Times*, December 24, 1965, 24.

Crowther, Bosley. "Mr. Kennedy and Mr. Reagan: New Cinema Playhouse Changes Its Fare. Picture Makes a Case for the Californian 'Operation Kid Brother.'" *New York Times*, November 23, 1967, 58.

Crowther, Bosley. "Population Explosion Victims: Secret Agents Abound in *Casino Royale* Impersonators of Bond at Two Theaters." *New York Times*, April 29, 1967, 25.

Crowther, Bosley. "Romantic Middle-Aged Men and Women." *New York Times*, September 12, 1963, 32.

Crowther, Bosley. "Sayonara, 007: Connery Is at It Again as Whatshisname." *New York Times*, June 14, 1967, 40.

Crowther, Bosley. "Venetian Affair." *New York Times*, January 19, 1967, 36.

Cullen, Tom A. "James Bond Undies? What's Next 007." *Delaware County Times* (Chester, Pennsylvania), April 8, 1965, 20.

Cullen, Tom A. "Judo Societies, Too. Masculine Women Too Much for Boys." *La Crosse Tribune* (La Crosse, Wisconsin), March 5, 1964, 9.

Cullen, Tom A. "Tarantulas in Bed Is Routine Fare." *Carroll Daily Times Herald* (Carroll, Iowa), June 5, 1962, 8.

"Current Movies: Fathom." *Pittsburgh Press*, August 30, 1967, 42.

"Curtis Helps Out." *Crowley Post-Signal* (Crowley, Louisiana), September 4, 1968, 5.

"Danger Route." *Monthly Film Bulletin* 35, no. 408 (January 1, 1968): 8.

Dawson, Sam. "James Bond Gadgets Just around Corner." *Daily Item* (Sunbury, Pennsylvania), July 5, 1966, 2.

"Dean Martin Looks at Success." *Charlotte Observer*, March 12, 1967, 87.

Dederer, Douglas Morgan. "The LO Heist." *Evening Tribune* (Cocoa, Florida), March 1, 1966, 8.

"Dell Best Seller List." *Newsday* (Nassau Edition), February 18, 1967, 122.

Deppa, Joan. "Davis, Lawford Touted as Next Abbott, Costello." *Pittsburgh Press*, October 22, 1967, 99.

"Designing Parisians Unveiled." *New York Times*, February 17, 1966, 29.

Devane, James. "TV's 'Espionage' Was Foredoomed to Failure," *Cincinnati Enquirer*, November 15, 1963, 17.

Dial, Bill. "*Fathom* Really Hard to Fathom." *Atlanta Constitution*, September 12, 1967.

"Dino Hits Career Heights but Still 'Stays Loose.'" *Hartford Courant*, August 18, 1968, 24.

"Disappointed Fans of James Bond Mob a Theater in Boston." *New York Times*, May 7, 1967, 58.

"Dispute over Copyright: James Bond Novel." *Daily Telegraph* (London, England), March 25, 1961, 9.

"007 Hit Also Beer Profit Blasted Urge New Sponsor." *Sault Star* (Sault Saint Marie, Ontario, Canada), December 28, 1965, 4.

"007 Lives On to Fight Another Day." *Birmingham Evening Mail* (Birmingham, England), March 31, 1983, 8.

"007 the Second." *Daily News* (New York, New York), January 31, 1966, 38.

"007's Helicopter in Rescue." *Birmingham Evening Mail* (Birmingham, West Midlands, England). March 17, 1969, 9.

"006-¾." *Time* 89, no. 26 (June 30, 1967): 73.

Dr. No advertisement. *The Item* (Sumter, South Carolina), June 14, 1963, 15.

"Dr. Who?" *Oakland Tribune*, September 8, 1965, 19.

Driscoll, Edgar, Jr. "*Caprice* Pits Doris Day and Spy-Spoof Formula." *Boston Globe*, May 25, 1967, 59.

Driscoll, Edgar, Jr. "Yul Brynner Scores as 'The Double Man.'" *Boston Globe*, May 9, 1968, 69.

"Dubbing Removes Barriers." *Evening Sun* (Baltimore, Maryland), November 14, 1968, 23.

DuBrow, Rick. "Spy Series Slump in New TV Season." *Honolulu Star-Bulletin* (Honolulu, Hawaii), July 27, 1967, 36.

Dulles, Allen W, interview with Thomas Braden. December 5–6, 1964. *John F. Kennedy Oral History Collection.*

Dunne, Irene. "What Happened to Sonny Tufts." *Los Angeles Times*, September 20, 1965, 73.

"Easy to *Fathom* Raquel's New Film." *Miami Herald*, August 22, 1967, 36.

Ebert, Roger. "Caprice." *Chicago Sun-Times*, June 30, 1967.

Ebert, Roger. "Casino Royale." *Chicago Sun-Times*, May 1, 1967.

Ebert, Roger. "The Chairman." *Chicago Sun-Times*, August 19, 1969.

Ebert, Roger. "Fathom." *Chicago Sun-Times*, December 13, 1967.

Ebert, Roger. "In Like Flint Review." *Chicago Sun-Times*, April 10, 1967.

Ebert, Roger. "Salt and Pepper." *Chicago Sun-Times*, October 25, 1968.

Edwards, Nadine M. "Excitement Colors Connery's New Film." *Valley Times* (North Hollywood, California), June 16, 1967, 14.

Edwards, Nadine M. "Exciting Vehicle for Agent Mike Caine." *Los Angeles Evening Citizen News*, December 23, 1966, 14.

Edwards, Nadine M. "*That Man in Istanbul* Seems Familiar." *Los Angeles Evening Citizen News*, March 25, 1966, 9.

Edwards, Nadine M. "Unemotional Film Stars Gregory Peck." *Valley Times* (North Hollywood, California), August 1, 1969, 18.

Eichelbaum, Stanley. "Doris Flirts Wholesomely with the Undercover Game." *San Francisco Examiner*, July 28, 1966, 26.

Estes, William. "Actor Weighs 375 but Says He's Too Skinny." *Los Angeles Times*, September 5, 1965, 124.

"Europe's Teen-Age Diplomats Arrive." *Press-Telegram* (Long Beach, California), November 23, 1962, 8.

"Even with the Temperature." *Press Democrat* (Santa Rosa, California), August 4, 1966, 7.

"Fall Preview 1966–1967 Shows." *TV Guide*, September 10–16, 1966.

"*Fat Spy* to Be Filmed in 27 Days. Jayne Mansfield, Other Stars Will Make Movie at Cape Coral." *News-Press* (Cape Coral, Florida), May 25, 1965, 1.

"Feature Page Catches Stars 'The Fat Spy' Spied On." *Orlando Evening Star*, June 19, 1965, 15.

Fenton, Lynn. "James Bond Is No Gentleman Even on Screen." *The Journal* (Newcastle, England), October 6, 1962, 10.

"50 Top-Grossing Films." *Variety*. January 14, 1970. 9.

"Film Fans Flock to 4 A.M. Fest of Our Man Flint." *Sun-Tattler* (Hollywood, Florida). February 26, 1966. 11.

Filmfacts 1967. United States, 1967.

"Filming Begins on New Picture." *Eureka Humboldt Standard* (Eureka, California). February 14, 1963. 14.

"Film Made at Cape to Start Run Here." *News-Press* (Cape Coral, Florida), September 9, 1966, 24.

"Film with Midas Touch." *Coventry Evening Telegraph*. April 10, 1964. 10.

Fiset, Bill. "Escape from the Office." *Oakland Tribune* (Oakland, California), January 13, 1965, 34.

Fiset, Bill. "Misadventures in Paradox." *Oakland Tribune*, September 2, 1965, 15.

"Five Thousand Finns for Film Hockey Game." *Edmonton Journal*, March 6, 1967, 27.

Fleet, Patrick. "Back-Alley Accents and Formula 'X' in the Orient Express." *Evening Post* (Bristol, Avon, England), August 22, 1964, 6.

Fleming, Ian. *Moonraker*. Jonathan Cape, 1955.

"*Flint* Is In." *Daily News* (New York, New York). March 13, 1967, *331*.

"*Flint* Sparks New Spy Spoof." *Morning News* (Wilmington, Delaware), September 26, 1966, 17.

"*Flintstones* Will Be Made into Film." *Herald-News* (Passaic, New Jersey), January 26, 1966, 82.

Follow Me advertisement. *Sault Star* (Sault St. Marie, Ontario, Canada), May 23, 1970, 16.

"For What Ails Them." *Daily News* (New York, New York), September 18, 1966, 152.

"Ford Cars Star in Bond Film." *Brentwood Gazette and Mid-Essex Recorder*, March 14, 1969, 22.

"Former Konan Harold Sakata Wrestler Tosh Togo Turns Movie Actor." *Hawaii Tribune-Herald* (Hilo, Hawaii), July 9, 1964, 20.

"4th James Bond Film Planned." *New York Times*, June 15, 1964.

Fox, Burton. "Quiller Memorandum Takes on Overtones with Ex-Nazi's Election." *Ridgewood Herald-News* (Ridgewood, New Jersey), December 15, 1966, 61.

"Fox to Run New Bond Film 'Round the Clock." *Philadelphia Daily News*, June 6, 1967, 55.

Freeman, Alex. "Gotham Night Spot Has Frantic Air." *Hartford Courant*, January 28, 1965, 44.

Freeman, Alex. "Is Former Mouseketeer Expecting?" *Hartford Courant*, March 25, 1965, 20.

Freeman, Alex. "Robert Preston Buys House in Connecticut." *Hartford Courant*, July 4, 1966, 10.

Freeman, Alex. "Studio Betting $3 Million on Actor." *Hartford Courant*, February 18, 1965, 45.

Fremont-Smith, Eliot. "*Lady L*, a Disturbing Film." *New York Times*, May 19, 1966, 51.

Freund, Bob. "Hollywood Producers Find Spying Is Worth the Gamble." *Fort Lauderdale News*, March 7, 1965, 62.

"*From Russia, with Love*: Bond Is Branded a Nazi." *New York Times*, September 30, 1965, 2.

"From Sloop to Nuts." *The Tribune* (San Luis Obispo, California). December 11, 1965, 16.

Funeral in Berlin advertisement. *Chicago Tribune*, February 14, 1965, 247.

Funke, Phyllis. "Flintstones Try Hand at Spy Game." *Courier-Journal* (Louisville, Kentucky), August 11, 1966, 28.

Funke, Phyllis. "*Where the Spies Are*—Good Game of Intrigue." *Courier-Journal* (Louisville, Kentucky), February 10, 1966, 33.

Gaghan, Jerry. "Lack of Prompters Worry Danish Dish." *Philadelphia Daily News*, December 12, 1966, 33.

Gardiner, Sandy. "Television." *Ottawa Journal*, May 3, 1968, 34.

Gardner, R. H. "*Second Best Agent* Sequel." *Baltimore Sun*, November 25, 1966, 23.

Garrett, Gerard, and Cleave, Maureen. "The Man from South of the Border." *Evening Standard* (London, England), April 19, 1963, 10.

Gelmis, Joseph. "Bugs, Bad Guys Plague Maharis but He's No 007." *Newsday* (Nassau Edition), April 15, 1965, 106.

"George Lazenby: Arrogant Egotist." *The Tribune* (San Luis Obispo, California), March 15, 1969, 42.

"Gert Frobe, an Actor, Dies at 75." *New York Times*, September 6, 1988, 14.

"Get More Out of Life . . . Go Out to a Movie." *Hartford Courant*, June 21, 1968, 16.

Gewertz, Beverly. "Alexandrian Is Movie Producer." *Town Talk* (Alexandria, Louisiana), June 21, 1967, 25.

Gibbs, Patrick. "In the Bed-Sitter Belt." *Daily Telegraph* (London, England), October 11, 1963, 13.

Gibbs, Patrick. "Old Cloak and Blunt Dagger." *Daily Telegraph* (London, England), March 6, 1964, 13.

Gilliatt, Penelope. "Laughing It Off with Bond." *The Observer* (London, England), October 13, 1963, 27.

"Goldfinger." *The Numbers.* January 25, 2008.

"Goldfinger Contest." *Miami News*, December 20, 1964, 22.

"Goldfinger Has Been Here." *Miami News* (Miami, Florida), November 5, 1964, 10.

Goldstein, Norman. "Comics Great Grist for the Movie Mill." *Herald-News* (Passaic, New Jersey), January 26, 1968, 23.

"Good Morning to You Too." *Daily Telegraph* (London, England), December 19, 1969, 10.

Goodlad, Douglas. "How Good Is Bad?" *Illustrated Chronicle* (Leicester, Leicestershire, England), August 14, 1964, 4.

Gough-Yates, Kevin. "Seth Holt Interview." *Screen* 10, no. 6 (November–December 1969): 17.

Gould, Jack. "Red Buttons in 2 Roles in New A.B.C. Series." *New York Times*, January 14, 1966, 79.

Gould, Jack. "TV: Spies, Space and the Stagestruck." *New York Times*, September 16, 1966.

Graham, Sheilah. "Amusement." *The News* (Paterson, New Jersey), January 4, 1966, 36.

Graham, Sheilah. "Anita Louise Takes Back House." *Indianapolis Star*, April 16, 1968, 16.

Graham, Sheilah. "Bette Davis to Play Vicious Mother." *Durham Morning Herald* (Durham, North Carolina), March 9, 1967, 34.

Graham, Sheilah. "Can Ava Gardner Help George Scott?" *Los Angeles Evening Citizen News*, November 15, 1965, 10.

Graham, Sheilah. "Charlie Chaplin's Daughter Adds Bullfighting to Agenda." *Los Angeles Evening Citizen News*, May 26, 1964, 13.

Graham, Sheilah. "Gleason Baking Off Pounds." *The News* (Paterson, New Jersey), March 16, 1963, 13.

Graham, Sheilah. "Graham's Grapevine." *Honolulu Advertiser*, January 2, 1966, 99.

Graham, Sheilah. "Hollywood." *Times-Tribune*, September 28, 1963, 5.

Graham, Sheilah. "Hollywood Everywhere." *Herald-Sun* (Durham, North Carolina), June 19, 1965, 13.

Graham, Sheilah. "Hollywood Move for Dyan Cannon." *Los Angeles Evening Citizen News*, May 30, 1968, 5.

Graham, Sheilah. "James Garner Out-Bonds Bond." *Los Angeles Evening Citizen News*, July 14, 1965, 46.

Graham, Sheilah. "Johnson Cheered by Many Friends." *Los Angeles Evening Citizen*, January 21, 1964, 8.

Graham, Sheilah. "Lawyers Battle as Burtons Relax." *Valley Times* (North Hollywood, California), July 23, 1968, 5.

Graham, Sheilah. "London Billboards Get Bonds Battle." *Miami News*, April 4, 1967, 22.

Graham, Sheilah. "Michael Caine: The Anti-Hero." *Los Angeles Evening Citizen News*, July 5, 1965, 8.

Graham, Sheilah. "Movie Attractions." *Times-Tribune* (Scranton, Pennsylvania), May 5, 1967, 23.

Graham, Sheilah. "The New James Bond." *Des Moines Tribune*, August 13, 1968, 17.

Graham, Sheilah. "Private Citizen." *News Tribune* (Tacoma, Washington), August 18, 1961, 14.

Graham, Sheilah. "Producer Allen Respects Martin." *Valley Times* (North Hollywood, California), November 10, 1969, 7.

Graham, Sheilah. "Saturday Sit-In at Club Aretusa." *Valley Times* (North Hollywood, California), October 12, 1968, 9.

Graham, Sheilah. "Sean Connery's Younger Brother." *Des Moines Tribune*, January 2, 1967, 10.

Graham, Sheilah. "Who Plays Bond Still Is a Good Question." *Indianapolis Star*, January 1, 1968, 39.

Graham, Sheilah. "*Women in Love* Next Screen Shocker." *Herald-Sun* (Durham, North Carolina), October 6, 1969, 17.

Gray, Tom. "Training Tiger Sharks for *Thunderball* Posed Great Many Problems." *Atlanta Constitution*, February 14, 1966, 43.

"Green in 'Wrecking.'" *Los Angeles Evening Citizen News*, May 20, 1968, 6.

Greenberg, Abe. "Of James Coburn on Stardom's Path." *Los Angeles Evening Citizen News*, February 17, 1965, 42.

Greenberg, Abe. "Of Stardom and Mary Ann." *Los Angeles Evening Citizen News*, April 20, 1965, 11.

Greenberg, Abe. "Shirley MacLaine to Raise Caine?" *Los Angeles Evening Citizen News*, December 8, 965, 27.

Hale, Wanda. "*Billion Dollar Brain* Lacking in Suspense." *Daily News* (New York, New York), December 23, 1967, 74.

Hale, Wanda. "*Strange Bedfellows* Tops Comedy Twin Bill." *Daily News* (New York, New York), March 11, 1965, 544.

Hale, Wanda. "2 Gals 'Deadlier Than Male.'" *Daily News* (New York, New York), February 22, 1967, 20.

Hall, Isabelle. "Group Files Test against TV Violence," *The Tennessean*, November 13, 1970, 15.

Hall, William. "It's 006 (Alias Mini-Bond)." *Liverpool Echo*, February 10, 1967, 5.

Hall, William. "Neil Connery—In His Brother's Footsteps with Stoicism." *San Francisco Examiner*, August 20, 1967, 223.

Harber, Joyce. "Jill Will Join Sean in New Bond Film." *Los Angeles Times*, March 4, 1971, 72.

Harford, Margaret. "*Goldfoot* Sparkling Comedy." *Los Angeles Times*, November 13, 1965, 19.

Harford, Margaret. "The Spies Have It: Too Many Gimmicks." *Los Angeles Times*, January 28, 1966, 7.

Haun, Harry. "A Bulldog in Bond-age: All Bite and No Bark." *Nashville Tennessean*, March 9, 1967, 20.

Haun, Harry. "A 'Spybrid' Both Beat and Bond." *The Tennessean* (Nashville, Tennessee), May 20, 1967, 7.

Head, Cliff. "Diller Serves Garbage Soup." *News-Press* (Cape Coral, Florida), June 13, 1965, 6.

"Hickman Back with Taurog." *Los Angeles Times*, September 13, 1965, 67.

Hinxman, Margaret. "Having Fun with a Spy." *Daily Herald*, March 6, 1964, 6.

Hoberman, J. "Jet-Setting in 'That Man from Rio,' and Chain Reactions in 'The Way Things Go.'" *New York Times*, April 23, 2015. https://www.nytimes.com/2015/04/26/movies/homevideo/jet-setting-in-that-man-from-rio-and-chain-reactions-in-the-way-things-go.html.

Hollander, Zander. "Watch Out, 007! Here Comes the Kid." *The Tennessean* (Nashville, Tennessee), December 11, 1966, 138.

"The Hollies Chart-Bound with New Disc." *Runcorn Weekly News* (Runcorn, Cheshire, England), October 6, 1966, 5.

Hopper, Hedda. "Bill Wellman Jr." *Daily News* (New York, New York), April 5, 1964, 87.

Hopper, Hedda. "Bond's Thunderball Film Deadlock Broken," *Chicago Tribune New York News Syndicate*. September 26, 1964.

Hopper, Hedda. "Colorful Stage Actor Gets Choice Film Role." *Hartford Courant*, April 10, 1965, 15.

Hopper, Hedda. "Curtis' Marriage Plans Indefinite." *Los Angeles Times*, January 9, 1963, 8.

Hopper, Hedda. "Edgar Bergen Family Has New Celebrity." *Chicago Tribune*, July 13, 1965, 31.

Hopper, Hedda. "Flintstones Join Spy Fad." *Los Angeles Times*, January 21, 1966, 60.

Hopper, Hedda. "Hollywood." *Daily News* (New York, New York), November 1, 1963, 13.

Hopper, Hedda. "Hollywood, February 18." *Daily News* (New York, New York), 42.

Hopper, Hedda. "Horton Throws Party for His 79th Birthday." *Memphis Press-Scimitar*, March 24, 1965, 31.

Hopper, Hedda. "Newcomer to Starsville." *Hartford Courant*, September 12, 1965, 142.

Horn, John. "Rating Shows on Quality." *Marion Star* (Marion, Ohio), March 31, 1967, 10.

"How Critics Assess New Shows—Part 3." *Broadcasting*, September 26, 1966, 74.

"How Critics See the New Season." *Broadcasting*, September 20, 1965, 39.

Howard, Edwin. "States's *Fat Spy* Is Thin Fare." *Memphis Press-Scimitar*, May 19, 1966, 22.

Howard, Edwin. "3 Marquees All Raising Caine." *Memphis Press-Scimitar*, December 21, 1966, 38.

"Hybrid Pix." *St. Louis Post-Dispatch*, October 3, 1965, 312.

"Ian Fleming Dies at 56; Wrote James Bond Tales." *Boston Globe*, August 12, 1964, 33.

Inman, Julia. "New Violence Study May End 18-Year-Old Video Standoff." *Indianapolis Star*, April 18, 1969, 25.

"The Ipcress File." *Variety*, December 31, 1964.

"*The Ipcress File* Is Mystery Thriller Starring Michael Caine." *Messenger-Inquirer* (Owensboro, Kentucky), November 28, 1965, 29.

"*Ipcress File* Shows Here." *Fairbanks Daily News-Miner* (Fairbanks, Alaska), December 24, 1965, 13.

"Israeli Queen in Spy Film." *Salt Lake Tribune*, October 28, 1968, 13.

"Israeli Star Will Visit Memphis." *Memphis Press-Scimitar*, January 10, 1966, 12.

"James Bond Comes Back for Christmas." *Pensacola News Journal* (Pensacola, Florida), December 20, 1964, 10.

"James Bond Said Too Expensive to Be Successor to Charlie Chan." *Star Tribune* (Minneapolis, Minnesota), April 26, 1964, 84.

"James Bond Spoof fff Film at Strand." *Delaware Gazette*, January 9, 1969, 9.

"James Bond's Bombshells." *Vancouver Sun*, January 16, 1965, 20.

"James Bond's Sixth Adventure." *Runcorn Weekly News* (Runcorn, Cheshire, England), May 2, 1968, 15.

"JFK's Favorite Thriller Writer, Creator of James Bond 'Flattered.'" *Racine Journal-Times* (Racine, Wisconsin), July 7, 1963, 12.

Johnson, Erskine. "Harem Dancers 'Frozen.'" *Eureka Humboldt* (Eureka, California), July 27, 1963, 2.

Johnson, Erskine. "Heart Thumper." *Star-Gazette* (Elmira, New York), April 2, 1963, 9.

Johnson, Erskine. "Sean Connery Heart-Thumper." *Odessa Star* (Odessa, Texas), March 24, 1963, 19.

"Joins *Thunderball* Cast." *Daily News* (New York, New York), April 18, 1965, 475.

Jordan, Turner. "Politicos, Election Special with Share Video Spot Here." *Birmingham News* (Birmingham, Alabama), March 28, 1963, 52.

"Joshua Logan Leads 'Wagon.'" *Los Angeles Times*, April 8, 1967, 18.

Kaliff, Joe. "Magic Carpet over Broadway." *Brooklyn Daily*, January 20, 1969, 2.

"Kathy Dunn Wows Columbia Executives in 'Candy Web.'" *Herald-News* (Passaic, New Jersey), December 22, 1962, 47.

Keely, Bob. "Nevada Scene." *San Francisco Examiner*, December 23, 1984, 243.

Kelly, Herb. "Movie 'Censorship' Now Up to Parents." *Miami News*, October 10, 1968, 16.

Kelly, Herb. "Parents Request Prom Party Tips, Here Are Some." *Miami News*, May 24, 1966, 12.

Ketridege, Chris "Give Me Some Gravy and I'm 'Swinging Fats.' Leonard Says He's a Bread Man." *News-Press* (Cape Coral, Florida), June 13, 1965, 6.

"Kildare Romance." *Buffalo News*, November 7, 1964, 61.

Kilgallen, Dorothy. "Connery Marriage in Trouble?" *Cincinnati Enquirer*, September 13, 1965, 24.

Kilgallen, Dorothy. "Off Stage." *South Bend Tribune*, September 26, 1965, 38.

Kilgallen, Dorothy. "Voice of Broadway." *Republican and Herald* (Pottsville, Pennsylvania), November 8, 1965, 6.

"Killer Legs." *Daily News* (New York, New York), May 7, 1969, 98.

Kirkley, Donald. "Look and Listen." *Baltimore Sun*, October 16, 1963, 28.

Kleiner, Dick. "Actress Is Gung Ho about Gung Foo." *Guam Daily News*, August 28, 1968, 18.

Kleiner, Dick. "Burr Gets Raise." *Ithaca Journal*, May 8, 1965, 14.

Kleiner, Dick. "Carol Channing—Loaded Dice Deal." *News-Press* (Fort Myers, Florida), March 6, 1967, 21.

Kleiner, Dick. "Dino Dryly Kids Role." *Wausau Daily Herald* (Wausau, Wisconsin), September 24, 1965, 15.

Kleiner, Dick. "Flint's Not a Bond." *Courier-News* (Bridgewater, New Jersey), September 6, 1966, 32.

Kleiner, Dick. "Hedy Shuffles Lineup in Legal Pursuit Game." *The Herald* (Rock Hill, South Carolina), October 24, 1966, 8.

Kleiner, Dick. "Hiding Cigarettes in a Bikini." *Mt. Vernon Register News* (Mt. Vernon, Illinois), August 28, 1965, 3.

Kleiner, Dick. "Hollywood Making Reappraisal." *Star-Phoenix* (Saskatoon, Saskatchewan, Canada), July 10, 1968, 30.

Kleiner, Dick. "Hollywood Today." *The Monitor* (McAllen, Texas), April 22, 1965, 4.

Kleiner, Dick. "Johnson in Hollywood." *Millville Daily* (Millville, New Jersey), December 5, 1964, 8.

Kleiner, Dick. "U.S. Idols, Stars on Japanese TV." *Philadelphia Daily News*, September 23, 1966, 34.

"Knows the Lingo." *Stockton Evening and Sunday Record* (Stockton, California), August 27, 1965, 28.

Koenig, Bill, compiler. Letters about Ian Fleming's U.N.C.L.E. involvement.

Kupcinet, Irv. "Super Brawl Poses Danger to Free TV." *Miami Herald*, March 10, 1971, 22.

Last of the Secret Agents? advertisement. *Kansas City Star*, July 24, 1966, 69.

"Laurence Harvey May Play Bond." *Birmingham Evening Mail* (Birmingham, England), January 7, 1964, 20.

Lazarus, George. "More Punch, Less Burp in 007 Beer." *Fort Worth Star-Telegram* (Fort Worth, Texas), March 17, 1967, 49.

"Lazenby Quits James Bond Role." *Tacoma News Tribune*, November 24, 1969, 27.

"Legion of Decency." *True Voice*, November 26, 1965, 5.

"Legion of Decency Rates Current Films." *The Tidings* (Los Angeles, California), November 5, 1965, 10.

"Legion of Decency: Recent Listings." *True Voice* (Omaha, Nebraska), June 12, 1964, 5.

Leino, Clarence. "*The Second Best Secret Agent* a Really Devil-May-Care Britisher." *Sun-Tattler* (Hollywood, Florida), November 25, 1965, 32.

Lenzi, Richard. "False Picture." Letter to the Editor. *Berkshire Eagle* (Pittsfield, Massachusetts), February 9, 1955, 18.

Leonard, Vince. "What's Out for Children." *Pittsburgh Press*, January 25, 1967, 78.

Lewis, Dan. "Caine Cases New York." *The Record* (Hackensack, New Jersey), September 9, 1965, 32.

Lewis, Dan. "Maharis as Superman." *The Record* (Hackensack, New Jersey), April 15, 1965, 42.

Lewis, Flora. "Unsecret Agent Even 'M' Would Cringe." *Virginian-Pilot* (Norfolk, Virginia), December 4, 1963, 30.

Liberty advertisement. *Times Recorder* (Zanesville, Ohio), January 15, 1966, 18.

"The Light Side." *Columbia Record* (Columbia, South Carolina), August 9, 1969, 10.

"Like Us All, Agents Face Dull Moments." *Central New Jersey Home News*, November 19, 1966, 6.

"Luscious Luciana Sean's Next Adversary." *Philadelphia Daily News*, March 3, 1965, 30.

Lyons, Leonard. "Pieces of Molding Bread for Penicillin." *Evening Standard* (Uniontown, Pennsylvania), March 8, 1962, 9.

"Making Debut in the Title Field." *Los Angeles Evening Citizen*, January 3, 1966, 10.

Man, Roderick. "Poor Boy Michael Caine Has Money Now." *Detroit Free Press*, October 17, 1965, 24.

"*Man Called Flintstone* Opens in Showcases." *New York Times*, November 25, 1967, 42.

"*Man from Rio* Premiere." *Daily News* (New York), May 22, 1964, 69.

"*Man Who Never Was* Filming in Berlin." *Sunday News* (Lancaster, Pennsylvania), July 10, 1966.

"The Man Who Never Wins." *Kansas City Star*, January 15, 1967, 117.

Manners, Dorothy. "Behind the Scenes in Hollywood." *Times Leader* (Wilkes-Barre, Pennsylvania), October 24, 1969, 9.

Manners, Dorothy. "Connery Not Amused by Film." *Columbus Ledger* (Columbus, Georgia), January 26, 1967, 40.

Manners, Dorothy. "Ladies Love Bob Hope." *San Francisco Examiner*, September 28, 1966, 53.

"Marlowe in Film." *Los Angeles Times*, December 24, 1962, 22.

Marth, Mike. "Buono Will Play Chinese Villain." *Van Nuys News and Valley Green Sheet*, August 26, 121.

Martin, Betty. "Delon to Return to France." *Los Angeles Times*, July 9, 1966, 21.

Martin, Betty. "Movie Call Sheet: Glenn Ford Set for 'El Mal.'" *Los Angeles Times*, August 20, 1965, 10.

Martin, Betty. "Operation: Lovebirds." *Los Angeles Times*, May 17, 1967, 66.

Martin, Betty. "Third Matt Helm Film Slated." *Los Angeles Times*, January 8, 1966, 17.

Martin, Betty. "*The Visitors* Film Roles Set." *Los Angeles Times*, April 13, 1966, D11.

Martin, Betty. "Warner to Film *Camelot*." *Los Angeles Times*, February 23, 1966, C9.

"Martin Returns to Columbia." *Calgary Herald*, April 22, 1965, 36.

"Martin's Happy with Matt Helm Parts; They're 'Up His Alley.'" *Star Press* (Muncy, Indiana), January 21, 1968, 19.

Mason, Todd. "*Planet of Apes* Set before Voting." *Pensacola News Journal*, June 11, 1967, 22.

Mastroianni, Tony. "*Kid Brother* Is Poor Relation." *Cleveland Press*, November 18, 1967, 42.

Matheson, Ed. "Talk of the Town." *Bangor Daily News*, September 13, 1965, 10.

"Mayhem on Males: British Actress Soars to Top with Violence." *Valley Morning Star* (Harlingen, Texas), February 2, 1964, 11.

McClure, Hal. "Fleming Autographs Mystery Thrillers for JFK." *The Progress-Index* (Petersburg, Virginia), July 17, 1963, 17.

McGrotha, Bill. "Big Season for Seminole." *Tallahassee Democrat*, November 19, 1965, 12.

McHarry, Charles. "Play for Bette." *Daily News* (New York, New York), June 1, 1966, 100.

McHarry, Charles. "Room for All." *Daily News* (New York, New York), March 13, 1967, 45.

McHenry Savings and Loan Association advertisement. *McHenry Plaindealer* (McHenry, Illinois), July 15, 1965, 13.

Mennella, Francesco. "What Next? A Jolly Mad Scientist!" *Hartford Courant* (Hartford Connecticut), March 6, 1966, 113.

"Metro-Goldwyn-Mayer Inc. Announces Acquisition of *Never Say Never Again* James Bond Assets." Metro-Goldwyn-Mayer Inc., December 4, 1997. Press Release.

"Mexican Star Kills Himself." *Morning News* (Wilmington, Delaware), June 19, 1963, 27.

"Michael Caine Proves That He Is Able." *Lincolnshire Echo* (Lincoln, Lincolnshire, England), August 24, 1965, 4.

Michelson, Herb. "That Glittering *Goldfinger*" *Oakland Tribune* (Oakland, California), December 30, 1964, 30.

Miller, Jeanne. "Another Secret Agent on Screen." *San Francisco Examiner*, January 20, 1966, 23.

Miller, Jeanne. "Bond's Latest Is Lavish." *San Francisco Examiner*, April 29, 1967, 8.

Miller, Lois. "Beautiful Girls, Humor Help the Wrecking Crew." *Kingston Whig-Standard* (Kingston, Ontario, Canada), December 27, 1968, 18.

"Miss Parker Gets Warning." *Los Angeles Times*, April 7, 1966, 92.

Mohbat, Joseph E. "TV Scored as Villain in 'Real-Life.'" *Cincinnati Enquirer*, September 25, 1969, 3.

Monahan, Kaspar. "Existentialism Is Delivered Crushing Blow." *Pittsburgh Press*, October 18, 1965, 36.

Monahan, Kaspar. "Noted Actors' Daughters Do Honor to Dads." *Pittsburgh Press*, January 11, 1967, 39.

Monahan, Kaspar. "Recalling Some Past Premieres." *Pittsburgh Press*, May 18, 1966, 48.

Monahan, Kaspar. "Second to *Navarone*." *Pittsburgh Press*, March 11, 1963, 28.

Moore, Sir Roger. *Bond on Bond: Reflections on 50 Years of James Bond Movies*. Rowman & Littlefield, 2013.

Mootz, William. "Bond Spoof, *Casino Royale*, Is a Losing Gambol." *Courier-Journal* (Louisville, Kentucky), April 29, 1967, 17.

Mootz, William. "James Bond Kills *Dr. No* on Island." *Courier-Journal* (Louisville, Kentucky), June 7, 1963, 22.

Mootz, William. "*Killed* Doesn't Dim Splendors of Mercouri." *Courier-Journal* (Louisville, Kentucky), May 5, 1966, 32.

Mootz, William. "*Man from Rio* Proves Irreverent and Delightful." *Courier-Journal* (Louisville, Kentucky), November 12, 1964, 42.

"Moral Evaluations of Current Movies." *The Tidings* (Los Angeles, California), November 4, 1966, 14.

"More Flint." *Cincinnati Post*, January 23, 1967, 17.

Morehouse, Ward. "Sean Connery Called 'Mr. Kiss-Kiss.'" *Calgary Herald*, July 10, 1963, 8.

Moss, Norman. "Bond Label Makes Sean Rich, Angry." *Press & Sun Bulletin* (Binghamton New York), March 5, 1966, 26.

"Most Popular Films of 1963." *The Times* (London, England), January 3, 1964, 4.

"Movie Directory." *Ottawa Citizen*, February 9, 1968, 31.

"Movie Filming Indoors." *Daily News* (New York, New York), July 11, 1965, 7.

"Movie Men to Visit Cape Area." *Orlando Sentinel*, March 1, 1966, 16.

"Movie Premiers." *Chicago Tribune*, February 12, 1966, 15.

"Movie Shot Over Two Continents." *Oakland Tribune,* May 7, 1963, 9.

"Movies for Everyone Fill El Paso Screens." *El Paso Times*, June 12, 1966, 65.

"Movies: *Salt and Pepper*." *Windsor Star* (Windsor, Ontario, Canada), December 17, 1968, 20.

"Much Derring-Do in *Some Girls Do*." *The Record* (Hackensack, New Jersey), February 12, 1971, 37.

Muir, Florabel. "Fess Takes Daniel to Mexico." *Akron Beacon Journal*, May 4, 1966, 69.

Muir, Florabel. "Looking at Hollywood." *Odessa American*, July 7, 1966, 27.

Munroe, Dale. "Gimmicks Abound in Spy Adventure." *Valley Times* (North Hollywood, California), January 12, 1967, 8.

Murdock, Henry T. "James Coburn Plays Hero in *Our Man Flint*." *Philadelphia Inquirer*, January 20, 1966, 12.

Murdock, Henry T. "*Kid Brother* Spoofs Bond." *Philadelphia Inquirer*, October 28, 1967, 11.

Murdock, Henry T. "Movie Spoofs Spy Plots." *Philadelphia Inquirer*, January 27, 1966, 10.

Musel, Robert. "New Fall TV Series Like James Bond on Horseback." *Oshkosh Northwestern* (Oshkosh, Wisconsin), August 9, 1965, 22.

"National Box Office Survey." *Variety*, August 9, 1967, 4.

"New Actor Picked for Agent 007 Role." *Bismarck Tribune*, October 3, 1968, 13.

"New Bond Movie Hailed in London." *Asbury Park Press*, September 17, 1964, 9.

"'New Bond,' Perhaps, in *Thunderball*." *Valley Times* (North Hollywood, California), December 27, 1963, 11.

"New Films in Review." *Knoxville News-Sentinel*, October 29, 1967, 64.

"New Hero Emerges in Spy Drama." *Miami Herald*, October 15, 1967, 207.

"New James Bond Had Never Acted." *Oakland Tribune*, October 9, 1968, 28.

"New Spy Thriller." *Sunday Gazette-Mail* (Charleston, West Virginia), September 4, 1966, 49.

"The Newsmakers." *Los Angeles Times*, December 14, 1969, 2.

Newton, Dwight. "Don't Lose Your Buttons." *San Francisco Examiner*, December 22, 1965, 17.

"Next at the Movies: The Adult Cartoon." *Calgary Herald*, September 12, 1966, 13.

Noe, Irving. "Noe News Is Show News." *Van Nuys News and Valley Green Sheet*, January 3, 1965, 43.

"Now Showing." *Detroit Free Press*, August 24, 1965, 31.

"Oldsters and Funsters in World of Wheels Show." *Daily News* (New York, New York), March 31, 1967, 873.

"On Location: Little Cleopatra." *Time*, May 6, 1966.

"*One Million Years B.C.* Presents a Nice Live Raquel Welch." *New York Times*, February 22, 1967, 21.

Operation: Lovebirds Double Feature advertisement. *Ottawa Citizen*, February 12, 1968, 27.

Oppenheimer, Peer J. "Failure Made Him a Success." *Denton Record-Chronicle* (Denton, Texas), November 21, 1965, 62.

Oppenheimer, Peer J. "Hollywood's Answer to James Bond." *Racine Journal-Times Sunday Bulletin* (Racine, Wisconsin), October 24, 1965, 63.

Oshinsky, Sy. "New Films in Review." *Knoxville News-Sentinel*, March 6, 1966, 62.

"*Our Man Flint* Sequel Scheduled." *Morning Call* (Allentown, Pennsylvania), November 11, 1965, 24.

"Out?" *The Age* (Melbourne, Victoria, Australia), January 27, 1966, 2.

"Owen Resigns as Director." *Morning Call* (Allentown, Pennsylvania), July 6, 1965, 15.

Owen, Roslyn. "Dressed to Kill." *TV Week* (Australia), January 8, 1966, 22.

Pack, Harvey. "NBC Signs Britain's 'The Saint,'" *Journal News* (White Plains, New York), January 10, 1966, 22.

"Palace Haunts 'Dr. Goldfoot.'" *Los Angeles Evening Citizen*, August 12, 1965, 10.

Palmer, Stephen. "*Satan Bug* Found Provocative." *Lexington Herald-Leader* (Lexington, Kentucky), May 9, 1965, 62.

Paramount Theater advertisement. *Daily News* (New York, New York), December 20, 1965, 145.

Parsons, Louella. "Ann-Margret May Have Date Set." *Indianapolis Star*, February 15, 1965, 13.

Parsons, Louella. "Bikini Wins Modest Gila Golan Lead Role." *Indianapolis Star*, March 10, 1965, 24.

Parsons, Louella. "*Human Bondage* Returning with Laurence Harvey." *Buffalo Evening News*, November 13, 1962, 16.

Parsons, Louella. "Rita Wins Top Role." *San Francisco Examiner*, April 1, 1963, 19.

Pearson, Drew. "Reappraising TV Violence." *Beatrice Daily Sun* (Beatrice, Nebraska), July 1, 1968, 6.

"People in the News." *Great Falls Tribune* (Great Falls, Montana), December 14, 1969, 2.

"Pert, Blonde Beautician Turned Down Movie Work." *News-Press* (Cape Coral, Florida), December 14, 1965, 11.

Petzold, Charles. "An Adventurous Briton." *Courier-Post* (Camden, New Jersey), July 24, 1967, 18.

"Phyllis Diller Arrives to Work in *The Fat Spy* at Cape Coral." *News-Press* (Cape Coral, Florida), June 10, 1965, 1.

"Pier Making Italian Film." *Spokesman-Review* (Spokane, Washington), June 13, 1965, 52.

Pisoni, R. "Kill Baby Kill." In *Un mondo aparte*, edited by Gabriele Acerbo and Roberto Pisoni. Rome, 2007.

"Plane Stowaway Lands Movie Role." *Buffalo Evening News*, November 15, 1962, 40.

"Pointers on Passing." *Memphis Press-Scimitar*, August 24, 1966, 31.

Porter, Reed. "*Billion Dollar Brain* Million-Volt Thrill." *Valley Times* (North Hollywood, California), December 23, 1967, 8.

Portis, Charles. "Is Cloak-and-Dagger Balloon Bursting." *Los Angeles Times*, April 26, 1964, 437.

Potomac, Peter. "The James Bond Mania: 007, the Grownup's Beatle." *Berkshire Eagle* (Pittsfield, Massachusetts), April 1, 1964, 18.

Powers, Thomas. "Nephew of Broccoli Grower Is Busy with James Bond Movies." *Daily Herald* (Provo, Utah), July 10, 1968, 11.

Prelutsky, Burt. "Two Centerfolds." *Los Angeles Times*, December 24, 1972, 228.

"Presenting 'That Man from Rio.'" *Sandusky Register* (Sandusky, Ohio), June 7, 1966, 10.

"Press Fund Premiere for Bond's Latest." *Evening Chronicle* (Newcastle, England), February 27, 1970, 11.

"Prisoner to Be Freed from TV." *Leicester Mercury* (Leicester, Leicestershire, England), December 2, 1967, 11.

"Promising Starlet to Wed Hair Style Pace Setter." *Herald Times* (Passaic, New Jersey), February 13, 1967, 8.

Quinn, Frank. "Of Broadway." *Daily News* (Lebanon, Pennsylvania), August 30, 1963, 15.

Rasor, John. "Just Plain Jayne." *Tampa Tribune*, June 27, 1965, 142.

"Recent Movie Ratings." *True Voice* (Omaha, Nebraska), April 21, 1967, 10.

"Red Viewers Dig Popular Video Shows." *Chicago Tribune*, August 27, 1967, 10.

Reiter, Ed. "How Do Shore Psychiatrists Rate 007, Batman?" *Asbury Park Press* (Asbury Park, New Jersey), January 30, 1966, 41.

"Restaurateur Takes Trip to Far East." *Valley News* (Van Nuys, California), October 8, 1965, 21.

Richards, Denise. "The Three Men in My Life." *Evening Standard* (London, England), January 9, 1964, 14.

"Ritz to Offer *Secret Agent Super Dragon*." *Anniston Star* (Anniston, Alabama), May 14, 1967, 31.

"Robert Vaughn," Interview conducted by Ron Simon, Academy of Television Arts & Sciences, New York, May 18, 2007. https://interviews.televisionacademy.com/interviews/robert-vaughn.

"Rod Taylor." *Sydney Morning Herald* (Sydney, Australia), January 8, 1964, 3.

Ross, Maris. "Became an Actor by Accident Says Movie Villain Telly Savalas." *Daily News-Journal* (Murfreesboro, Tennessee), February 9, 1969, 8.

Roud, Richard. "New Films." *The Guardian* (London, England), October 11, 1963, 11.

Roud, Richard. "New Films." *The Guardian* (London, England), June 16, 1967, 9.

Roud, Richard. "New Films in London." *The Guardian* (London, England), March 6, 1964, 11.

Runnells, Charles. "'The Worst Movie Shot in Cape Coral': *The Fat Spy* and the Year Hollywood Came to Town." *News-Press* (Cape Coral, Florida), December 14, 2018.

Russell, Fred. "Passing Show." *Bridgeport Post* (Bridgeport, Connecticut), March 5, 1965, 12.

Sack Theaters advertisement. *Boston Globe*, October 22, 1967, 108.

Sar, Ali. "Buono's Current Popularity Owes to Single Film Role." *Van Nuys News and Valley Green Sheet*, October 26, 1965, 16.

Sar, Ali. "Sturges' *Satan Bug* Found Non-Communicable." *Van Nuys News and Valley Green Sheet*, May 7, 1965, 38.

"The *Satan Bug* Will Get You If You Don't Watch Out." *Buffalo News*, April 29, 1965, 54.

Savoy advertisement. *Boston Globe*, January 14, 1966, 29.

Scheuer, Philip K. "Action Galore in *Thunderball* but Cinematically It's a Dud." *Los Angeles Times*, December 20, 1965, 79.

Scheuer, Philip K. "Coburn Just Right for *Our Man Flint*." *Los Angeles Times*, February 5, 1965, 65.

Scheuer, Philip K. "Even Allen and Rossi Unable to Save 'The Secret Agents.'" *Los Angeles Times*, May 26, 1966, 79.

Scheuer, Philip K. "Gilbert to Direct *Khartoum*." *Los Angeles Times*, April 21, 1964, 9.

Scheuer, Philip K. "'Glass Boat' Draws Laughs." *Los Angeles Times*, August 17, 1966, 68.

Scheuer, Philip K. "Hit Raises Caine." *Philadelphia Inquirer*, January 9, 1966, 95.

Scheuer, Philip K. "Pair Acquire Rights to 'Spawn of Evil.'" *Los Angeles Times*, July 10, 1964, 65.

Scheuer, Philip K. "Paris Film at 3rd and Broadway." *Los Angeles Times*, September 20, 1966, C1.

Scheuer, Philip K. "Spy Foolishment in 'Man in Istanbul.'" *Los Angeles Times*, March 24, 1966, 79.

Scheuer, Philip K. "Story of Taj Mahal Set for $8 Million: Bombay and Beirut Report; Check List of 1964's Best." *Los Angeles Times*, December 29, 1964, 54.

Scheuer, Philip K. "Visitors Will See 'How Movies Made.'" *Los Angeles Times*, May 10, 1963, 69.

Schlesinger, Arthur M. "Papers of John F. Kennedy. Presidential Papers President's Office Files." February 1963.

Scott, John L. "*Goldfinger* Rousing Melodrama." *Los Angeles Times*, December 25, 1964, 17.

Scott, John L. "Hollywood Calendar: Her Art Belongs to Daddy." *Los Angeles Times*, January 16, 1966, 473.

Scott, John L. "Maureen's Tardy Spirit." *Los Angeles Times*, May 23, 1965, 525.

Scott, Vernon. "Actor James Coburn Wins the Hard Way." *Fresno Bee*, April 12, 1965, 12.

Scott, Vernon. "Glamor Gal Gains Fame on Her Own." *Republican and Herald* (Pottsville, Pennsylvania), June 15, 1967, 11.

Scott, Vernon. "Israeli Actress Different." *Lubbock Avalanche-Journal*, April 15, 1965, 67.

Scott, Vernon. "James Coburn Climber in Film Industry." *Tipton Daily Tribune* (Tipton, Indiana), April 12, 1965, 6.

Scott, Vernon. "Mini-Skirts Will Give 'Ambushers' Film a Lift." *Fresno Bee*, April 24, 1967, 9.

Scott, Vernon. "Ring Ding–Type Movies Here to Stay." *Boston Globe*, July 11, 1965, 111.

Scott, Vernon. "*Song of Norway* to Be Made Film." *Morning News* (Wilmington, Delaware), May 31, 1968, 12.

"Sean Connery to Be Back as James Bond." *St. Louis Post-Dispatch*, March 7, 1971, 107.

"Sean Could Make 007 Comeback." *Liverpool Echo* (Liverpool, England), February 24, 1971, 1.

"Sean's Doing Bond for Charity." *San Francisco Examiner*, March 4, 1971, 27.

2nd Best in the Whole Wide World advertisment. *Tampa Bay Times* (St. Petersburg, Florida), December 19, 1965, 10.

"2nd Best Definitely 2nd Rate." *Post-Standard* (Syracuse, New York), January 21, 1966, 16.

"Secret Agent Is Theme of Picture." *Longview Daily News* (Longview, Washington), May 13, 1966, 24.

Secret Agent Super Dragon advertisement. *Northwest Arkansas Times* (Fayetteville, Arkansas), October 31, 1966, 2.

"Sells in Millions." *Sun Times* (Owen Sound, Ontario, Canada), April 10, 1964, 4.

"Sensational Raquel Welch Co-Star of Action Drama." *Great Bend Tribune* (Great Bend, Kansas), November 5, 1967.

"Sequel 'I Was a Teen-Age Deadhead.'" *Fort Worth-Star Telegram*, August 10, 1965, 6.

"Shame, James Agent 007 Denounced by Vatican Paper." *Courier-Journal* (Louisville, Kentucky), May 18, 1962, 16.

Shearer, Lloyd. "She Claims She's the Luckiest Girl in the World." *Clarion-Ledger* (Jackson, Mississippi), October 30, 1966, 83.

Shearer, Lloyd. "This Summer's Fads: Knee Make-Up and Crew Shirts." *Miami Herald*, August 1, 1965, 183.

Shippy, Dick. "The Suspense Just Isn't." *Akron Beacon Journal*, May 7, 1965, 12.

Shippy, Dick. "We Don't Need Bad Imitations." *Akron Beacon Journal*, March 11, 1966, 14.

"Shooting Starts Wednesday. Cape Coral Is Film Site of 'Fat Spy.'" *Miami Herald*, June 4, 1965, 89.

"Show 'Nuf." *Charlotte News*, March 5, 1966, 26.

"Show Schedule Apache Drive In." *Tucson Daily Citizen* (Tucson, Arizona), November 4, 1968, 24.

"Silver Lining." *Daily Standard* (Sikeston, Missouri), May 6, 1967, 2.

6 Mile Theater advertisement. *Detroit Free Press*, January 22, 1966, 26.

Skolsky, Sidney. "Gossipel Truth for Hollywood." *Los Angeles Evening Citizen*, June 7, 1966, 6.

Smith, Ardis. "*Second Best Agent* Surely No Threat to Replace 007." *Buffalo News*, January 13, 1966, 57.

"Smith, Carr Buy Film Rights." *Los Angeles Times*, May 17, 1968, 87.

"*Some Girls Do* Arrives at the Victoria." *New York Times*, February 11, 1971, 55.

Sparks, Nancy. "From This Viewpoint . . . " *Wichita Beacon*, November 13, 1965, 31.

Sparks, Nancy. "Latest Bond Interestingly Enough Has Never Worked in Films Before." *Wichita Beacon*, October 28, 1968, 11.

Spencer, Walter. "TV's Vast Grey Belt." *Television* 24, no. 8 (August 1967): 54–55.

"Spiegel to Film 'Swimmer.'" *Los Angeles Times*, March 19, 1965, 81.

"Spies, Tarzan, Monster on Bridge Drive-In Bill." *Sunday News and Tribune* (Jefferson City, Missouri), August 14, 1966, 29.

"Spy Film Is Just Old Stuff." *Daily News* (New York, New York), February 12, 1971, 89.

The Spy in Lace Panties advertisement. *Sydney Morning Herald*, March 4, 1967, 25.

"Spy Spoof Coming to Palace Screen May 7." *Philadelphia Daily News*, April 30, 1969, 32.

"The Spy Who Came In from the Cold." *Variety*, December 31, 1965.

"Spy with a Mission in the Austrian Tyrol: Yul Brynner Stars in 'The Double Man'; 3 Other Films Open at Theaters Here." *New York Times*, May 2, 1968, 57

"Stanley Caine Will Bow in *Billion Dollar Brain*." *Atlanta Constitution*, February 25, 1967, 56.

"Stargazer's Cinema Round Up: *The Quiller Memorandum* Disturbingly Topical." *Bucks Examiner* (Chesham, Buckinghamshire, England), January 13, 1967, 6.

"Starlets Hope to Get Aboard 'Bond Express.'" *Commercial Appeal* (Memphis, Tennessee), February 7, 1965, 42.

Steel, Bert. "Let's Chat Movies." *Windsor Star* (Windsor, Ontario, Canada), April 1, 1967, 42.

Steele, Arthur. "From 'Idiot' Roles to Space Race Satire." *Birmingham Mail* (Birmingham, England), April 13, 1963, 3.

Stein, Herb. "Best of Hollywood." *Philadelphia Inquirer*, September 1, 1965, 18.

Steinem, Gloria. "Our Man Is 'Real Boss.'" *New York Times*, August 28, 1966, 109.

"Stella Stevens in *Silencers*." *Morning Call* (Allentown, Pennsylvania), June 16, 1965, 14.

Stern, Harold. "'Anti-Hero' Aspires to Movie Stardom." *Indianapolis Star*, September 6, 1965, 10.

Stern, Harold. "This Star Not Looking for Series." *Paducah Sun* (Paducah, Kentucky), May 25, 1965, 19.

Sterngold, James. "Sony Pictures, in an Accord with MGM, Drops Its Plan to Produce New James Bond Movies." *New York Times*, March 30, 1999, 11.

Stevens, Dale. "Phyllis Diller's First Movie Seen Here Soon." *Cincinnati Post*, May 9, 1966, 22.

Strobel, Bill. "Drummond Back—Hefner-Styled." *Oakland Tribune*, March 18, 1967, 9.

Swaebly, Fran. "Duggan Happy Grind of TV Series Is Over." *Miami Herald*, July 15, 1966, 84.

Talbert, Bob. "The 007th Heaven of James Bond." *The State* (Columbia, South Carolina), January 16, 1966, 63.

"'Teen Diplomats' Star in New Film." *Van Nuys News and Valley Green Sheet*, December 28, 1962, 12.

"Teenage Latin Hopeful." *Odessa American* (Odessa, Texas), November 25, 1962, 41.

"Teen-Talizers." *The Charlotte News* (Charlotte, North Carolina), April 29, 1966, 19.

Terry, Clifford. "Budget Goes Up in Bond Venture." *The Guardian* (London, England), June 18, 1967, section 2, page 22.

Terry, Clifford. "Star-Laden Bond Film Sags." *Chicago Tribune*, May 2, 1967, 39.

That Man from Rio advertisement. *Los Angeles Times*, January 20, 1965, 58.

That Man from Rio advertisement: The Paris Theater. *Daily News* (New York, New York), June 12, 1964, 76.

"Theater Open 24 Hours for *Goldfinger* Showings." *New York Times*, December 23, 1964, 22.

"Theater Schedule Announced." *Orlando Sentinel*, December 18, 1966, 67.

"*Thigh Spy* Ad." *Philadelphia Inquirer*, November 5, 1967, 122.

Thomas, Bob. "Female 'James Bond' Set Tough-Gal Clothes Fad." *Arizona Daily Star* (Tucson, Arizona), December 2, 1964, 36.

Thomas, Bob. "Hollywood Highlights." *Spokane Daily Chronicle*, December 20, 1965, 15.

Thomas, Bob. "James Bond, Ian Fleming, Hero, Popular in England." *Petaluma Argus-Courier* (Petaluma, California), February 27, 1964, 10.

Thomas, Bob. "Latest James Bond Movie Has Typical Ingredients." *Arizona Daily Star* (Tucson, Arizona), December 1, 1964, 3.

Thomas, Bob. "Michael Caine Treated as Star in Hollywood." *Corsicana Daily Sun*, January 11, 1966, 1.

Thomas, Bob. "Movies Bet $200 Million on 1966." *Oakland Tribune*, January 3, 1966, 15.

Thomas, Bob. "Newest James Bond Star Is Real; Says He Took Job Only for Money." *San Bernardino County Sun*, October 25, 1968, 43.

Thomas, Bob. "Producers Seeking New James Bond Character." *Belleville News-Democrat* (Belleville, Illinois), July 27, 1967, 20.

Thomas, Bob. "Robert Culp Happy Many Off James Bond Bandwagon." *Indiana Gazette* (Indiana, Pennsylvania), February 28, 1967, 32.

Thomas, Bob. "Sean Connery in U.S. as James Bond." *Wausau Daily Herald* (Wausau, Wisconsin), March 18, 1963, 6.

Thomas, Bob. "SMERSH Holds No Terror." *Hillsdale News* (Hillsdale, Michigan), October 26, 1968, 3.

Thomas, Kevin. "*Fat Spy* Lean Fare for Comedy Devotees." *Los Angeles Times*, May 13, 1966, 71.

Thomas, Kevin. "*Kona, Double Man* Playing Citywide." *Los Angeles Times*, May 22, 1968, 68.

Thomas, Kevin. "Pair of Suspense Movies Set a Dizzy Action Pace." *Los Angeles Times*, January 13, 1967, 66.

Thomas, Kevin. "Second 'Dr. Goldfoot' Film Really a Bomb." *Los Angeles Times*, December 2, 1966, 92.

Thomas, Kevin. "*Tiger Lily* a Spoof to End All Spoofs." *Los Angeles Times*, November 18, 1966, 84.

Thompson, Bish. "*Khartoum* Labeled Good." *Evansville Press* (Evansville, Indiana), October 13, 1966, 12.

Thompson, Howard. "British Double Bill." *New York Times*, June 6, 1968, 54.

Thompson, Howard. "Kiss the Girls." *Sacramento Bee* (Sacramento, California), February 5, 1967, 134.

Thompson, Howard. "An Original Spy!: David Niven Film Owes James Bond Naught." *New York Times*, January 27, 1966, 29.

Thompson, Howard. "Pale Bond Copy." *New York Times*, January 6, 1966, 20.

Thompson, Howard. "Peck in Thriller." *New York Times*, June 26, 1969, 44.

Thompson, Howard. "Super-Agent Martin and the Ambushers." *New York Times*, December 23, 1967, 24.

"*Thunderball*, Bond Film, to Be Produced in Bahamas." *San Bernardino County Sun*, September 23, 1964, 28.

"*Thunderball* on Way to New Record in Japan; 'Poppins' Also Clicks." *Variety*, December 29, 1965, 5.

"*Thunderball* to Open on December 21." *Los Angeles Times*, November 29, 1965, 79.

Tinsley, Anne Miller. "No Escape Here: *King Rat* Ruled Top POV Movie." *Fort Worth Star-Telegram* (Fort Worth, Texas), March 1, 1966, 20.

"Tonight in Television." *Kokomo Tribune*, January 18, 1966, 9.

"Top Hero Role Goes to Little-Known Actor." *The Providence* (Vancouver, Canada), November 13, 1961, 8.

Tower Drive-In Theater advertisement. *News and Observer* (Raleigh, North Carolina), August 7, 1970, 15.

"Tricky Film Comes Over Rather Sadly." *Lincolnshire Echo* (Lincolnshire, England), November 8, 1966, 4.

"The Trust—Scottish International Educational Trust." Scottish International Educational Trust, November 17, 2021, https://scotinted.org.uk/the-trust.

"TV Linked to Violence; Improvement Noted." *Roanoke Times* (Roanoke, Virginia). September 25, 1969, 3.

"TV Program Listings." *The Chillicothe Constitution-Tribune* (Chillicothe, Missouri). January 19, 1968, 5.

"TV Provides Features for Film Houses." *Ogden Standard-Examiner* (Ogden, Utah), January 11, 1967, 19.

"TV Violence Continues." *Herald and Review* (Decatur, Illinois), October 22, 1968, 8.

"20th Century Fox Ending Year with 16 Films, Including 3 Roadshow Attractions in 70mm." *Rocky Mount Telegram* (Rocky Mount, North Carolina), November 22, 1964, 7.

"Unique Spy Thriller Opens Sunday at Moon-Lit." *Leaf-Chronicle* (Clarksville, Tennessee), May 7, 1967, 29.

"Universal Changes Title of Picture." *Morning Call* (Allentown, Pennsylvania), June 15, 1965, 23.

"Unrewarding Spy Story." *New York Times*, May 12, 1966, 51.

"Unusual Sets for James Bond." *Cincinnati Post*, October 4, 1969, 46.

Van Gelder, Lindsy. "Roger Moore: 'The Saint's' Halo Is Almost Apparent," *Times Recorder* (Zanesville Ohio), June 25, 1967, 10D.

Variety Film Reviews 1907–1980. Vol. 11. Garland Publishing Inc., 1983.

Veysey, Arthur. "Man behind Secret Agent 007." *Chicago Tribune*, November 18, 1962, 248.

Victory. "Agent from H.A.R.M." *Sydney Morning Herald*, September 25, 1966, 87.

"Virna Signs for New Film." *Fort Lauderdale News*, October 8, 1965, 45.

Wale, Michael. "Steering Clear of Trouble." *Daily Herald* (London, England), June 5, 1964, 5.

Walker, Alexander. "Wham! Now Bond Is Superman." *Evening Standard* (London, England), December 28, 1965, 9.

Wallace, Kenneth G. "Nicely, Nicely Bet On 'Guy.'" *The Record* (Hackensack, New Jersey), November 5, 1965, 62.

Wallenstein, Marcel. "James Bond Starts a Flood of Wealth." *Kansas City Star*, November 10, 1963, 31.

"Wanted: A Young Greta Garbo." *Los Angeles Times*, February 25, 1963, 59.

Ward, Alan. "*Fathom* a Spy Film Spoof for All Raquel Welch Fans." *Oakland Tribune*, August 16, 1967, 47.

Watts, Granville. "$8 Million First Movie Doesn't Faze New James Bond." *Fort Lauderdale*, March 23, 1969, 50.

Watts, Stephen. "An 007 Movie without Connery? Get Headquarters!" *New York Times*, May 22, 1966, 129.

Wedman, Les. "That Man from Rio Review." *Vancouver Sun*, December 23, 1964, 18.

"Weighty Menace." *Tampa Tribune*, March 28, 1967, 11.

Weiler, A. H. "'Best Film' Award Winning Team Will Try to Repeat for MGM." *New York Times*, January 3, 1966, 46.

Weiler, A. H. "Comedians and Others Enlisted in Future Film Wars: More about Movie Matters." *New York Times*, January 30, 1966.

Weiler, A. H. "Dean Martin and (Shapely) Company Arrive in 'The Silencers.'" *New York Times*, March 17, 1966, 35.

Weiler, A. H. "New James Bond: George Lazenby Follows the Connery Pattern." *New York Times*, December 19, 1969, 68.

Weiler, A. H. "*Salt and Pepper* Opens." *New York Times*, September 19, 1968, 62.

Weiler, A. H. "Shooting for 'Sixpence': More on Movies." *New York Times*, November 14, 1965.

"What the Networks Are Showing This Summer." *Broadcasting*, July 11, 1966, 58.

Where the Spies Are advertisement. *Paris News* (Paris, Texas), January 23, 1966, 19.

"Whither James Bond? It's Up to Next Film." *Stockton Evening and Sunday Record* (Stockton, California), March 12, 1968, 19.

Willey, George. "TV to Become More Animated." *Redwood City Tribune* (Redwood City, California), February 17, 1966, 18.

William Goldman Randolph Theater advertisement. *Philadelphia Daily News*, January 19, 1966, 35.

Wilson, Earl. "Another James Bond Spoof about Secret Agent Oy-Oy 7." *Reno Gazette-Journal*, August 30, 1965, 8.

Wilson, Earl. "Barbra's Missing Letter." *San Francisco Examiner*, November 21, 1965, 35.

Wilson, Earl. "Bond Star Explains 'Insanity.'" *Detroit Free Press*, December 12, 1969, 15.

Wilson, Earl. "Boyer Thinks O'Toole Is Great: He's Not Afraid to Take Chances" *Honolulu Advertiser*, September 18, 1965, 17.

Wilson, Earl. "Gleason's Score—A Par 72." *Detroit Free Press*, June 27, 1964, 11.

Wilson, Earl. "It Happened Last Night." *Courier-Post* (Camden, New Jersey), April 26, 1967, 6.

Wilson, Earl. "It Happened Last Night." *The Tribune* (Scranton, Pennsylvania), January 15, 1965, 9.

Wilson, Earl. "The Midnight Earl. . . ." *Evansville Press*, August 4, 1966, 36.

Wilson, Earl. "Nancy Sinatra Well on Way to First Million." *Charlotte News*, August 8, 1966, 14.

Wilson, Earl. "North Carolinian Acts." *News and Observer* (Raleigh, North Carolina), July 26, 1963, 26.

Wilson, Earl. "That's Earl for Today." *Evening Standard* (Uniontown, Pennsylvania), November 27, 1963, 2.

Wilson, Earl. "Troy Donahue Hopes for Active New Year." *Herald-Sun* (New York, New York), December 19, 1965, 56.

Wilson, Wayne. "Capsule Reviews of Current Movies." *Valley News* (Van Nuys, California), January 27, 1967, 38.

Winchell, Walter. "The Broadway-Hollywood Cast." *Durham Sun*, December 18, 1962, 4.

Winchell, Walter. "Gina, Mate 'Splituation' in Air." *Orlando Evening Star*, June 26, 1964, 22.

Winchell, Walter. "It Takes All Kinds." *Terre Haute Tribune*, September 22, 1965, 4.

Wister, Emery. "Squeaky Don's Voice Is Loud." *Charlotte News*, August 27, 1966, 28.

Witbeck, Charles. "Flintstones' Swan Song." *Morning Call* (Allentown, Pennsylvania), June 29, 1966, 40.

Withers, F. Leslie. "What, No Kitchen Sink?" *Sunday Mercury* (Birmingham, England), October 7, 1962, 18.

"Woody-Allenized: *Tiger Lily*, Innovation of Sorts, Is Here the Cast." *New York Times*, November 18, 1966, 33.

The Wrecking Crew advertisement. *The Province* (Vancouver, British Columbia, Canada), December 30, 1968, 19.

"Yes, Virginia, There Is a Soviet SMERSH." *Lompoc Record* (Lompoc, California), March 24, 1964, 9.

Zenou, Theo. "JFK's Secret Weapon in the Cold War: James Bond." *Washington Post*, October 9, 2021.

Zubryn, Emil. "Latin America's Challenge to Bond." *Dayton Daily News* (Dayton, Ohio), February 4, 1968, 128.

INDEX